D0891655

Applying **Quality**

Management

IN HEALTHCARE

Patrice L. Spath
Diane L. Kelly

FOURTH EDITION

Applying Quality Management

IN HEALTHCARE

A SYSTEMS APPROACH

AUPHA

Health Administration Press, Chicago, Illinois

Association of University Programs in Health Administration, Washington, DC

Your board, staff, or clients may also benefit from this book's insight. For more information on quantity discounts, contact the Health Administration Press Marketing Manager at (312) 424-9450.

21   20   19   18   17   5   4   3   2   1

Library of Congress Cataloging-in-Publication Data

Names: Spath, Patrice L., author. | Kelly, Diane L., author.
Title: Applying quality management in healthcare : a systems approach /
  Patrice L. Spath, Diane L. Kelly.
Description: Fourth edition. | Chicago, Illinois : Health Administration
  Press ; Washington, DC : Association of University Programs in Health
  Administration, [2017] | Revision of: Applying quality management in
  healthcare / Diane L. Kelly. | Includes bibliographical references and
  index.
Identifiers: LCCN 2016055038 (print) | LCCN 2017001695 (ebook) | ISBN
  9781567938814 (print : alk. paper) | ISBN 9781567938821 (Ebook) | ISBN
  9781567938838 (Xml) | ISBN 9781567938845 (Epub) | ISBN 9781567938852
  (Mobi)
Subjects: LCSH: Medical care—Quality control. | Health services
  administration. | Total quality management.
Classification: LCC RA399.A1 K455 2017 (print) | LCC RA399.A1 (ebook) | DDC
  362.1068—dc23
LC record available at https://lccn.loc.gov/2016055038

The paper used in this publication meets the minimum requirements of American National Standard for Information Sciences—Permanence of Paper for Printed Library Materials, ANSI Z39.48-1984. ♾™

Acquisitions editor: Jennette E. McClain; Project manager: Theresa L. Rothschadl; Cover designer: James Slate; Layout: Virginia Byrne

Found an error or a typo? We want to know! Please e-mail it to hapbooks@ache.org, mentioning the book's title and putting "Book Error" in the subject line.

For photocopying and copyright information, please contact Copyright Clearance Center at www.copyright.com or at (978) 750-8400.

Health Administration Press
A division of the Foundation of the American
  College of Healthcare Executives
One North Franklin Street, Suite 1700
Chicago, IL 60606-3529
(312) 424-2800

Association of University Programs
  in Health Administration
1730 M Street, NW
Suite 407
Washington, DC 20036
(202) 763-7283

To my lifelong friend and companion, my husband Robert O. Brown.
—P. S.

To Isabella.
—D. K.

BRIEF CONTENTS

DETAILED CONTENTS

A NOTE FROM DIANE L. KELLY

The quality landscape has changed dramatically since the first edition of *Applying Quality Management in Healthcare: A Process for Improvement* (2003). At that time, the Institute of Medicine reports *To Err Is Human* (1999) and *Crossing the Quality Chasm* (2001) were still relatively new and patient safety was in its early stages. The Premier Hospital Quality Incentive Demonstration, the precursor to today's value-based purchasing initiatives, was just getting started. Transparency was in its infancy.

Fast-forward to today. The concept of systems is widely embraced in healthcare and has become a cornerstone for driving improvements toward achieving the Institute for Healthcare Improvement's Triple Aim. Perverse financial incentives, which punished organizations for reducing utilization by improving care, are being challenged with a wide array of innovative payment models that reward improvements in quality, safety, and health promotion. The numerous and often disparate parts of the US healthcare system are working together to improve the health of populations, not just to care for sick individuals. The quality, safety, and systems concepts discussed in this book have become foundational, essential, and timeless. They may be applied to any type, size, level, or complexity of organizational forms.

I would like to thank the many students whom I have had the privilege to get to know, work with, and learn from as a result of writing and teaching with this text. I would also like to thank my mentor and friend, Dr. Arnold Kaluzny. I am delighted that Patrice Spath is collaborating on this fourth edition so that the book may continue to bring value to future students.

Diane L. Kelly, DrPH, MBA, RN
Principal Consultant
Quantix Health Capital
Columbus, OH

PREFACE

everal years ago, I partnered with a physician, Dr. William Minogue, to respond to an article in a medical journal that bemoaned the lack of successful patient safety improvement initiatives. The article's authors suggested a new model was needed for conducting patient safety investigations because the current way of doing things was not working. At the time, I was facilitating training workshops for the Maryland Patient Safety Center, where Dr. Minogue was the medical director. We both agreed that a new safety investigation model was not the answer. This belief resulted in our coauthoring an article on the subject for WebM&M, an online case-based forum on patient safety sponsored by the Agency for Healthcare Research and Quality.

Our article began by reminding readers of the insights of Louis Pasteur, who, throughout his career, "insisted that germs were the cause of disease, not the body." Near the end of his life, Pasteur changed his opinion and "declined treatment for potentially curable pneumonia, reportedly saying, 'It is the soil, not the seed.' In other words, a germ (the seed) causes disease when our bodies (the soil) provide a hospitable environment" (Spath and Minogue 2008).

This lesson, discovered by Pasteur so many years ago, has application to all quality improvement activities and is reinforced by the topics covered in this book. The systems in health services organizations must be carefully nurtured to create a hospitable environment for the many tools and techniques of improvement to thrive. If the soil is not properly prepared, the seeds of improvement will not take root or be sustainable. Dr. Diane Kelly, author of the first three editions of this book, was insightful in taking a systems approach to quality improvement. Dr. Kelly understood that preparing the "soil" of the organization is just as important as learning how to use the various quality tools. I am honored to have the opportunity to build on Dr. Kelly's contributions in this fourth edition.

This book is intended for managers—anyone who influences the design of healthcare systems for the purpose of improving quality. It is not necessary to hold the official title of *manager* in an organization to be instrumental in creating and supporting higher-quality services. Many frontline, nonmanagerial clinical and administrative staff members are directly or indirectly involved in shaping patient care systems and in using improvement techniques to design more efficient, safer processes. Although the word *manager* is used liberally throughout this book, it is not intended to narrow the audience or the purpose. Anyone interested in making improvements in the quality and safety of health services will benefit from the learning in these pages.

Changes from the Third Edition

The emphasis on systems in the third edition is still evident in this fourth edition. What has changed is an expansion of information about quality tools, data analysis techniques, and patient safety. As with all editions of this book, concepts covered in the chapters are supported by real-life examples, illustrations, and thought-provoking end-of-chapter exercises. Some chapters have been added and others reordered. The book is now divided into three major sections instead of two.

Section 1 provides students with the foundational principles of healthcare quality and explains how systems affect an organization's ability to accomplish quality goals. The chapter on the role of policy in advancing quality (chapter 8 in the third edition) was moved to this section so students can better appreciate how external forces affect system behavior and relationships as well as the quality methods used by health services organizations (covered in later chapters). Some of the material relevant to reliability and patient safety covered in this section in the third edition has been moved to a new chapter dedicated solely to the topic of patient safety.

Section 2 contains three chapters designed to illustrate what health services organizations must do to set the stage for success in quality management efforts. Because teamwork and collaboration are essential for advancing healthcare quality, the teamwork chapter at the end of the third edition has been expanded and moved to this section (chapter 8, "Fostering a Culture of Collaboration and Teamwork"). Much of the information from chapter 10 has been moved to chapter 9 ("Measuring Process and System Performance"), and some topics have been shifted to other related chapters.

The nuts and bolts of quality management are found in section 3. The chapters in this section are expansions of topics covered in the third edition. Instructors using the third edition in a quality course indicated the need for more detailed explanations of quality models and the tools and techniques of healthcare quality management. In addition, a new chapter has been added (chapter 10, "Using Data Analytics Techniques to Evaluate Performance"). This chapter covers basic concepts of healthcare data analytics, including how to use various statistical and graphical methods for reporting and evaluating performance data. Some of these methods were covered briefly in the third edition, and some of the discussion is new to the fourth edition.

Materials on improvement models, project teams, and quality tools are greatly expanded from the third edition and now covered in two separate chapters (chapter 11, "Designing and Implementing Improvements," and chapter 12, "Using Improvement Teams and Tools"). In the third edition, the various topics related to patient safety were dispersed among several different chapters. Now, most of the material concerning patient safety is in a new chapter (chapter 13, "Making Healthcare Safer for Patients"). This chapter is focused entirely on systems issues affecting patient safety and methods for reducing mistakes and preventing patient harm.

Health Administration Press now offers educators the opportunity to build custom textbooks comprising chapters from several different books. To accommodate this service, the chapters in the fourth edition of this book have been written to stand alone as much as possible. Within each chapter, references to material in other chapters have been minimized, or the concepts summarized and repeated when necessary. Where there are linkages between materials in various chapters, instructors are encouraged to point out these relationships because the connections are not as clearly stated as in the third edition.

Resources

Listed at the end of each chapter are companion readings and web resources. Instructors can expand students' learning experience by assigning a companion reading or directing them to explore one or more of the online resources. These readings and websites are particularly useful in the chapter on data analysis techniques, if instructors want to cover more than just basic concepts. The web resources also provide instructors and students with sources of the most current information on relevant quality management and patient safety topics.

Patrice L. Spath, MA, RHIT
President
Brown-Spath & Associates
Forest Grove, OR

Instructor Resources

This book's Instructor Resources include explanations of the exercises, a test bank, and PowerPoint slides.

For the most up-to-date information about this book and its Instructor Resources, go to ache.org/HAP and browse for the book's title or author names.

This book's Instructor Resources are available to instructors who adopt this book for use in their course. For access information, please e-mail hapbooks@ache.org.

Student Resources

For students, end-of-chapter exercises and web resources are available on this book's companion website at ache.org/books/qualitymanagement4.

Reference

Spath, P., and W. Minogue. 2008. "The Soil, Not the Seed: The Real Problem with Root Cause Analysis." *Perspectives on Safety*. Agency for Healthcare Research and Quality. Published July. https://psnet.ahrq.gov/perspectives/perspective/62/the-soil-not-the-seed-the-real-problem-with-root-cause-analysis.

ACKNOWLEDGMENTS

The primary person that I must thank is Diane Kelly, author of the first three editions of this book. Her contributions to the learning experience of innumerable students and seasoned professionals have been outstanding. I am also grateful to the many people over the years who afforded me opportunities to share knowledge through my books and journal articles. In particular, I'd like to thank Janet Davis and Audrey Kaufman (the current and former acquisitions managers at Health Administration Press, respectively) and Richard Hill (senior editor at Health Forum, a unit of the American Hospital Association).

QUALITY MANAGEMENT: A SYSTEMS APPROACH

QUALITY MANAGEMENT FUNDAMENTALS

Learning Objectives

After completing this chapter, you should be able to

- describe the vital role of management in achieving quality patient and client health services;
- differentiate among key healthcare quality characteristics, common approaches to quality improvement, and total quality principles; and
- recognize management practices and traits as organizations mature along the quality continuum.

A mother arrives at the pediatrician's office for her daughter's six-month well-child checkup. As she has for previous checkups, she arrives 10 minutes early. Her daughter's scheduled appointment time of 10:00 am passes and she is still waiting at 11:30 am. The front desk receptionist politely tells the mother that the pediatrician has been called to an emergency, saying, "I'm sure you understand. If it was your child, you would want the doctor to attend to her." Although the mother understands the reason for the delay, this explanation does not change the fact that she has to pick up her son from preschool at noon. The mother asks if her daughter can at least get the immunizations today and have the rest of her checkup at another time. A clinic nurse hurriedly administers the child's immunizations while quietly complaining to the mother that she is often too busy to get a lunch break.

Dissatisfied with the hours wasted at the pediatrician's office and disappointed with the need to return to finish her daughter's checkup, the mother begins to investigate other healthcare options for her children. While the doctor at her current pediatric clinic seems highly trained and knowledgeable, the mother has concerns about the organization in which the doctor practices. The organizational aspects of the pediatric clinic are not meeting the mother's expectations. In the broadest definition, an **organization** is a structured system designed to accomplish a goal or set of goals. In this example, the care providers and office staff are a pediatric health services organization designed to deliver healthcare to children.

organization
a structured system designed to accomplish a goal or set of goals

This book focuses on managing the quality of the structured system in which health services are delivered. Like any organization, the structured system in the pediatric clinic is a by-product of numerous variables that affect the design and execution of many interrelated factors. What are the specific goals of the healthcare organization and how are they determined? Does everyone in the organization understand and agree with these goals? How are patient appointments, office workflow, and staff hours scheduled to enable the practice to meet these goals? How are patient and family needs and expectations taken into account? How are clinic employees recruited, hired, trained, and evaluated? Does the pediatrician devote all of her time to the office or does she also have hospital commitments? How is the pediatrician compensated for services? How does reimbursement influence the office structure and work systems? Does the practice operate according to a budget? Does the practice employ an office manager? If so, how is the manager's role defined? How do the pediatrician and the staff communicate with each other and with patients and their families?

These are just some of the questions that influence managerial decisions about how the structured system will operate. In the example, the mother's experience resulted from how her pediatrician's practice addressed such organizational questions. This mother's perception of quality had nothing to do with the quality of the *medical* care. It had everything to do with the organizational quality of the health services. The focus of this text is on managing the structured systems of health-related services—within and between organizations—to provide the highest-quality and safest healthcare.

Why Focus on Managing Systems?

Providing the medical care (e.g., performing cardiac surgery) and producing the service (e.g., maintaining a clean environment) are functions of the clinical and technical professionals. Creating and managing the structured system in which clinical and technical professionals work is the role of management. The manager's perspective and tactics may vary depending on his organizational level (e.g., senior administrative, middle management, frontline supervisory) and his scope of responsibilities (e.g., team, project, department, division, agency, organization-wide). Regardless, all persons holding management responsibilities in an organization are charged with finding ways to carry out, coordinate, and improve the organizational functions.

As illustrated by the mother's experience at the pediatric clinic, patients may not receive the benefits of good medical care when the system of delivery is poorly managed. Quality is not simply the obligation of clinical and technical professionals. The task of achieving quality outcomes from healthcare organizations is a shared responsibility belonging to those who provide medical care and produce services and the management professionals who oversee the system. Management determines how and what organizational goals are set; how human, fiscal, material, and intellectual resources are secured, allocated, used, and preserved; and how activities in the organization are designed, carried out, coordinated, and improved. The material presented in this book is intended to assist managers in the decision-making processes related to quality and safety in health services organizations.

What Are Quality and Safety?

A widely accepted definition of **quality** as given by the Institute of Medicine (IOM) is this: "The degree to which health services for individuals and populations increase the likelihood of desired health outcomes and are consistent with current professional knowledge" (Lohr 1990, 21). To further clarify the concept of quality, the IOM (2001) identified the **key components of quality care**: safe, effective, patient centered, timely, efficient, and equitable. **Patient safety**, a key component of quality care, is defined as, "freedom from accidental or preventable injuries produced by medical care" (Agency for Healthcare Research and Quality [AHRQ] 2016b).

The way managers in health services organizations define and prioritize quality in the context of their daily responsibilities is often influenced by their own background and experiences. For example, a physician manager may emphasize the importance of achieving optimal patient outcomes through implementation of evidence-based medicine. A nurse manager or pharmacist may stress the importance of interpersonal skills, teamwork, and patient-centered care. A manager with public health credentials may take a population-based approach to improving healthcare quality. Likewise, the educational focus of nonclinical managers may influence the preferred quality definition and priorities. A manager educated in a business school may emphasize operations management, whereas someone trained as an accountant may focus on how quality affects the financial bottom line. A manager with a health services administration background may stress the importance of organizational structures and stakeholder relationships.

These examples illustrate the assortment of perspectives and preferences about health services quality and the numerous ways quality concerns may be expressed in healthcare organizations. The multifaceted nature of quality poses several additional questions and challenges for healthcare managers: What is quality in healthcare? Which approach is best? How are the approaches related?

Since the early 1970s, Avedis Donabedian's work has influenced the prevailing medical paradigm for defining and measuring quality. In his early

quality
"the degree to which health services for individuals and populations increase the likelihood of desired health outcomes and are consistent with current professional knowledge" (Lohr 1990, 21)

key components of quality care
quality care is safe, effective, patient centered, timely, efficient, and equitable (IOM 2001)

patient safety
"freedom from accidental or preventable injuries produced by medical care" (AHRQ 2016b)

writings, Donabedian (1980) introduced the two essential components—the technical and the interpersonal—that comprise quality medical care. He also identified three ways to measure quality (structure, process, outcome) and the relationships among them. Donabedian (1980, 79, 81–83) described the measures in the following way:

process of care
"a set of activities that go on within and between practitioners and patients" (Donabedian 1980, 79)

structure
"the relatively stable characteristics of the providers of care, of the tools and resources they have at their disposal, and of the physical and organizational settings in which they work" (Donabedian 1980, 81)

outcome
"a change in a patient's current and future health status that can be attributed to antecedent healthcare" (Donabedian 1980, 83)

patient experience
a patient's "report of observations of and participation in health care, or assessment of any resulting change in their health" (AHRQ 2016a)

I have called the **"process" of care** . . . a set of activities that go on within and between practitioners and patients. . . . Elements of the process of care do not signify quality until their relationship to desirable health status has been established. By **"structure"** I mean the relatively stable characteristics of the providers of care, of the tools and resources they have at their disposal, and of the physical and organizational settings in which they work. . . . Structure, therefore, is relevant to quality in that it increases or decreases the probability of good performance. . . . I shall use **"outcome"** to mean a change in a patient's current and future health status that can be attributed to antecedent healthcare. The fundamental functional relationships among the three elements are shown schematically as follows: Structure → Process → Outcome.

For example, in a family medicine group practice, the number and credentials of physicians, nurse practitioners, physician's assistants, nurses, medical technicians, and office staff are considered structure measures. The percentage of elderly patients who appropriately receive an influenza vaccine is considered a process measure, and the percentage of elderly patients who are diagnosed and treated for influenza is considered an outcome measure for this practice. The staff members in the office (structure) influence the ability of the practice to appropriately identify patients for whom the vaccine is indicated and to correctly administer the vaccine (process), which in turn affects the number of patients developing influenza (outcome). If a process measure has a clearly demonstrated link to an outcome, the process measure may be used as a proxy measure for an outcome (Parast et al. 2015)

When the IOM recognized patient-centered care as a key component of twenty-first-century healthcare quality in 2001, the Donabedian model for measuring quality expanded to include patient experience. **Patient experience** measures are a subcategory of outcomes that represent the voice of patients— their "report of observations of and participation in health care, or assessment of any resulting change in their health" (AHRQ 2016a). For example, a family practice clinic may have a good process for identifying patients needing an influenza vaccine and qualified staff to correctly administer the vaccine, yet patients may report their experience to be unsatisfactory if caregivers do not listen to their concerns and adequately answer questions about the vaccination.

While a health services manager can easily become overwhelmed by the complexity and extensive range of views on the topic of healthcare quality, she may also consider this array of perspectives as a vast pool from which to draw quality-related knowledge and lessons.

Creating a Common Understanding of Quality Methods

As with most elements of management, the subject of quality in healthcare organizations has been the object of numerous trends, fads, and attempts at quick fixes. Because departments and professionals with "quality" responsibilities may change their job titles with the latest trend, managers must understand what is behind the label; in other words, they must understand the philosophy and actions used to promote quality in an organization. The first step for managers is to develop a common understanding of quality terminology. Definitions of frequently used terms to describe quality are provided here.

Quality control. Mostly used in the manufacturing setting, **quality control (QC)** encompasses "the operational techniques and activities used to fulfill requirements for quality" (American Society for Quality [ASQ] 2016). In health services, quality control activities usually refer to equipment maintenance and calibration, such as for point-of-care and laboratory testing, imaging machines, and sterilization procedures.

Quality assurance. A **quality assurance (QA)** approach is focused on the outputs of a process. Products are inspected after they are produced, and imperfect products are discarded. In some cases, the defect may not be readily noticeable and is replaced at a later time, as with a new automobile warranty. In service organizations fields such as healthcare, defects refer to unsatisfactory or defective outputs from a received service. The quality of the service is inspected after it is received and, if not acceptable, the customer may ask for the service to be repeated. For example, when the customer discovers that a retail pharmacy includes only half the number of tablets in a prescription refill, he asks for the refill to be corrected. Sometimes the service defect is not readily noticeable, as in the case of a surgical sponge left in a patient after an operation. As the patient's condition deteriorates, tests are performed to identify causes of the defective output. The patient must return to surgery for the defect to be corrected.

Hearing QA and QC used interchangeably when "referring to the actions performed to ensure the quality of a product, service or process" is not uncommon (ASQ 2016).

Quality improvement. A **quality improvement (QI)** approach, also referred to as *continuous quality improvement* (CQI), is focused on the ongoing improvement of processes as a way to improve the quality of the outputs (i.e.,

quality control (QC)
"the operational techniques and activities used to fulfill requirements for quality" (ASQ 2016)

quality assurance (QA)
actions performed to eliminate defective outputs

quality improvement (QI)
"ongoing improvement of products, services or processes through incremental and breakthrough improvements" (ASQ 2016)

reduce the number of defective outputs). Preoperative checklists, sponge counts, and team briefings are examples of operating room process improvements designed to prevent defective outputs or surgical complications. By implementing incremental and breakthrough improvements, QI seeks to produce defect-free outputs and provide consistent high-quality services.

Total quality. The term **total quality (TQ)**, also referred to as *total quality management* or TQM, is often used interchangeably with "QI" and "CQI." This tendency can cause students and managers to be confused by the two related but different concepts. Total quality is "a philosophy or an approach to management that can be characterized by its principles, practices, and techniques. Its three principles are customer focus, continuous improvement, and teamwork . . . each principle is implemented through a set of practices . . . the practices are, in turn, supported by a wide array of techniques (i.e., specific step-by-step methods intended to make the practices effective)" (Dean and Bowen 2000, 4–5).

As shown by this definition, TQ is a strategic concept, whereas CQI is one of three principles that support a TQ strategy. Numerous techniques—including performance management, Six Sigma, and Lean—are available for managers in implementing the principles of CQI on a tactical level and an operational level. A brief description of these techniques is provided in the following section with more detail in subsequent chapters.

Performance management. The business literature defines **performance management** as "an umbrella term that describes the methodologies, metrics, processes and systems used to monitor and manage the business performance of an enterprise" (Buytendijk and Rayner 2002). Performance management is also referred to as *enterprise performance management* (EPM), *corporate performance management* (CPM), and *business performance management* (BPM).

Six Sigma. **Six Sigma** is a rigorous and disciplined approach using process improvement tools, methods, and statistical analysis. Its precepts are based on the philosophy "that views all work as processes that can be defined, measured, analyzed, improved and controlled" (Muralidharan 2015, 528). *Six sigma* is a statistical term referring to the goal of achieving zero defects or failures. Six Sigma quality is considered a "rate of less than 3.4 defects per million opportunities, which translates to a process that is 99.99966 percent defect free" (Spath 2013, 125). Although the technique originated in manufacturing, the use of Six Sigma is being encouraged in health services organizations as a way of achieving high reliability (Chassin and Loeb 2013).

Lean. Sometimes called *Lean thinking*, **Lean** "is about finding and eliminating waste in all processes" (Black 2016, 6). This quality philosophy and set of tools, which also originated in manufacturing, is used to remove wasted effort from healthcare processes without compromising quality (Chassin and Loeb 2013). Lean techniques have helped health services organizations

---

total quality (TQ)
"a philosophy or an approach to management that can be char-acterized by its principles, practices, and techniques. Its three principles are customer focus, continuous improvement, and teamwork . . . each principle is imple-mented through a set of practices . . . the practices are, in turn, supported by a wide array of techniques (i.e., specific step-by-step methods intended to make the practices effective)" (Dean and Bowen 2000, 4–5)

performance management
"an umbrella term that describes the methodologies, metrics, processes and systems used to monitor and manage the business performance of an enterprise" (Buytendijk and Rayner 2002)

Six Sigma
a rigorous and dis-ciplined process improvement approach using defined tools, methods, and statisti-cal analysis with the goal of improving the outcome of a process by reducing the fre-quency of defects or failures

Lean (or Lean thinking)
an improvement phi-losophy and set of tools that "is about finding and eliminating waste in all processes" (Black 2016, 6)

increase patient staff satisfaction, create more efficient processes, lower expenses, reduce patient wait times, improve capacity management, and make many other value-added, customer-focused enhancements (Black 2016). The **Toyota Production System** (TPS) is a common method of applying Lean in health services organizations.

Organizational effectiveness. Several models or definitions of effectiveness in management literature exist, and the meanings are derived from the values and preferences of evaluators (Cameron 2015). From the perspective of TQ, **organizational effectiveness** means accomplishing goals.

Change management. Whether quality improvement is aimed at reducing defects, removing wasteful process steps, or achieving better patient outcomes, the work people do in the organization will be modified in minor and sometimes major ways. **Change management** is a "systematic approach that prepares an organization to accept, implement, and sustain the improved processes" (Chassin and Loeb 2013, 481). A structure for managing the changes that result from quality improvement efforts is essential for ensuring that quality does not deteriorate as time passes, staff turnover occurs, and new priorities emerge. Components of this strategy can include human resources planning, financial and resource management, and implementation of a control system that involves measurement and oversight of performance results (McLaughlin and Olson 2012). A phrase often associated with change management is "sustain the gains."

Exhibit 1.1 provides a summary of the quality-related terms described in this section and the influence these concepts have on the actions of healthcare managers.

Quality management. Continuously improving products and services to achieve better performance is often referred to as **quality management**. In this book, the term *quality management* is used to describe the manager's role and contribution to organizational effectiveness. Quality management, for our purposes, refers to how managers working in various types of health services organizations and settings understand, explain, and continuously improve their organizations to allow them to deliver quality and safe patient care, promote quality patient and organizational outcomes, and improve health in their communities.

Three Principles of Total Quality

Total quality is based on three principles: customer focus, continuous improvement, and teamwork. While these topics are explored in depth in later chapters, a brief introduction to these principles is provided in this section.

Toyota Production System
a common method of applying Lean in health services, first developed at the Toyota Motor Company

organizational effectiveness
the ability to accomplish goals

change management
a "systematic approach that prepares an organization to accept, implement, and sustain the improved processes" (Chassin and Loeb 2013, 481)

quality management
the manager's role and contribution to organizational effectiveness; how managers working in various types of health services organizations and settings understand, explain, and continuously improve their organizations to allow them to deliver quality and safe patient care, promote quality patient and organizational outcomes, and improve health in their communities

EXHIBIT 1.1
Quality-Related
Terms

Quality-Related Term	Relevant Manager Actions
Quality control	Fulfill process requirements
Quality assurance	Find and repair faulty processes causing defective outputs
Quality improvement/continuous quality improvement	Incrementally and continuously improve processes
Performance management	Continuously review, evaluate, and improve performance to meet changing customer, stakeholder, and regulatory requirements
Six Sigma	Aggressively improve processes and reduce variation to achieve zero defects
Lean/Lean thinking	Seek better ways to organize human actions and processes to eliminate waste
Total quality/total quality management	Manage using a customer focus, continuous improvement, and teamwork
Organizational effectiveness	Understand and improve the system to achieve goals
Change management	Use systematic methods to transition individuals, teams, and the organization

customer
the user or
potential user
of services or
programs

external customer
a user outside the
organization

internal customer
a user inside the
organization

stakeholder
"all groups that
are or might be
affected by an
organization's
services, actions
or success" (BPEP
2015, 53)

Customer. A **customer** is defined as a user (or potential user) of services or programs. Patients are customers, as are referring healthcare providers, as well as payers such as patients' family members and health plans (Baldrige Performance Excellence Program [BPEP] 2015).

External customers are the parties outside the organization, and the primary external customers for health services providers are patients, families and partners, clients, insurers and other third-party payers, and communities. An **internal customer** is a user inside of the organization. Internal customers have been described as "someone whose inbox is your outbox." For example, in a hospital, when patient care is handed off from one provider to another at shift change, the incoming provider is considered the internal customer of the outgoing provider. Completing the requisite shift responsibilities in a timely manner, communicating relevant information, and leaving a tidy work space demonstrate one's recognition of coworkers as internal customers.

The contemporary view of quality management expands the concept of "customer" to include stakeholders and markets in which the organization operates. The term **stakeholder** is used to refer to "all groups that are or might be affected by an organization's services, actions or success" (BPEP 2015, 53). In healthcare organizations, key stakeholders may include "customers, the community, employers, health care providers, patient advocacy groups, departments of health, students, the workforce, partners, collaborators, governing boards, stockholders, donors, suppliers, taxpayers, regulatory bodies, policy makers, funders, and local and professional communities" (BPEP 2015, 53).

customer-focused quality
a type of quality in which key patient and other customer requirements and expectations are identified and drive improvement efforts

Customer-focused quality means that key patient and other customer requirements and expectations are identified and drive improvement efforts (BPEP 2015). Defining customers and stakeholders is a prerequisite to determining their requirements and, in turn, to designing organizational processes that meet these requirements.

Continuous improvement. When the manager of an environmental services department in a large hospital picks up something from the hallway floor and throws it away in the nearest trash can, her action exemplifies the principle of continuous improvement. While other hospital employees might walk past the trash, the environmental services manager realizes the importance of being committed to continuous improvement for her department and for the hospital; if at any time the manager sees something that needs fixing, improving, or correcting, she takes the initiative. If managers want to achieve continuous improvement in their organizations, they must demonstrate continuous improvement through their everyday actions.

The principle of continuous improvement may also be expressed through managers' execution of their managerial functions. Managing by fact and depending on performance data to inform decisions is requisite to this principle. Though they might vary according to the nature of the work and the scope of management responsibility, performance data may be reported at various time intervals. For example, a shift supervisor for the patient transportation service in an 800-bed academic medical center watches the electronic dispatch system that displays a minute-by-minute update on transportation requests, indicators of patients en route to their destinations, and the number of patients in the queue. By monitoring the system, the supervisor is immediately aware when a problem occurs and, as a result, is able to take action quickly to resolve the problem. If the number of requests unexpectedly increases, the supervisor can reassign staff breaks to maximize staff availability and minimize response times.

Each day, the supervisor posts the total number of transports performed the previous day, along with the average response times. This way, the patient transporters are aware of the department's statistics and their own individual statistics, which helps the transporters take pride in a job that is typically underappreciated by others in the organization. The daily performance data also enable the supervisor to quickly identify documented complaints and to address them within 24 hours, which in turn increases employee accountability and improves customer relations. On a monthly basis, the department manager and the shift supervisors review the volume of requests by hour of the day to determine whether employees are scheduled appropriately to meet demand.

The manager also reviews the statistics sorted by patient unit (e.g., nursing unit, radiology department) to identify any issues that need to be explored directly, manager to manager. The manager reviews the monthly statistics with his administrator, and the annual statistics are used in the budgeting process. A performance management system such as this promotes **continuous improvement**, which is defined as steady, incremental improvement in the organization's overall performance.

continuous improvement
steady, incremental improvement in the organization's overall performance

teamwork
a team process involving the "knowledge, skills, experience, and perspectives of different individuals" (Health Resources and Services Administration 2011, 3)

Teamwork. When the terms **teamwork** and *quality* are used together, management is usually referring to cross functional or interdisciplinary project teams. Healthcare organizations seeking to make changes in complex processes or activities that involve more than one discipline or work area often use a team approach. Quality improvement is fundamentally a team process in which significant and lasting improvements rely on the "knowledge, skills, experience, and perspectives of different individuals" (Health Resources and Services Administration 2011, 3).

In relation to quality management, managers should also consider teamwork when they carry out functions inherent in the managerial role—in particular, organizational design, resource allocation, and communication. Designing and implementing decision-making, documentation, and communication processes (which ensure individuals and teams have the information they need, when they need it, to make effective and timely clinical and organizational decisions) reflect a manager's understanding of the quality management principles. For example, in one hospital, the manager of the materials management department negotiates with a supplier to obtain surgical gloves at a discounted rate compared with the rate of the current supplier. The decision is made based on vendor and financial input. The first time the new gloves are used, however, the surgeon rips out the fingers of the gloves while inserting his hand. Had the manager embraced the concept of teamwork in her approach to decision making, she would have sought out information and input from the patient care team—the people who actually use the product and know the advantages and disadvantages of different brands of gloves.

Quality Continuum for Organizations

Quality management is not a single event; rather, it is an organizational journey. Progress along the journey may be viewed on a continuum, with one end representing traditional or early attempts at quality and the other end representing more mature approaches (exhibit 1.2). Regulatory, accreditation, and cost-control pressures, as well as consumer activism, are accelerating the quality journey of health services organizations. These external factors are described in more detail in the next chapter.

Less Mature	Developing		More Mature
Quality priorities	Complying with quality requirements of external stakeholders is an operational imperative	Internal quality improvement is one of three or four strategic priorities	Internal quality improvement is the organization's top strategic priority
Quality scope	Internal customers	Internal and external customers and stakeholders	Internal and external customers and stakeholders and the community served
Quality transparency	Key quality measures not reported internally throughout the organization and not reported publicly	Key quality measures reported internally throughout the organization; few reported publicly	Key quality measures reported internally and publicly; reports include benchmark data from best practice organizations
Quality methods	No organization-wide approach to quality improvement	Data-driven, statistical methods used in some improvement initiatives	Managers trained in data-driven, statistical methods that are used for all improvement initiatives
Performance measures	Only measures used are those required by external stakeholders	In addition to measures required by external stakeholders, internal measures are used to evaluate quality priorities of managers	In addition to measures required by external stakeholders, internal measures linked to the quality goals of the organization are used
Information technology (IT)	There is little or no IT support for quality activities	IT supports some quality activities, but many are still paper based	IT support is provided for all quality activities

EXHIBIT 1.2
Quality Continuum for Healthcare Organizations

Source: Adapted from Chassin and Loeb (2013).

Although a healthcare organization may occupy a point anywhere along this maturity continuum, the goal of quality management is to continually strive toward the most mature end of the continuum. An understanding of the quality continuum in health services organizations begins to explain differences in operations and outcomes in organizations that all claim to be "quality organizations," such as

- how an organization can be successful at quality projects but not attain a quality organizational culture;
- why some organizations have adjusted better than others to current oversight practices of regulatory groups and accreditation agencies;
- why implementing clinical practice guidelines does not in itself guarantee healthcare quality;
- why operations management efforts, independent of clinical context, may not yield expected results; and
- why, without leadership's involvement in establishing a quality philosophy and strategy for the entire organization, only pockets of excellence may be found in an organization.

Summary

Achieving organizational effectiveness requires leaders to combine the knowledge of management and quality to understand and improve the organization. This chapter has introduced various terms and approaches to help managers establish a common vocabulary for quality in their organizations. The path to becoming a mature, quality organization is a process characterized by transitions in managerial philosophy, thinking, and action.

Exercise 1.1
Objective: To explore the current state of healthcare quality in the United States.

Instructions:

- Go to the AHRQ website (https://nhqrnet.ahrq.gov/inhqrdr) and find the most current version of the National Healthcare Quality and Disparities report.
- Read the Executive Summary.
- Browse the rest of the report.

- Based on your brief review of this report, summarize the state of healthcare quality and disparities in the United States in one or two paragraphs.

Companion Readings

Health Resources and Services Administration. 2011. *Quality Improvement.* US Department of Health and Human Services. Published April. www.hrsa.gov/quality/toolbox/508pdfs/qualityimprovement.pdf.

Institute of Medicine (IOM). 2001. *Crossing the Quality Chasm: A New Health System for the 21st Century.* Washington, DC: National Academies Press.

Web Resources

Agency for Healthcare Research and Quality: www.ahrq.gov
American Society for Quality: www.asq.org
National Association for Healthcare Quality: www.nahq.org
Public Health Foundation: www.phf.org

References

Agency for Healthcare Research and Quality (AHRQ). 2016a. "Domain Framework and Inclusion Criteria: Domain Definitions." Updated March 17. www.quality measures.ahrq.gov/about/domain-definitions.aspx.

————. 2016b. "Patient Safety Network Glossary." Accessed June 25. www.psnet .ahrq.gov/glossary.aspx.

American Society for Quality (ASQ). 2016. "Quality Glossary." Accessed June 25. www.asq.org/glossary/index.html.

Baldrige Performance Excellence Program (BPEP). 2015. *2015–2016 Baldrige Excellence Framework: A Systems Approach to Improving Your Organization's Performance (Health Care).* Gaithersburg, MD: US Department of Commerce, National Institute of Standards and Technology.

Black, J. 2016. *The Toyota Way to Healthcare Excellence: Increase Efficiency and Improve Quality with Lean,* 2nd ed. Chicago: Health Administration Press.

Buytendijk, F., and N. Rayner. 2002. "A Starter's Guide to CPM Methodologies." Research Note TU-16-2429. Stamford, CT: Gartner, Inc.

Cameron, K. 2015. "Organizational Effectiveness." In *Wiley Encyclopedia of Management*, vol. 11, 1–4. Published January. http://onlinelibrary.wiley.com/doi/10.1002/9781118785317.weom110202/abstract.

Chassin, M. R., and J. M. Loeb. 2013. "High-Reliability Health Care: Getting There from Here." *The Milbank Quarterly* 91 (3): 459–90.

Dean, J. W., Jr., and D. E. Bowen. 2000. "Management Theory and Total Quality: Improving Research and Practice Through Theory Development." In *The Quality Movement and Organization Theory*, edited by R. E. Cole and W. R. Scott, 3–22. Thousand Oaks, CA: SAGE Publications.

Donabedian, A. 1980. *Explorations in Quality Assessment and Monitoring.* Vol. 1 in *The Definition of Quality and Approaches to Its Assessment.* Chicago: Health Administration Press.

Health Resources and Services Administration. 2011. *Quality Improvement.* US Department of Health and Human Services. Published April. www.hrsa.gov/quality/toolbox/508pdfs/qualityimprovement.pdf.

Institute of Medicine (IOM). 2001. *Crossing the Quality Chasm: A New Health System for the 21st Century.* Washington, DC: National Academies Press.

Lohr, K. N. (ed.). 1990. *Medicare: A Strategy for Quality Assurance.* Washington, DC: National Academies Press.

McLaughlin, D. B., and J. R. Olson. 2012. *Healthcare Operations Management*, 2nd ed. Chicago: Health Administration Press.

Muralidharan, K. 2015. *Six Sigma for Organizational Excellence: A Statistical Approach.* New York: Springer.

Parast, L., B. Doyle, C. L. Damberg, K. Shetty, D. A. Ganz, N. S. Wenger, and P. G. Shekelle. 2015. "Challenges in Assessing the Process–Outcome Link in Practice." *Journal of General Internal Medicine* 30 (3): 359–64.

Spath, P. L. 2013. *Introduction to Healthcare Quality Management*, 2nd ed. Chicago: Health Administration Press.

ROLE OF POLICY IN ADVANCING QUALITY

Learning Objectives

After completing this chapter, you should be able to

- describe the types of oversight organizations that influence healthcare quality;
- recognize how public and private policies encourage quality improvement at the organizational, community, and national levels; and
- identify resources to maintain current knowledge about policy changes, new initiatives, and updates on current initiatives.

The most visible or well-known topics of healthcare policy tend to be those related to funding, payment, and access. Examples include Titles XVIII and XIX, the Social Security Act amendments of 1965 that created Medicare and Medicaid; the Balanced Budget Act of 1997 that created the Children's Health Insurance Program (CHIP); and the Patient Protection and Affordable Care Act of 2010 (ACA). There are many other public and private policies that play an integral role in ensuring the quality of healthcare services.

Licensure is an example of how healthcare quality is affected by public health policies. Physicians, nurses, nurse practitioners, pharmacists, physical therapists, and other care providers must have licenses to practice their professions. These requirements are guided by the statutes and rules outlined in the professional practice acts and occupational licensing bodies of their respective states. There are many other examples of how public and private policies influence healthcare quality. The Americans with Disabilities Act requires health facilities to have ramped sidewalks to the front door and Braille numbers on the elevator buttons. Sprinklers in the ceilings, signs labeled "fire exit," and alarm-activated doors that close automatically are mandated by state building codes and the fire safety requirements of state regulations and private health facility oversight groups. Inappropriate or excessive radiation exposure to patients and healthcare personnel during diagnostic exams is prevented when facilities comply with the requirements of the Occupational Safety and

Health Administration and private oversight entities. The safety and efficacy of medications are investigated by the US Food and Drug Administration before they are released for patient use.

Considering the Donabedian (1980) model for measuring quality (structure, process, outcome), policy initiatives have historically targeted the quality of the structural elements of the healthcare delivery system, such as people, physical facilities, equipment, and drugs. Outcome measures, such as infant mortality rates and life expectancy, and aggregate process measures, such as immunization rates, have been collected for many years by the public health infrastructure at state, national, and international levels. Current health quality policy initiatives target outcomes and processes at the organization, provider, and population levels.

This chapter discusses the increasingly important role of public and private policies on healthcare quality by providing a brief overview of health policy concepts, explaining the role of quality oversight bodies, and introducing several healthcare quality initiatives that demonstrate the use of public and private policies to drive system change and improvement.

licensure
status granted by a governmental body and confirming minimum standards

accreditation
"a public recognition by a healthcare accreditation body of the achievement of accreditation standards by a healthcare organization, demonstrated through an independent external peer assessment of that organization's level of performance in relation to the standards" (Smits, Supachutikul, and Mate 2014, 66)

certification
a form of external quality review for health services professionals and organizations; when applied to individuals, it represents advanced education and competence; when applied to organizations, it represents meeting predetermined standards for a specialized service provided by the organization (Rooney and van Ostenburg 1999).

External Stakeholders Affecting Quality

A variety of external stakeholders—federal, state, and local government agencies and private organizations—set quality expectations and assess and monitor services delivered by health plans, health facilities, integrated delivery systems, and individual practitioners. Types of quality oversight organizations are summarized in exhibit 2.1.

External stakeholders use three primary approaches to influence healthcare quality: licensure, accreditation, and certification. **Licensure** is granted by a governmental body and represents *minimum* quality standards, while **accreditation** and **certification** are granted by nongovernmental

EXHIBIT 2.1
Types of Healthcare Quality Oversight Organizations in the United States

State licensing bodies. States, typically through their health departments, have long regulated healthcare delivery through the licensure of healthcare institutions such as hospitals, long-term care facilities, and home health agencies, as well as individual healthcare practitioners such as physicians and nurses. States also license, through their insurance and health departments, financial "risk-bearing entities," including both indemnity insurance products and those managed care products that perform the dual function of bearing risk (like an insurer) and arranging for or delivering healthcare services (like healthcare-providing entities).

(continued)

EXHIBIT 2.1

Types of
Healthcare
Quality
Oversight
Organizations
in the United
States
(continued)

Private sector accrediting bodies. Accrediting bodies set standards for healthcare organizations and assess compliance with those standards. They also focus on the operation and effectiveness of internal quality improvement systems. In some functional areas, state and federal governments rely on or recognize private accreditation for purposes of ensuring compliance with licensure or regulatory requirements.

Medicare and Medicaid compliance. For a healthcare entity to receive Medicare or Medicaid reimbursement, the entity must meet certain federally specified conditions of participation (CoPs) or other standards. The Centers for Medicare & Medicaid Services (CMS) promulgates CoPs for hospitals, home health agencies, nursing facilities, hospices, ambulatory surgical centers, renal dialysis centers, rural health clinics, outpatient physical therapy and occupational therapy, and rehabilitation facilities. CMS also establishes standards for the participation of managed care organizations contracting under the Medicare program.

US Department of Labor. Oversight of certain aspects of employer-provided health plans is performed by the US Department of Labor. The Employee Retirement Income Security Act of 1974 sets minimum federal standards for group health plans maintained by private-sector employers, by unions, or jointly by employers and unions. The department oversees plan compliance with the following legal requirements of plan administration: reporting and disclosure of plan features and operations, fiduciary obligations for management of the plan and its assets, handling benefit claims, continuation coverage for workers who lose group health coverage, limitations on exclusions for preexisting conditions, prohibitions on discrimination based on health status, renewability of group health coverage for employers, minimum hospital stays for childbirth, and parity of limits on mental health benefits.

Individual certification and credentialing organizations. The American Board of Medical Specialties (an umbrella for 24 specialty boards) and the American Osteopathic Association have certification programs that designate certain medical providers as having completed specific training in a specialty and having passed examinations testing knowledge of that specialty. The Accreditation Council for Graduate Medical Education, sponsored by the American Medical Association and four other organizations, accredits nearly 7,700 residency programs in 1,600 medical institutions across the United States. For nursing, the American Board of Nursing Specialties sets standards for the certification of nursing specialties. The largest numbers of nurses, both in generalist and specialist practice, are certified by the American Nurses Credentialing Center on the basis of practice standards established by the American Nurses Association.

Source: Data from President's Advisory Committee on Consumer Protection and Quality in the Health Care Industry (1998).

organizations. Accreditation and certification represent *optimal* quality standards for organizations or *advanced* education and competence for individuals.

Quality oversight organizations are vital stakeholders of health services organizations. Their standards, regulations, and conditions of participation (CoPs) increasingly drive system change and improve quality of care and services. Details on the specific laws, regulations, and impact of healthcare quality may be found in other texts dedicated to health policy and healthcare management. In the next sections, a few key examples of external stakeholders (public and private) and how they influence healthcare quality are provided. Because the priorities and expectations of external stakeholders are constantly changing, students and managers charged with quality responsibilities will need additional resources to learn about the most current requirements of all stakeholder groups affecting their organization. The web resources at the end of this chapter are useful for this purpose.

Federal Health Policies and Oversight

The federal government is a vital stakeholder of health services organizations. Its regulations, CoPs, and health policy priorities are increasingly being used to drive system change and improve quality of care and services. Details on specific laws and regulations that affect healthcare quality may be found in other texts dedicated to health policy. This section presents a few key examples that illustrate the role of policy in system improvement. A brief background on the evolution of these initiatives is also provided so readers may appreciate the influence of history on the current healthcare quality landscape.

public policy
"authoritative decisions made in the legislative, executive, or judicial branches of government that are intended to direct or influence the actions, behaviors, or decisions of others" (Longest 2010, 5)

The US government serves the following generic purposes: "to provide for those who cannot provide for themselves, to supply social and public goods, to regulate the market, and to instill trust and accountability" (Tang, Eisenberg, and Meyer 2004, 48). To accomplish these purposes, the government uses **public policy** or "authoritative decisions made in the legislative, executive, or judicial branches of government that are intended to direct or influence the actions, behaviors, or decisions of others" (Longest 2010, 5). Some of these public policies are considered **health policies** because they "pertain to health or influence the pursuit of health" (Longest 2010, 6). Health policies are crafted to influence health determinants, which in turn influence health. The ACA (US Department of Health and Human Services [HHS] 2015) was the most significant legislation resulting from public health policy since enactment of the Medicare and Medicaid programs in 1965.

health policies
policies that "pertain to health or influence the pursuit of health" (Longest 2010, 6)

However, the federal government's influence extends beyond the ACA. In 2011, the HHS published *National Strategy for Quality Improvement in Health Care*. This document outlined the National Quality Strategy, a road map for achieving affordability, better care, and healthy people and communities. The recommendations in this document affect all healthcare stakeholders—patients; providers; employers; health insurance companies; academic researchers; and local, state, and federal governments (HHS 2011). Each year, the road map is reviewed and revised as needed to reflect current priorities and performance results (Agency for Healthcare Research and Quality [AHRQ] 2016b).

The three broad aims of *National Strategy for Quality Improvement in Health Care* guide the local, state, and national efforts to improve health and the quality of healthcare. These aims include the following (AHRQ 2014):

- *Better care.* Improve overall quality by making healthcare more patient-centered, reliable, accessible, and safe.
- *Healthy people/healthy communities.* Improve the health of the US population by supporting proven interventions to address behavioral, social, and environmental determinants of health in addition to delivering higher-quality care.
- *Affordable care.* Reduce the cost of quality healthcare for individuals, families, employers, and the government.

The many legislative, regulatory, and reimbursement changes necessary to support the National Quality Strategy are affecting quality management at the provider level. Two notable changes came from federal legislation passed before the National Quality Strategy. The Health Information Technology for Economic and Clinical Health Act, enacted as part of the American Recovery and Reinvestment Act of 2009, promoted the adoption and meaningful use of health information technology (Jha 2012). This legislation has influenced the transition to electronic health records to improve the quality and safety of the healthcare system. The large federal subsidies for adopting this technology and financial disincentives have made the conversion from paper to electronic records possible in many organizations.

The ACA may also support the National Quality Strategy by encouraging healthcare organizations to form **accountable care organizations (ACOs)** to bring about efficiencies in consumption of services while lowering overall costs. An ACO is a network of providers (primarily doctors and hospitals) that share financial and medical responsibilities for providing coordinated care to patients in hopes of limiting unnecessary spending (Gold 2015).

Knowledge Acquisition

Public policy at the federal level creates formal structures and mechanisms for acquiring new knowledge so that public and private policymakers may make informed, evidence-based decisions about health quality practices. For example,

accountable care organization (ACO) a network of providers (primarily doctors and hospitals) that share financial and medical responsibilities for providing coordinated care to patients in hopes of limiting unnecessary spending (Gold 2015)

the AHRQ sponsors and conducts research and disseminates information to advance healthcare quality (see exhibit 2.2).

Another example is the Innovation Center at CMS (2016a), which the ACA created "for the purpose of testing innovative payment and service delivery models to reduce program expenditures . . . while preserving or enhancing the quality of care for those individuals who receive Medicare, Medicaid, or Children's Health Insurance Program (CHIP) benefits." Best practices and lessons learned from these tests are made available to all healthcare organizations to support quality improvement throughout the healthcare system at large. Several of the innovation models being tested have the potential to greatly affect quality and safety improvement activities at the provider level (see exhibit 2.3).

One initiative of the CMS Innovation Center is a nationwide public–private collaboration called Hospital Engagement Networks (HEN). These networks work at the regional, state, national, or hospital-system level to help identify solutions already working and disseminate them to other hospitals and providers. Initially, the CMS Innovation Center formed 26 HENs in 2012 as part of a campaign to reduce harm and improve the quality and safety of healthcare. Many of these networks were successful at achieving this goal. For instance, the 127 hospitals participating in the Iowa-based HEN prevented potential harm to more than 4,300 patients in 2013 and reduced healthcare costs by more than $51 million according to data released by the Iowa Healthcare Collaborative (Iowa Hospital Association 2014), which administers

---

EXHIBIT 2.2

Agency for Healthcare Research and Quality

Mission. To support research designed to improve the quality, safety, efficiency, and effectiveness of healthcare for all Americans. The research sponsored, conducted, and disseminated by AHRQ provides information that helps people make better decisions about healthcare.

Created. The agency was founded in December 1989 as the Agency for Health Care Policy and Research, a public health service agency in the HHS. Reporting to the HHS secretary, the agency was reauthorized on December 6, 1999, as the Agency for Healthcare Research and Quality. Sister agencies include the National Institutes of Health, the Centers for Disease Control and Prevention, the Food and Drug Administration, the Centers for Medicare & Medicaid Services, and the Health Resources and Services Administration.

Main functions. AHRQ sponsors and conducts research that provides evidence-based information on healthcare outcomes; quality; and cost, use, and access. The information helps healthcare decision makers—patients and clinicians, health system leaders, purchasers, and policymakers—make more informed decisions and improve the quality of healthcare services.

Source: Adapted from AHRQ (2016a).

Accountable care. Accountable care organizations and similar care models are designed to incentivize healthcare providers to become accountable for a patient population and to invest in infrastructure and redesigned care processes that provide for coordinated care, high quality, and efficient service delivery.

Episode-based payment initiatives. Under these models, healthcare providers are held accountable for the cost and quality of care that beneficiaries receive during an episode of care, which usually begins with a triggering healthcare event (such as a hospitalization or chemotherapy administration) and extends for a limited time thereafter.

Primary care transformation. Primary care providers are a key point of contact for patients' healthcare needs. Strengthening and increasing access to primary care is critical to promoting health and reducing overall healthcare costs. Advanced primary care practices—also called *medical homes*—use a team-based approach while emphasizing prevention, health information technology, care coordination, and shared decision making among patients and their providers.

Initiatives focused on Medicaid and CHIP populations. Medicaid and CHIP are administered by the states but are jointly funded by the federal government and the states. Initiatives in this category are administered by the participating states.

Initiatives focused on Medicare and Medicaid enrollees. The Medicare and Medicaid programs were designed with distinct purposes. Individuals enrolled in both Medicare and Medicaid (called *dual eligibles*) account for a disproportionate share of the programs' expenditures. A fully integrated, person-centered system of care that ensures all enrollees' needs are met could better serve this population in a high-quality, cost-effective manner.

Initiatives to accelerate the development and testing of new models. Many innovations necessary to improving the healthcare system will come from local communities and healthcare leaders from across the country. By partnering with these local and regional stakeholders, CMS can help accelerate the testing of models today that may be the next breakthrough tomorrow.

Initiatives to speed the adoption of best practices. Recent studies indicate that it takes nearly 17 years, on average, before best practices (practices backed by research) are incorporated into widespread clinical practice—and even then the application of the knowledge is very uneven. The CMS Innovation Center is partnering with a broad range of healthcare providers, federal agencies, professional societies, and other experts and stakeholders to test new models for disseminating evidence-based best practices and significantly increasing the speed of adoption.

EXHIBIT 2.3

Categories of New Payment and Service Delivery Models Being Tested by the CMS Innovation Center

Source: Data from CMS (2016b).

the network. To sustain this national progress and momentum, in 2015 CMS awarded a second round of contracts to 17 HENs, which include more than 3,200 hospitals (CMS 2015a).

CMS also promotes local implementation of quality practices through its network of Quality Improvement Organizations (QIOs). The Medicare QIO Program (formerly referred to as the Medicare Utilization and Quality Control Peer Review Program) was created by statute in 1982 to improve quality and efficiency of services delivered to Medicare beneficiaries (Leavitt 2006, 2). Today, the QIO Program comprises 14 regional Quality Innovation Networks designed to "bring Medicare beneficiaries, providers, and communities together in data-driven initiatives that increase patient safety, make communities healthier, better coordinate post-hospital care, and improve clinical quality" (Quality Improvement Organizations 2016).

Transparency

Transparency is a vital component of an efficient and effective healthcare system, as it fosters improved management of the cost and quality of health services (Wetzel 2014). In 1987, an unprecedented effort at nationwide healthcare performance transparency occurred when the Health Care Financing Agency (HCFA), now known as CMS, produced its first annual report of "observed hospital-specific mortality rates for Medicare acute care hospitals" (Cleves and Golden 1996, 40). The goal of this HCFA transparency initiative was to produce "better information to guide the decisions of physicians, patients, and the agency, thus improving outcomes and the quality of care" (Roper et al. 1988, 1198).

This initial transparency strategy set the stage for using federal policy to systematically develop and implement expectations, requirements, methodology, and infrastructure to collect, publish, and disseminate performance data measuring beneficiaries' quality of care. The mortality data reports were discontinued in 1994 and the focus turned to gathering and reporting performance data for high-volume, high-cost clinical conditions and patient experiences.

The specific performance data that healthcare organizations are required to report to CMS change each year. Many of the organization-specific quality performance data currently being reported can be found on the Medicare website (www.medicare.gov). In addition to quality measures for hospitals, the public has access to performance data for nursing homes, home health providers, and dialysis facilities. Making performance results more transparent—enabling stakeholders to assess healthcare quality and compare providers—is intended to encourage healthcare organizations to take steps toward improving health services. Refer to the web resources box for more information about these measurement and reporting initiatives.

Financial Incentives

The inpatient prospective payment system (IPPS) implemented by CMS in the 1980s focused on containing the increasing costs of hospital care. The next phase of financial incentives is focusing on improving the **value** of health services. Value is the ratio of quality to cost (value = quality/cost). Section 5001(c) of Deficit Reduction Act of 2005 required CMS to identify conditions that "could reasonably have been prevented through the application of evidence-based guidelines" (CMS 2015b). As of October 1, 2008, CMS denied additional payment for these **hospital-acquired conditions** (HACs), also known as **never events**, when patients developed one during a hospital stay (CMS 2015b). For example, when a patient got a HAC, such as a surgical-site infection following coronary artery bypass graft, the hospital would be paid as though this infection were not present.

To understand how CMS has refocused the IPPS on value, consider the historical role of clinical complications and hospital payment. If a surgical sponge was accidently left inside the patient after surgery and the patient required another surgery to remove it, both surgeries were billed to the payer. The HAC financial incentive in the IPPS was designed to ensure that CMS would not pay for complications that should not have occurred in the first place. In addition, it was intended to encourage hospitals to adopt evidence-based practices to prevent never events from occurring.

To date, the success of this approach to financially incentivizing hospital quality improvements has been mixed. Waters and colleagues (2015) studied the association between Medicare's nonpayment policy and four of the more common HACs: central line–associated bloodstream infections (CLABSIs), catheter-associated urinary tract infections (CAUTIs), hospital-acquired pressure ulcers (HAPUs), and injurious inpatient falls. "Medicare's nonpayment policy was associated with an 11% reduction in the rate of change in CLABSIs . . . and a 10% reduction in the rate of change in CAUTIs, but was not associated with a significant change in injurious falls . . . or HAPUs" (Waters et al. 2015, 347). The authors concluded that reductions in the rates of CLABSI and CAUTI resulted from implementation of better hospital processes, whereas little evidence exists that changing hospital processes can lead to reductions in HAPUs or injurious inpatient falls (Waters et al. 2015).

A continued focus on value is the theme of contemporary healthcare quality policy at the federal level. The Medicare Access and CHIP Reauthorization Act of 2015 introduced two value-based payment models for physicians that have an impact on quality management: a Merit-Based Incentive Payment System and alternative payment models. These value-based payment models are intended to strengthen the relationship between physician payment and quality practices such as efficient use of healthcare resources and clinical improvements. These changes to the Medicare payment system for physicians

value
the ratio of quality to cost (value = quality/cost)

hospital-acquired conditions (or never events)
medical conditions that "could reasonably have been prevented through the application of evidence-based guidelines" (CMS 2015b)

are not expected to be implemented for several years. It will be essential for physicians and healthcare facilities to understand how these payment models work so they can determine how and where to focus a systems approach to improving performance (Bassett 2016).

Private Health Policies and Oversight

Accreditation bodies are private, nongovernmental groups with policies and standards that encourage healthcare quality and safety improvement. Accreditation is voluntary, which means that, unlike public policies and oversight, healthcare organizations can choose whether to comply with an accreditation group's private policies and be subject to its oversight.

The Joint Commission is a nongovernmental accreditation organization for several types of health services organizations: ambulatory care, behavioral health care, critical access, home care, hospitals, laboratory services, nursing care, and office-based surgery. The Joint Commission also offers certification for disease-specific services for conditions such as chronic kidney disease and stroke and for programs such as palliative and perinatal care and primary care medical homes. For more information, see its website at www.jointcommission.org.

The National Committee for Quality Assurance (NCQA) offers accreditation programs for health plans and related organizations and programs such as wellness and health promotion and disease management. The NCQA also offers a variety of certifications; for a fuller description, see www.ncqa.org.

The national Public Health Voluntary Accreditation Board was established to "improve and protect the health of the public by advancing the quality and performance of Tribal, state, local, and territorial public health departments" (Public Health Accreditation Board 2016). Additional accreditation organizations are listed in the web resources box.

Organizations seeking CMS approval to participate in federally funded insurance programs such as Medicare and Medicaid may undergo state surveys on behalf of CMS or be surveyed by an accrediting body approved by CMS. Some private accreditation groups such as The Joint Commission, DNV GL, the Healthcare Facilities Accreditation Program, and the Institute for Medical Quality have been granted *deemed authority* by CMS. An organization accredited by one of these groups "would have 'deemed status' and would not be subject to the Medicare survey and certification process because it has already been surveyed by the accrediting organization" (American Society for Healthcare Engineering 2016). Because of this private–public relationship, the policies and standards of accreditation organizations with deeming authority necessarily support and, in many instances, parallel the federal regulations governing the healthcare organizations they accredit.

Knowledge Acquisition

Accreditation bodies, like public agencies, work to identify and disseminate best practices that support healthcare quality and safety improvements. For example, since 1996, accredited facilities have been encouraged to report sentinel events to The Joint Commission. A **sentinel event** is a patient safety event that affects a patient and results in death, permanent harm, or severe temporary harm and intervention required to sustain life (Joint Commission 2016). "Reporting of the event enables 'lessons learned' from the event to be added to The Joint Commission's Sentinel Event Database, thereby contributing to the general knowledge about sentinel events and to the reduction of risk for such events" (Joint Commission 2016). As of June 2016, The Joint Commission had published 56 sentinel event alerts describing process changes healthcare organizations can make to improve prevention.

> **sentinel event**
> a patient safety event that affects a patient and results in death, permanent harm, or severe temporary harm and intervention required to sustain life (Joint Commission 2016)

Knowledge sharing is common practice in other accreditation and certification bodies. For example, more than 1,500 cancer care programs accredited by the Commission on Cancer report data to the National Cancer Database (NCDB). Data in the NCDB, jointly sponsored by the American College of Surgeons and the American Cancer Society, are used to analyze and track patients with malignant neoplastic diseases, their treatments, and their outcomes (American College of Surgeons 2016). This information is available to healthcare organizations to encourage the spread of cancer care best practices.

Laboratories accredited by the College of American Pathologists offer complimentary online access to resource guides that present new and evolving technologies in pathology and assist pathologists with ways to better understand, evaluate, and implement these technologies into their practices. For more information, see the group's website at www.cap.org.

Transparency

Since 2002, healthcare organizations accredited by The Joint Commission have been required to gather and report data for various performance measures. In 2002, hospitals reported data for eight measures of care provided for patients with heart failure, pneumonia, and myocardial infarction. By 2014, hospitals reported data for up to 49 different measures of disease-specific care as well as surgical care, venous thrombosis, and immunization care (Baker and Chassin 2016).

The Joint Commission's performance measure project is intended to assist facilities in identifying important quality gaps and help them improve their care (Baker and Chassin 2016). This aim is achieved, in part, by making facility-specific data and comparative state and national data for various measures publicly available on The Joint Commission's Quality Check website (www.qualitycheck.org). Several performance improvements have resulted from The Joint Commission's transparent quality measurement efforts, including reduction of medically unnecessary early elective deliveries from 13.6 percent in 2011 to 3.3 percent in 2014 (Joint Commission 2015).

Financial Incentives

Private accrediting bodies lack the authority to impose financial incentives on healthcare organizations to influence quality improvements. However, private sector health plans and business groups are encouraging payment strategies similar to those being advanced by CMS in order to improve the value of healthcare services.

Summary

This chapter discusses the role of quality oversight organizations and introduces public and private groups whose policies and initiatives target system change. These initiatives fall into three areas: knowledge acquisition, transparency, and financial incentives. Because of the dynamic and rapidly changing nature of healthcare quality policy, both public and private, readers are encouraged to review the accompanying Internet resources as a means to keep current on changes, new initiatives, and plans for the future.

Exercise 2.1

Objective: To become familiar with the current CMS quality initiatives and how they support the National Quality Strategy and organizational performance improvement.

Instructions:

- Based on your work setting or an area of interest, select and explore one of the CMS quality initiatives (e.g., hospitals, home health, nursing home, end-stage renal disease) at www.cms.gov/center/quality.asp and review the current National Quality Strategy report (www.ahrq.gov/workingforquality).
- In two or three paragraphs, answer the following questions in reference to the quality initiative you selected:
  a. What does the CMS quality initiative include? Describe the initiative and its relationship to the National Quality Strategy.
  b. How can the data publicly available on the compare site for the quality initiative benefit a healthcare organization? Describe how the measurement data can be used in the setting you are interested in to improve performance.

Exercise 2.2

Objective: To become familiar with the current quality measurement initiatives of The Joint Commission.

Instructions: Explore the current ORYX performance measures of The Joint Commission (www.jointcommission.org/performance_measurement.aspx). For each measure, describe which system or systems in your chosen setting will be improved by the use of the measure.

Companion Readings

Callender, A. N., D. A. Hastings, M. C. Hemsley, L. Morris, and M. W. Peregrine. 2007. *Corporate Responsibility and Health Care Quality: A Resource for Health Care Boards of Directors.* US Department of Health and Human Services Office of Inspector General and American Health Lawyers Association. Published September 13. http://oig.hhs.gov/fraud/docs/complianceguidance/CorporateResponsibilityFinal%209-4-07.pdf.

Chassin, M. A., J. M. Loeb, S. P. Schmaltz, and R. M. Wachter. 2010. "Accountability Measures—Using Measurement to Promote Quality Improvement." *New England Journal of Medicine* 363 (7): 683–88.

Commonwealth Fund. 2013. "Better Care at Lower Cost: Is It Possible?" Published November 21. www.commonwealthfund.org/publications/health-reform-and-you/better-care-at-lower-cost.

Partnership for Sustainable Health. 2013. *Strengthening Affordability and Quality in America's Health Care System.* Robert Wood Johnson Foundation. Published April. www.rwjf.org/content/dam/farm/reports/reports/2013/rwjf405432.

Skyve, P. M. 2009. *Leadership in Healthcare Organizations: A Guide to Joint Commission Leadership Standards.* Governance Institute. Published Winter. www.jointcommission.org/leadership_in_healthcare_organizations.

Web Resources

Accreditation

Accreditation Association for Ambulatory Health Care (AAAHC): www.aaahc.org

Accreditation Commission for Education in Nursing (ACEN): www.acenursing.org

(continued)

Accreditation Council for Graduate Medical Education (ACGME): www.acgme.org

Accreditation Council for Pharmacy Education (ACPE): www.acpe-accredit.org/

Center for Improvement in Healthcare Quality (CIHQ): http://cihq.org

College of American Pathologists (CAP): www.cap.org

Commission on Accreditation of Rehabilitation Facilities (CARF): www.carf.org

Commission on Cancer: www.facs.org/quality-programs/cancer/coc

Commission on Collegiate Nursing Education (CCNE): www.aacn.nche.edu/Accreditation/index.htm

Community Health Accreditation Program (CHAP): www.chapinc.org

DNV GL: http://dnvglhealthcare.com

Healthcare Facilities Accreditation Program (HFAP): www.hfap.org

Institute for Medical Quality: www.imq.org

The Joint Commission: www.jointcommission.org

National Committee for Quality Assurance (NCQA): www.ncqa.org

National Public Health Performance Standards Program (NPHPSP): www.cdc.gov/od/ocphp/nphpsp/index.htm

Public Health Accreditation Board (PHAB): www.phaboard.org

URAC (formerly the Utilization Review Accreditation Commission): www.urac.org

Reports

CMS Quality of Care Center (with links to compare websites): www.cms.gov/center/quality.asp

The Joint Commission Quality Check: www.qualitycheck.org

National Cancer Databases: www.facs.org/quality%20programs/cancer/ncdb

Federal Policymakers

CMS Innovation Center: https://innovation.cms.gov

CMS Partnership for Patients: https://partnershipforpatients.cms.gov

CMS Quality Improvement Programs: www.qioprogram.org

National Quality Strategy: www.ahrq.gov/workingforquality

Patient Protection and Affordable Care Act of 2010: www.hhs.gov/healthcare

US Department of Health and Human Services, priority goals and objectives: www.performance.gov/agency/department-health-and-human-services

References

Agency for Healthcare Research and Quality (AHRQ). 2016a. "About AHRQ." Reviewed March. www.ahrq.gov/cpi/about/index.html.

———. 2016b. "NQS Reports and Annual Updates." Accessed June 25. www.ahrq.gov/workingforquality/reports.htm.

———. 2014. "The National Quality Strategy: Fact Sheet." Revised September. www.ahrq.gov/workingforquality/nqs/nqsfactsheet.htm.

American College of Surgeons. 2016. "National Cancer Database." Retrieved June 27. www.facs.org/quality-programs/cancer/ncdb.

American Society for Healthcare Engineering. 2016. "Deemed Status." Retrieved June 25. www.ashe.org/advocacy/orgs/deemedstatus.shtml.

Baker, D. W., and M. R. Chassin. 2016. "Measuring and Improving Quality." *Journal of the American Medical Association* 315 (24): 27–33.

Bassett, M. 2016. "MACRA, MIPS: Slated to Make an M-pressive Impact." *For the Record*, May, 17–19.

Centers for Medicare & Medicaid Services (CMS). 2016a. "About the CMS Innovation Center." US Department of Health and Human Services. Updated July 8. https://innovation.cms.gov/about/index.html.

———. 2016b. "Innovation Models." Retrieved June 26. https://innovation.cms.gov/initiatives.

———. 2015a. "Hospital-Acquired Conditions." Last modified August 19. www.cms.gov/medicare/medicare-fee-for-service-payment/hospitalacqcond/hospital-acquired_conditions.html.

———. 2015b. "Partnership for Patients and Hospital Engagement Networks: Continuing Forward Momentum on Reducing Patient Harm." Published September 25. www.cms.gov/Newsroom/MediaReleaseDatabase/Fact-sheets/2015-Fact-sheets-items/2015-09-25.html.

Cleves, M. A., and W. E. Golden. 1996. "Assessment of HCFA's 1992 Medicare Hospital Information Report of Mortality Following Admission for Hip Arthroplasty." *Health Services Research* 31 (1): 39–48.

Donabedian, A. 1980. *Explorations in Quality Assessment and Monitoring*. Vol. 1 in *The Definition of Quality and Approaches to Its Assessment*. Chicago: Health Administration Press.

Gold, J. 2015. "Accountable Care Organizations, Explained." *Kaiser Health News*. Published September 14. http://khn.org/news/aco-accountable-care-organization-faq.

Iowa Hospital Association. 2014. "Iowa Initiative Reduces Medical Errors, Saves $51M." Published February 25. http://blog.iowahospital.org/2014/02/25/iowa-initiative-reduces-medical-errors-saves-51m/.

Jha, A. K. 2012. "Health Information Technology Comes of Age." *Archives of Internal Medicine* 172 (9): 737–38.

Joint Commission. 2016. "Sentinel Event Policy and Procedures." Published January 6. www.jointcommission.org/sentinel_event_policy_and_procedures.

———. 2015. *America's Hospitals: Improving Quality and Safety: The Joint Commission's Annual Report.* Retrieved June 27. www.jointcommission.org/assets/1/18/TJC_Annual_Report_2015_EMBARGOED_11_9_15.pdf.

Leavitt, M. O. 2006. *Report to Congress: Improving the Medicare Quality Improvement Organization Program—Response to the Institute of Medicine Study.* Retrieved June 25, 2016. www.cms.gov/QualityImprovementOrgs/downloads/QIO_Improvement_RTC_fnl.pdf.

Longest, B. B. 2010. *Health Policymaking in the United States,* 5th ed. Chicago: Health Administration Press.

President's Advisory Committee on Consumer Protection and Quality in the Health Care Industry. 1998. "Quality First: Better Health Care for All Americans." US Department of Health and Human Services. Revised July 18. http://archive.ahrq.gov/hcqual/final.

Public Health Accreditation Board. 2016. "What Is Accreditation?" Accessed June 26. www.phaboard.org/accreditation-overview/what-is-accreditation.

Quality Improvement Organizations. 2016. "About QINs-QIOs." Retrieved June 27. www.qioprogram.org/about/why-cms-has-qios.

Rooney, A. L., and P. R. van Ostenburg. 1999. *Licensure, Accreditation, and Certification: Approaches to Health Service Quality.* USAID Quality Assurance Project. Published April. www.usaidassist.org/sites/assist/files/accredmon.pdf.

Roper, W. L., W. Winkenwerder, G. M. Hackbarth, and H. Krakauer. 1988. "Effectiveness in Health Care: An Initiative to Evaluate and Improve Medical Practice." *New England Journal of Medicine* 319 (18): 1197–202.

Smits, H., A. Supachutikul, and K. S. Mate. 2014. "Hospital Accreditation: Lessons from Low- and Middle-Income Countries." *Globalization and Health* 10: 65.

Tang, N., J. M. Eisenberg, and G. S. Meyer. 2004. "The Roles of Government in Improving Health Care Quality and Safety." *Joint Commission Journal on Quality and Safety* 30 (4): 47–55.

US Department of Health and Human Services (HHS). 2015. "Read the Law" HHS.gov. Reviewed August 28. www.hhs.gov/healthcare/about-the-law/read-the-law.

———. 2011. *National Strategy for Quality Improvement in Health Care.* Published March. www.ahrq.gov/workingforquality/nqs/nqs2011annlrpt.pdf.

Waters, T. M., M. J. Daniels, G. J. Bazzoli, E. Perencevich, N. Dunton, V. S. Staggs, C. Potter, N. Fareed, M. Liu, and R. I. Shorr. 2015. "Effect of Medicare's Nonpayment for Hospital-Acquired Conditions: Lessons for Future Policy." *Journal of the American Medical Association: Internal Medicine* 175 (3): 347–54.

Wetzel, S. 2014. *Transparency: A Needed Step Towards Health Care Affordability.* American Health Policy Institute. Published March. www.americanhealthpolicy.org/Content/documents/resources/Transparency%20Study%201%20-%20The%20Need%20for%20Health%20Care%20Transparency.pdf.

CHARACTERISTICS OF COMPLEX SYSTEMS

Learning Objectives

After completing this chapter, you should be able to

- discuss how a systems perspective can explain recurrent organizational problems,
- recognize different types of systems and the role of systems thinking,
- describe system characteristics that contribute to dynamic complexity, and
- explain the influence of dynamic complexity on managerial decision making.

As people accumulate years of experience in the healthcare field, they begin to see recurring problems—sometimes in an individual organization and sometimes across the entire field. Problems thought to be solved by one manager may come back at a later time for a different manager. The vice president of nursing at a large hospital may centralize and cross-train nurse educator positions to meet necessary budget cuts for the year; three years later, the new vice president of nursing at the same hospital adds unit-based nurse educator positions to address the unmet clinical orientation needs of its new hires. Consider the following situation (Georgopoulos and Mann 1962, 549–51):

> The hospital faces a number of problems concerning the nursing staff . . . one major problem is . . . attracting and retaining a sufficient professional nursing staff, especially non-supervisory nursing staff. . . . The problem lies in the fact that the number of professional nurses being trained in nursing schools is much too low to meet an ever increasing demand for professional nurses by hospitals and other sources. . . . Being understaffed, hospitals often assign to the professional nurse a rather heavy workload that is not seen as normal or reasonable by many nurses. . . . Another important problem . . . involves the composition of the total nursing staff, the question of optimum balance in the proportions of staff members who are registered nurses, practical nurses, and aides.

Although this situation may appear to address a manager's current challenges with nursing shortages, the excerpt was taken from the book *The Community General Hospital*, which was published in 1962! During the more than 50 years since that book was written, health services organizations seem to have made little headway in issues related to workforce planning and management. Nursing shortages, for example, appeared and disappeared in waves in the 1960s, 1970s, 1980s, early 1990s, and again in the early decades of the twenty-first century. Worker shortages are not limited to nursing. In the 2013 AMN Clinical Workforce Survey, 78 percent of hospital executives report a physician shortage, 66 percent a shortage of nurses, 50 percent shortages of nurse practitioners and physician assistants, and 43 percent a shortage of allied healthcare professionals (AMN Healthcare 2013).

The projected supply of healthcare workers will not meet the demand associated with future population growth and aging (Anderson 2014). Compounding this problem, the Affordable Care Act of 2010 has flooded the already-strained healthcare delivery system with newly insured patients. Individuals are facing longer wait times to see physicians, difficulties accessing specialty care, reduced appointment duration, inadequate services, and overall frustration as a result of workforce shortages. Being short-staffed requires careful management of an organization's healthcare resources. For example, the lack of experienced registered nurses is causing acute care facilities, such as the Rapid City Regional Hospital in South Dakota, to adjust the number of available beds every day on the basis of the number of nurses available for each shift (Grant 2016).

Regardless of how healthcare systems might change in the future, one constant remains. Organizations still need people on the front lines of healthcare delivery—physicians, nurses, advanced practitioners, and allied health professionals. As healthcare delivery systems become more complex, organizations without a sufficient number of skilled and dedicated workers will find it difficult to achieve quality goals.

Why do budget problems and workforce shortages remain nagging issues for health services managers? The reasons lie in the complex nature of healthcare, healthcare organizations, and the healthcare field. In healthcare, as in other sectors, "systems thinking is needed more than ever because we are being overwhelmed with complexity" (Senge 1990, 69). Today, one may rephrase Senge's 1990 comment to read, "Systems thinking is imperative in health services organizations because they are much more complex than they were in 1990."

complex
having a large number of variables that interact with each other in innumerable, and often unpredictable, ways

In healthcare systems, the term **complex** refers to the presence of a large number of variables that interact with each other in countless and often unpredictable ways. Considering the multiple determinants of health and the vast number of components composing health services organizations, the possible interactions are mind-boggling. Health and health services organizations are also characterized by situations in which "cause and effect are subtle, and where the effects over time of interventions are not obvious" (Senge 2006, 71). This characteristic represents another type of complexity, known as **dynamic complexity**. In the presence of dynamic complexity, "the same action has dramatically different effects in the short run and the long run . . . an action has one set of consequences locally and a very different set of consequences in another part of the system . . . and obvious interventions produce nonobvious consequences" (Senge 2006, 71).

When faced with dynamic complexity, managers must select interventions that alter the fundamental behavior of the system that is causing the problem; otherwise, the solution is only temporary. As seen in the nursing shortage example, although interventions may offer temporary relief, the problems resurface again and again.

The starting point for altering fundamental system behavior is always a mystery. Every system improvement we now know as being successful started out as a puzzle in which the variables that mattered were unknown and the cause-and-effect relationships unclear (Martin 2013). Once relevant variables are understood, cause-and-effect relationships can be defined and managed. With study, the mysteries of the dynamic complexities in healthcare systems are becoming clearer. The relevant variables are still not entirely understood and subtleties of the cause-and-effect relationships have yet to be unraveled, but we are not at the mystery stage. This chapter introduces a systems perspective on quality management that is based on the concepts of systems thinking and dynamic complexity.

Systems Thinking

Just as there are a variety of perspectives surrounding the term *quality*, the term *system* brings with it numerous connotations and perceptions. While "system change" is often heard in the quality and safety discourse, "system" may be defined and perceived in a variety of ways. In this book, **system** refers to "a set of connected parts that fit together to achieve a purpose" (Langabeer and Helton 2016, 477).

A healthcare system contains a complex variety of interdependent organizations, as illustrated by the diagram of the public health system in exhibit 3.1. Such a **megasystem** of connected parts is necessary for the purpose of advancing the vision of healthy communities (Institute of Medicine 1996). The importance of understanding these megasystems as interrelated parts of a whole cannot be overstated.

dynamic complexity
complexity in which "cause and effect are subtle, and where the effects over time of interventions are not obvious" (Senge 2006, 71)

system
"a set of connected parts that fit together to achieve a purpose" (Langabeer and Helton 2016, 477)

megasystem
a complex variety of interdependent organizations

EXHIBIT 3.1
The Public
Health System

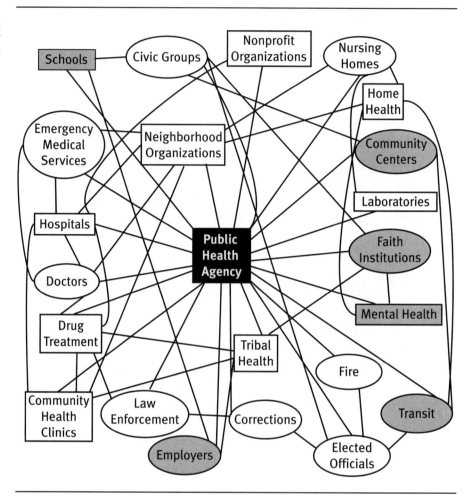

Source: Data from Centers for Disease Control and Prevention (2014).

macrosystems
organizations
providing health
services, such as
hospitals, nursing
homes, community
health clinics,
and emergency
medical services

microsystems
"people, machines,
and data at the
level of direct
patient care (the
treatment team
within the hospital
or the physician
office practice, for
example)" (Schyve
2005, 2)

In the public health system are many macrosystems that provide input to the larger system. **Macrosystems** are the organizations providing health services, such as hospitals, nursing homes, community health clinics, and emergency medical services. These macrosystems are "connected via individuals and teams, regulations and rules, and technology" (Johnson, Miller, and Horowitz 2008, 3). The many health organization mergers, partnerships, and affiliations following passage of the 2010 Affordable Care Act have created a number of regional healthcare delivery systems comprising multiple macrosystems (PricewaterhouseCoopers 2016).

In each macrosystem are innumerable microsystems. **Microsystems** are made up of the "people, machines, and data at the level of direct patient care (the treatment team within the hospital or the physician office practice, for example)" (Schyve 2005, 2). Just like the parts of a macrosystem, the parts of a microsystem interact with each other to form an interdependent whole. During research into the frontline clinical teams in various healthcare settings, Godfrey, Nelson, and Batalden (2004, 5) coined the phrase **clinical microsystem** to describe "a small group of people who work together on a regular basis to provide care to discrete subpopulations of patients." These clinical microsystems are "the place where patients, families, and care teams meet. . . . They are living units that change over time and always have a patient (person with a health need) at their center" (Microsystem Academy 2016).

> **clinical microsystem** a "small group of people who work together on a regular basis to provide care to discrete subpopulations of patients" (Godfrey, Nelson, and Batalden 2004, 5)

An example of a microsystem (or clinical microsystem, as some would call it) is the team of people working in the cardiac catheterization lab during a coronary angiography procedure. This team often consists of a cardiologist, one or more nurses monitoring the patient's vital signs, a scrub nurse and a circulating nurse, an X-ray technician, and one or more nurses or cardiovascular invasive specialists assisting with recording and other duties. These people have different responsibilities, yet the angiography procedure cannot get done without each of them working interactively with other team members.

A system reflects the whole, and "**systems thinking** is a view of reality that emphasizes the relationships and interactions of each part of the system to all the other parts" (McLaughlin and Olson 2012, 39). Rather than considering each part of the system to be unique and separate, systems thinking acknowledges the infinite number of unique parts and the ways in which the parts interact, as well as the nature of the interactions. Recognizing how each part functions within the system as a whole and how an individual's actions affect all other aspects of the system is vital to unlocking the power of systems thinking.

> **systems thinking** "a view of reality that emphasizes the relationships and interactions of each part of the system to all the other parts" (McLaughlin and Olson 2012, 39)

The importance of developing a clear understanding of the parts of a system and how they interact is illustrated by the ancient parable from India about the blind men and the elephant. There are many versions of this story; however, the common denominator is that each man feels a different part of the animal, and only that part, to learn what an elephant is. When the men compare their understandings of an elephant, they are in complete disagreement. This parable demonstrates what can happen when people have distinctly different perceptions about the same system. In these situations, identifying relationships between the elements and understanding how they are connected is more challenging.

Dynamic Complexity

Several system characteristics contribute to the presence of dynamic complexity (Sterman 2000). Five characteristics, predominant in healthcare and health services organizations, are described in this section: change, trade-offs, history dependency, tight coupling, and nonlinearity (see exhibit 3.2).

Change

Systems are dynamic—that is, constantly changing. Change occurs at different rates and scales within and among systems, especially in healthcare. Consider three levels of this characteristic of dynamic complexity in health services. First, the human body changes continuously. This fact means that key inputs (patients with a clinical problem) to and outputs (patients' status after clinical intervention) of healthcare systems are moving targets. Second, the organizational contexts in which health services are carried out are dynamic in nature. Employees move in and out of organizations, research provides an ongoing stream of new evidence, and technological advances offer new clinical and management approaches. Third, the communities and political environments in which we live and in which healthcare organizations operate change—that is, the environment changes with economic cycles, political ideologies, and election cycles. Unlike other complex systems, such as aviation, the level of change and the degree of uncertainty that characterizes many of the problems faced by practitioners make healthcare a particularly hazardous complex system (Runciman, Merry, and Walton 2007).

Implications for Healthcare Managers

From the day a person is born to the day she dies, she is in a constant state of change, growing and developing physiologically and emotionally. No two

EXHIBIT 3.2
System Characteristics Contributing to Dynamic Complexity

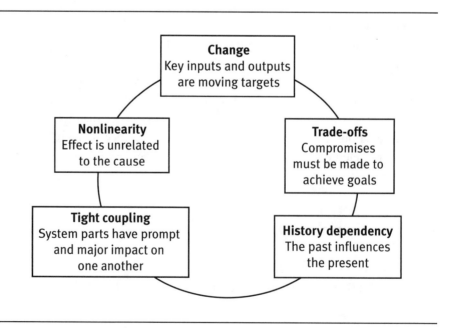

human systems are alike or precisely predictable in their responses to a medical intervention. As a result, functions that may seem straightforward in other industries, such as product standardization, become more difficult for healthcare managers. For example, the practice of using a standardized list of drug names and brands (i.e., a hospital formulary) to reduce medication expenses is accepted practice. However, when the dynamic nature of patient physiology is introduced, the manager recognizes that in addition to the question, "What are the set of drug names and brands that will be most cost-effective?" he also needs to ask, "How should the approved drugs be selected, and what are the consequences to patients?"

To aid in grasping the subtle but important nuances involved in individualizing treatment plans, consider the process of trying on a pair of blue jeans. People have their own favorite brand of blue jeans that fit well, even though another brand may be advertised as having a similar size and style. The hospital formulary essentially dictates to doctors that the patient may buy only slim-cut size 10 jeans and not relaxed-fit size 10 jeans (Kelly and Pestotnik 1998). Studies on variations in genetic makeup and the nature of gene–environment interactions promise to shed light in yet unimaginable ways on why certain treatments or medications may work better for one person than another. The emerging field of **pharmacogenomics** may permit drug selection in the future to be based on an individual's unique genetic makeup, altering the paradigm on which health services organizations manage **pharmacotherapeutics** (Medline Plus and Merriam-Webster 2016). Preemptive medicine—"removing the initial molecular event—precluding the possibility of that thing even happening" (Culliton 2006, W96)—will likely alter the fundamental role of healthcare delivery organizations in the future.

Trade-Offs

The need to understand the nature of trade-offs may seem unnecessary for managers taught to weigh pros versus cons or opportunities versus risks as they consider organizational decision options. Trade-offs may be seen as an accepted attribute of management situations. However, an understanding of dynamic complexity fosters an appreciation for the system consequences of local management trade-off decisions. "Time delays in feedback channels mean the long-run response of a system to an intervention is often different from its short-run response. High leverage policies often cause worse-before-better behavior, while low leverage policies often generate transitory improvement before the problem grows worse" (Sterman 2000, 22).

Implications for Healthcare Managers

Classic examples of low-leverage policies are found in the studies of attempts to reduce health system costs by reducing the length of hospital stays. One

pharmaco-genomics
"a biotechnological science that combines the techniques of medicine, pharmacology, and genomics and is concerned with developing drug therapies to compensate for genetic differences in patients which cause varied responses to a single therapeutic regimen" (Medline Plus and Merriam-Webster 2016)

pharmaco-therapeutics
"the study of the therapeutic uses and effects of drugs" (Medline Plus and Merriam-Webster 2016)

study reported that healthy newborns discharged from the hospital 48 hours or sooner after delivery, saving the costs of a longer stay, had a significantly higher risk for readmission, morbidity, and neonatal mortality (Farhat and Rajab 2011). Another analysis found that hospitals with shorter lengths of stay were more likely to discharge Medicare patients to nursing facilities and inpatient rehabilitation facilities, suggesting that some hospitals may be using post-acute care as a substitute for inpatient care (Sacks et al. 2016).

If a manager in these cases viewed the healthcare system as a microsystem (e.g., the hospital department where patients received care) or the hospital administrator viewed it as a macrosystem (e.g., this hospital), the interventions chosen to reduce system costs might have been viewed as successful. However, if one views the healthcare system as a megasystem that includes not only the acute phase of care (e.g., the department where patient care occurred, the hospital) but also the downstream providers (e.g., other hospitals, emergency services, clinic services, nursing and rehabilitation facilities) and takes into account how the relationships among all providers influence patient outcomes, the longer-term behavior of the system can be observed.

From a systems perspective, the acute care manager is responsible for the acute care unit or hospital and also for the effect those local decisions have on the rest of the system of which the manager's component is a part. This perspective does not mean that the manager of a hospital department or the hospital administrator should not strive to reduce hospital costs. It does mean that managers, financial officers, CEOs, and policymakers should be aware of how decisions made and implemented in their domains of responsibility affect other parts of the healthcare system positively and negatively. When a negative impact on another part of the system is anticipated, the manager should be proactive in the short term to help minimize the negative effects and preserve positive patient outcomes. With the emergence of accountable care organizations, managers must learn how to optimize the macrosystems of healthcare delivery while improving the microsystems.

Other common trade-off challenges for healthcare managers surround the differences between expense and investment decisions within organizations and departments. The long-term effect of a manager's short-term decision may not be felt by another component in the macrosystem, but perhaps it will surface in the future in the manager's own department or organization. For example, does the manager sacrifice capital improvements to fund contract workers in the short term? Do managers reduce staff education expenditures to lower current expenses? Although choosing contract workers and reducing staff development activities may meet short-term financial priorities, these efforts fall into the category of low-leverage policies because the problems of facility aging, staff shortages, and the need for a competent workforce will surely be faced by the manager in the future. Without an appreciation of system consequences, one manager may be rewarded for short-term "success" with a promotion, while his successor inherits the longer-term problem.

In the formulary example, the organization may be willing to trade the rare adverse medication event for dollar savings realized from product standardization. However, this decision could compromise patient outcomes and unintentionally contribute to polarization and conflict between clinicians and managers.

History Dependency

Systems are history dependent. In other words, what has happened in the past influences what is happening right now. "We have always done it this way" methods of healthcare delivery are often perpetuated, despite research-supported knowledge that points to more effective practices. Some of these dated practices include (Melnyk 2016)

- recording vital signs every four hours at night on stable patients, despite their need for undisrupted sleep for recovery;
- removing urinary catheters only on a physician's orders, though the removal of catheters according to a nurse-driven protocol is more efficient and may prevent urinary tract infections; and
- continuing the practice of 12-hour nursing shifts, when findings from research indicate adverse outcomes for nurses and patients.

Some actions taken in the past are reversible, while some cannot be easily overturned. For example, a strategic decision by a hospital to convert some inpatient beds to skilled nursing beds could be difficult to reverse when more inpatient beds are needed.

Implications for Healthcare Managers

History dependency may be seen in the patient and the organization. Because of advancements in the care of chronic illnesses, rather than succumb to complications of one illness, elderly adults are often under treatment for several chronic illnesses concurrently. Persons with cystic fibrosis or born with congenital heart defects now enjoy a life expectancy into adulthood; previously, these conditions usually were fatal in childhood. Unhealthy behaviors, such as excessive alcohol, drugs, or cigarettes, even when discontinued, may have long-lasting health consequences. Understanding a patient's history is important not only for clinical providers but also for health services managers. For example, a patient's health history influences resources required for his care. An obese patient being treated for asthma, hypertension, and diabetes requires more labor-intensive care when having his gallbladder removed than an otherwise healthy athlete undergoing the same surgery. In recognition of these differences, managers must be willing to make nurse staffing adjustments for patient acuity (Huston 2013).

The manager must realize not only how past events have shaped current events but also how past decision-making strategies and directions may influence her ability to successfully achieve current and future goals. Using the nursing staff issue example, if the organization has historically rewarded managers for staying within budgetary expectations, a significant increase in nurse salary costs associated with caring for sicker patients without corresponding increases in patient care revenue might be difficult to sell given the organization's history of rewards and decision making.

Tight Coupling

tightly coupled relating to a system in which the parts "exhibit relatively time-dependent, invariant, and inflexible connections with little slack" (Scott 2003, 358)

A system is characterized as **tightly coupled** when its "parts exhibit relatively time-dependent, invariant, and inflexible connections with little slack" (Scott 2003, 358). An example is an elegantly crafted configuration of dominoes that can be set in motion by a push to the first piece. In a tightly coupled system, it can be difficult for people to recognize and correct mistakes to prevent an undesirable outcome. Tight coupling is also present when "the actors in the system interact strongly with one another" (Sterman 2000, 22).

Implications for Healthcare Managers

Organizations in industries outside of health services that are most commonly identified as tightly coupled include nuclear power plants and aircraft carriers (Dlugacz and Spath 2011). Healthcare organizations often demonstrate loosely coupled social structures such as departments, divisions, and professional groups, yet the tasks carried by the microsystems in the organizations are often tightly coupled. For example, cardiologists, nurses, and X-ray technicians belong to separate, distinct, loosely coupled professional groups and departments within the structure of the organization. Yet, when these people come together as a microsystem in the cardiac catheterization lab, the tasks they perform while conducting an angiogram procedure are tightly coupled. In this tightly coupled system, an undetected patient identity mistake or the administration of a wrong medication can quickly lead to disastrous consequences because the link between actions and outcomes is more direct.

Numerous interactions among and between people, processes, and departments in individual organizations and interactions among services along the continuum of care require managers to be attentive to the concept of coupling. Identifying, designing, and institutionalizing tools that promote task alignment, communication, collaboration, coordination, and strengthened relationships among players are required competencies for contemporary health services managers. Checklists that detail proper patient management practices, bar-coded patient identification mechanisms, and standardized handoffs between caregivers are just three of the many tools used to improve the quality of patient care in tightly coupled systems (Dlugacz and Spath 2011).

Nonlinearity

The term **nonlinear**, as it refers to a system characteristic, means that the "effect is rarely proportional to the cause" (Sterman 2000, 22). Because the parts in nonlinear systems may interact in numerous ways, these interactions often follow "unexpected sequences that are not visible or not immediately comprehensible" (Scott 2003, 358). In a nonlinear system, small deviations may have huge, unpredictable, and irregular effects.

nonlinear
relating to a system in which the "effect is rarely proportional to the cause" (Sterman 2000, 22)

Implications for Healthcare Managers

Here is an example of the nonlinear nature of healthcare systems. A respiratory therapist just starting the afternoon shift is the object of an outburst of anger from a patient's family. The therapist relates the encounter to a colleague at the nurse's station: "All I did was say, 'Hello'!" This situation may bring to mind the old idiom "the straw that broke the camel's back." In fact, this cliché is an accurate description of the encounter.

The patient and her family had accumulated a sequence of unsatisfactory experiences during the hospital stay, so all it took was one more encounter to trigger their anger. Although this time was the first that the afternoon therapist had met the family, his was the last in a series of interactions between the patient and the healthcare system that caused this family grief. If the patient complains to the manager about this therapist, what should the manager do? Without an appreciation for the nonlinear nature of systems, the manager may be tempted to discipline the employee. However, if the manager does have such an appreciation, she may try to investigate the sequence of events that culminated in the family's dissatisfaction. Although each event was relatively harmless when considered individually, when linked together with the family's overall experiences, they contributed to an unacceptable encounter. From this investigation, the manager may identify areas that can be improved to enhance the patient's overall experience with the care delivery process.

Another example of the nonlinear nature of systems may be seen in strategies used to reduce personnel expense in healthcare organizations. Because personnel expenses make up such a large percentage of operating budgets, changing the staff mix—that is, reducing the number of professional staff (e.g., registered nurses, medical technologists, pharmacists) and increasing the proportion of assistive personnel (e.g., nurse aides, laboratory assistants, pharmacy technicians)—is a common cost-cutting intervention. When this intervention is studied from a systems perspective, however, the resulting sequences of activities and their interrelationships are more readily seen. The unplanned consequences of this cost-cutting strategy in one organization included an increase in the overall employee turnover rate because of the frequency with which entry-level, assistive personnel left their jobs. Because this cost-cutting strategy was used by managers across different types of professions and departments, the stress and cost of continuously recruiting, hiring, and training new employees more than offset the savings hoped for from lowering the average hourly wage. When viewed from one department's point of view, the cost-reduction strategy may appear to be reasonable; however, when the compounding effect of this cost-cutting strategy is viewed across the entire organization, the strategy designed to reduce costs actually undermines the organization's ability to do so (Kelly 1999).

Summary

Like "quality," "system" can carry a variety of connotations. In this text, a system refers to a set of connected parts that fit together to achieve a purpose. The connected parts may be a health system that contains many organizations (a megasystem), an organization (a macrosystem), or a small unit or clinical team in an organization (a microsystem).

Systems thinking, a management discipline, acknowledges the large number of parts in a system, the infinite number of ways in which the parts interact, and the nature of the interactions. The healthcare system, whether the term refers to a single patient care unit, a facility, or all providers in a state or throughout the nation, is dynamically complex. The five system characteristics contributing to the presence of dynamic complexity are change, trade-offs, history dependency, tight coupling, and nonlinearity.

Exercise 3.1

Objective: To practice identifying dynamic complexity.

Instructions: Describe how the following example illustrates one or more of the system characteristics that contribute to dynamic complexity.

Example: Medical Associates is a for-profit medical group of 40 physicians that operates two facilities and offers services in several medical specialties, including cardiology; ear, nose, and throat; family medicine; gastroenterology; general surgery; pediatrics; and obstetrics and gynecology. Medical Associates is open six days a week in each location from 8:00 am until 6:00 pm. Plans are being developed to extend its hours to 9:00 pm two days a week. For several years, Medical Associates discounted its listed fees by 3 percent to 5 percent for its managed care contracts, but a few years ago, it had to accept larger discounts to remain in the networks of health plans. Lower reimbursements led

> Medical Associates to change its staffing from relying solely on registered nurses (RNs) to hiring medical assistants (MAs) as well. Currently, all physicians assigned to primary care service are assigned one RN or MA to assist with patient care. Physicians assigned to surgery are assigned one RN for every two physicians. As RNs retire or reassign, they have been replaced with MAs. On five recent occasions, when an RN assigned to a senior physician resigned, the senior physician demanded that the RN assigned to a junior physician be reassigned to him and that a new MA be hired to fill the vacancy with the junior physician. This ad hoc system of job switching has caused internal turmoil between the senior and junior physicians and has led to the subsequent resignation of two RNs who did not want to be reassigned. . . . Confusion exists around staff reporting relationships and who has the authority to change job assignments. (Seidel and Lewis 2014, 215)

Companion Readings

Anderson, A. 2014. "The Impact of the Affordable Care Act on the Health Care Workforce." The Heritage Foundation. Published March 18. www.heritage.org/research/reports/2014/03/the-impact-of-the-affordable-care-act-on-the-health-care-workforce.

Coutou, D. L. 2003. "Sense and Reliability: A Conversation with Celebrated Psychologist Karl E. Weick." *Harvard Business Review* 81 (4): 84–90.

Lipsitz, L. A. 2012. "Understanding Health Care as a Complex System: The Foundation for Unintended Consequences." *Journal of the American Medical Association* 308 (3): 243–44.

Nelson, E. C., M. Godfrey, P. B. Batalden, S. A. Berry, A. E. Bothe, K. E. McKinley, C. N. Melin, S. E. Muething, G. Moore, J. H. Wasson, and T. W. Nolan. 2008. "Clinical Microsystems, Part 1: The Building Blocks of Health Systems." *The Joint Commission Journal on Quality and Patient Safety*. Published July. http://clinicalmicrosystem.org/wp-content/uploads/2014/05/jc_quality_safety_01.pdf.

New England Complex System Institute. 2016. "About Complex Systems." Accessed November 8. www.necsi.edu/guide.

Peters, D. H. 2014. "The Application of Systems Thinking in Health: Why Use Systems Thinking?" *Health Research Policy and Systems*. Published August. https://health-policy-systems.biomedcentral.com/articles/10.1186/1478-4505-12-51.

Senge, P. M. 1990. "The Leader's New Work: Building Learning Organizations." *Sloan Management Review* (Fall): 149–65.

Web Resources

Applied Systems Thinking: http://appliedsystemsthinking.com

Dartmouth Institute Microsystem Academy: https://clinicalmicro
system.org

Society of Organizational Learning: www.solonline.org

System Dynamics Society: www.systemdynamics.org

References

AMN Healthcare. 2013. *Clinical Workforce Survey*. Retrieved June 30, 2016. www
.amnhealthcare.com/uploadedFiles/MainSite/Content/Healthcare_Industry_
Insights/Industry_Research/executivesurvey13.pdf.

Anderson, A. 2014. "The Impact of the Affordable Care Act on the Health Care
Workforce." The Heritage Foundation. Published March 18. www.heritage
.org/research/reports/2014/03/the-impact-of-the-affordable-care-act-
on-the-health-care-workforce.

Centers for Disease Control and Prevention. 2014. "The Public Health System and
the 10 Essential Public Health Services." Updated May 29. www.cdc.gov/
nphpsp/essentialservices.html.

Culliton, B. J. 2006. "Extracting Knowledge from Science: A Conversation with Elias
Zerhouni." *Health Affairs* 25 (3): W94–W103.

Dlugacz, Y. D., and P. L. Spath. 2011. "High Reliability and Patient Safety." In *Error
Reduction in Health Care: A Systems Approach to Improving Patient Safety*,
edited by P. L. Spath, 35–56. San Francisco: Jossey-Bass.

Farhat, R., and M. Rajab. 2011. "Length of Postnatal Hospital Stay in Healthy
Newborns and Re-hospitalization Following Early Discharge." *North American
Journal of Medical Sciences* 3 (3): 146–51.

Georgopoulos, B. S., and F. C. Mann. 1962. *The Community General Hospital*. New
York: MacMillan Company.

Godfrey, M. M., E. C. Nelson, and P. Batalden. 2004. *Clinical Microsystem Action
Guide: Improving Healthcare by Improving Your Microsystem*. Dartmouth
College. Revised September 2. http://clinicalmicrosystem.org/wp-content/
uploads/2014/07/CMAG040104.pdf.

Grant, R. 2016. "The U.S. Is Running Out of Nurses." *The Atlantic*. Published February
3. www.theatlantic.com/health/archive/2016/02/nursing-shortage/459741.

Huston, C. J. 2013. *Professional Issues in Nursing: Challenges and Opportunities*. New
York: Lippincott Williams & Wilkins.

Institute of Medicine. 1996. *Healthy Communities: New Partnerships for the Future of Public Health*. Washington, DC: National Academies Press.

Johnson, J. K., S. H. Miller, and S. D. Horowitz. 2008. "Systems-Based Practice: Improving the Safety and Quality of Patient Care by Recognizing and Improving the Systems in Which We Work." In *Advances in Patient Safety: New Directions and Alternative Approaches*, vol. 2: *Culture and Redesign*, edited by K. Henriksen, J. B. Battles, M. A. Keyes, and M. L. Grady. Agency for Healthcare Research and Quality. Published August. www.ncbi.nlm.nih. gov/books/NBK43731/pdf/Bookshelf_NBK43731.pdf.

Kelly, D. L. 1999. "Systems Thinking: A Tool for Organizational Diagnosis in Healthcare." In *Making It Happen: Stories from Inside the New Workplace,* no editor, 89–98. Waltham, MA: Pegasus Communications.

Kelly, D. L., and S. L. Pestotnik. 1998. "Using Causal Loop Diagrams to Facilitate Double Loop Learning in the Healthcare Delivery Setting." Unpublished manuscript.

Langabeer, J. R., and J. Helton. 2016. *Healthcare Operations Management: A Systems Perspective*, 2nd ed. Burlington, MA: Jones & Bartlett Learning.

Martin, R. L. 2013. "Our Self-Inflicted Complexity." *Harvard Business Review*. Published September 6. https://hbr.org/2013/09/our-self-inflicted-complexity.

McLaughlin, D. B., and J. R. Olson. 2012. *Healthcare Operations Management*, 2nd ed. Chicago: Health Administration Press.

Medline Plus and Merriam-Webster. 2016. *Medical Dictionary*. Retrieved June 30. www.merriam-webster.com/medlineplus/pharmacotherapeutics.

Melnyk, B. 2016. "Evidence-Based Practice vs. Doing It the Way We've Always Done It." *Medscape Nurses*. Retrieved June 30. www.medscape.com/viewarticle/860627.

Microsystem Academy. 2016. "Transforming Microsystems in Healthcare." Dartmouth Institute for Health Policy and Clinical Practice. Retrieved June 26. https:// clinicalmicrosystem.org.

PricewaterhouseCoopers. 2016. *US Health Services Deals Insights: Analysis and Trends in US Health Services Activity: 2015 and 2016 Outlook*. Published February. www.pwc.com/us/en/healthcare/publications/assets/pwc-health-services-deals-insights-q4-2015.pdf.

Runciman, B., A. Merry, and M. Walton. 2007. *Safety and Ethics in Health Care: A Guide to Getting It Right*. Burlington, VT: Ashgate.

Sacks, G., E. Lawson, A. Dawes, R. Weiss, M. Russell, R. Brook, D. Zingmond, and C. Ko. 2016. "Variation in Hospital Use of Postacute Care After Surgery and the Association with Care Quality." *Medical Care* 54 (2): 172–79.

Schyve, P. 2005. "Prologue: Systems Thinking and Patient Safety." In *Advances in Patient Safety: From Research to Implementation*, vol. 2: *Concepts and Methodology*, edited by K. Henriksen, J. B. Battles, E. S. Marks, and D. I. Lewin. Agency for Healthcare Research and Quality. Published February. www.ncbi.nlm.nih .gov/books/NBK20523.

Scott, R. A. 2003. *Organizations: Rational, Natural, and Open Systems*, 5th ed. Upper Saddle River, NJ: Prentice Hall.

Seidel, L. F., and J. B. Lewis. 2014. *The Middleboro Casebook: Healthcare Strategy and Operations*. Chicago: Health Administration Press.

Senge, P. M. 2006. *The Fifth Discipline: The Art and Practice of the Learning Organization*, 2nd ed. New York: Doubleday Currency.

———. 1990. *The Fifth Discipline: The Art and Practice of the Learning Organization*. New York: Doubleday Currency.

Sterman, J. D. 2000. *Business Dynamics: Systems Thinking and Modeling for a Complex World*. Boston: Irwin McGraw-Hill.

UNDERSTANDING SYSTEM BEHAVIOR

Learning Objectives

After completing this chapter, you should be able to

- explain systemic structure from the perspective of the iceberg metaphor;
- describe how an understanding of systemic structure guides managerial questions about performance problems;
- identify the influence of mental models on managerial behaviors, decisions, and effectiveness; and
- apply learning strategies to better understand how systemic structures affect performance.

On Thursday, respiratory therapist (RT) Ahmed volunteers to work a double shift in the internsive care unit (ICU). The next day, he misses his regularly scheduled shift when he calls in sick. The following month, RT Martinez, who works in the same ICU, volunteers to work a double shift. Two days later, she misses her regularly scheduled shift when she calls in sick. When the RT manager mentions this "coincidence" to two nurse manager colleagues, they also describe similar situations with their staff members. As the RT manager gathers more information about employee staffing practices, he realizes that although the work schedule policies help staffing in the short term, the same policies inadvertently contribute to increased sick calls and more overtime in the long run. The manager discovers that well-intended efforts such as the carefully written staffing policies and procedures for his department may not yield the expected results. Likewise, well-intended change or improvement interventions often yield disappointing results. This chapter explores how better understanding the dynamics of system behavior can help managers plan and execute improvement interventions in their organizations.

A Systems Metaphor for Organizations

Metaphors provide a concrete picture of a theoretical concept. Thinking of an organization as an iceberg is one metaphor that illustrates the subtle but powerful systems principles at work in organizations (Innovation Associates 1995). Those forces that cause an organization to function the way it does and the people in the organization to behave the way they do are like the nine-tenths of an iceberg hidden underwater. The essence of an organization is not visible to most observers; what is below the organizational "waterline" can undermine well-intended change initiatives, improvement efforts, and clinical interventions, just as the part of the iceberg beneath the water's surface can sink a passing ship.

The triangular shape in exhibit 4.1 represents the iceberg, and the wavy, thick line represents the waterline. The tip of the iceberg (the top layer of the triangle) represents the events that occur daily in the organization. The middle layer of the iceberg represents a deeper understanding of the organization as a system that links events into patterns of behavior. The bottom level of the iceberg, which is underwater, represents the deepest understanding of the behavior of the organization as a system. This level represents relationships among system variables that cause the events and patterns to occur.

In the staffing example at the beginning of this chapter, the managers saw the RTs and nurses working double shifts and calling in sick as unique events in each of their areas. However, while comparing notes, they identified a pattern of similar behavior across different patient care services. Although the act of identifying patterns is above the organizational waterline, it is the first step toward systems thinking. The RT manager began to go below the

EXHIBIT 4.1
The Iceberg
Metaphor

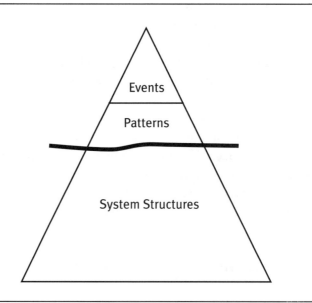

Source: Reprinted with permission from Innovation Associates (1995).

waterline when he started linking his observations into patterns. By telling a "story" of his discoveries, the relationships and underlying causes of the problems began to emerge:

> The hospital policies were supposed to promote adequate staffing and discourage sick calls; however, the day shifts were often overstaffed and the evening and nights shifts were understaffed.
>
> Employees were paid overtime and often an additional "premium" for working a double shift. When professional staff volunteered for a double shift, they were positively perceived as "helpful" and "team players." The employees helped out with a shift that was short-staffed and did not cause staffing difficulties on their next shift.
>
> By working a double shift and calling in sick later in the week, the employees were able to work the same amount of hours but get paid more than if they had worked their regular scheduled shifts.

The RT manager began to identify the key system variables at work: scheduling policies, individual employee incentives and compensation, informal rewards, policy on calling in sick, individual unit operations, and float-pool operations. Although individually the policies and operations seemed reasonable, their interactions contributed to the underlying systemic structure. The perceived benefit to professional staff (i.e., the opportunity to help out peers and patients and earn more money while working the same hours) and the frequency of these staff members volunteering for a double shift and calling in sick later in the week were related in a way that reinforced the behavior; that is, as the number of employees who perceived this benefit increased, the number of times the behavior occurred increased. Note that the staff members had no malicious intent in this case; they were simply following the policies as they were crafted. As this reinforcing relationship occurred across several nursing and clinical support departments, an overall increase in salary expense became the unintended consequence to the hospital.

When the RT manager understood each of the policies in the context of how they made up the human resources system, he and the other managers were able to redesign the system to achieve the intended result of staffing the hospital in a dependable and cost-effective manner. Some of the changes this organization made to break the reinforcing cycle included reviewing the distribution of nurses and other clinical staff during the day, evening, and night shifts to better balance staffing across the 24-hour period; improving coordination between the RT and nursing schedules and the float-pool schedules; and changing the overtime criteria (consistent with legal labor requirements) from hours worked in excess of 8 hours per day to hours worked in excess of 40 hours per week.

Lessons for Healthcare Managers

systemic structure
the interrelationships among key elements in the system and the influence of these interrelationships on the system's behavior over time (Senge 2006)

organizational structure
the manner in which responsibility and authority are distributed throughout an organization (Shortell and Kaluzny 2006)

In the iceberg metaphor for organizations, above-the-waterline activities are daily events and the patterns that make up these events. The term **systemic structure** refers to what is found below the waterline. The systemic structure involves the interrelationships among key elements in the system and the influence of these interrelationships on the system's behavior over time (Senge 2006). Systemic structure refers to interrelationships among elements, components, and variables that make up the system, not to interpersonal relationships among people (Senge 2006). Systemic structure should also be differentiated from **organizational structure**, which refers to how responsibility and authority are distributed throughout an organization (Shortell and Kaluzny 2006), although organizational structure may act as a systemic structure.

Understanding systemic structure helps a manager to better understand the organization. Based on this understanding, the manager may choose high-leverage interventions to improve the organization's performance. Valuable insights about one's organization may be gained by understanding the concept of systemic structure. This section offers four lessons for healthcare managers:

1. Systemic structure influences behavior.
2. Systemic structure is not readily visible.
3. Information is essential to identifying systemic structure.
4. Successful change requires going below the waterline.

Lesson 1: Systemic Structure Influences Behavior

Consider the following story from an anonymous author:

> A college student spent an entire summer going to the football field every day wearing a black-and-white striped shirt, walking up and down the field for 10 or 15 minutes, throwing birdseed all over the field, blowing a whistle, and then walking off the field. At the end of the summer, it came time for the first home football game. The referee walked onto the field and blew the whistle. The game had to be delayed for a half hour to wait for the birds to get off the field.

Everyone laughs at this story. However, if one were sitting in the stadium stands without a clue about the events of the summer, one would probably be annoyed and blame those darn birds. The birds were not right or wrong. They were doing what they were supposed to be doing based on the underlying systemic structures: the relationships between feeding time and the football field, the striped shirt and the birdseed, the whistle and their hunger.

"Every organization is perfectly designed to get the results that it gets. To get different results you need to improve the design of the organization"

(Hanna 1988, 36). This expression has almost become a cliché in quality improvement presentations and articles. However, what is not commonly heard or read is that improvements must be targeted at issues below the waterline, not simply above the waterline. An understanding of the iceberg metaphor prompts improvement questions to be asked from all levels of the iceberg to reveal the underlying structures that cause the patterns and events to occur.

Consider how the improvement interventions change depending on the level from which the improvement questions are asked. An events-level improvement question might focus on what *the individual* needs to do differently and usually results in the desire to blame an individual in response to unsatisfactory performance or a medical error. A patterns-level question moves from the individual to the group and focuses on what *we* need to do differently. Interventions at this level may target the collective actions of a team, a department, or an organization and may include implementing clinical guidelines, streamlining office scheduling systems, or installing new computers. The below-the-waterline question focuses on how we can best understand why we are getting the results we are getting (see exhibit 4.2).

The iceberg metaphor adds insight to issues on the sector level and the organizational level. For example, after passage of the Affordable Care Act in 2010, traditional roles, responsibilities, and authority of various healthcare stakeholders were altered. One notable change has been increased costs for consumers covered by high-deductible health plans, including spending more on medications. Many consumers now exhibit cost-conscious behaviors such as asking for generic drugs instead of brand names, checking the price of a service before getting care, and requesting more information about treatment

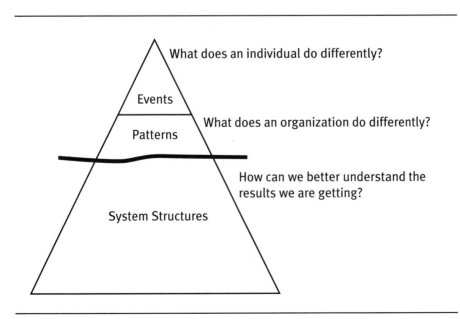

EXHIBIT 4.2
Improvement
Questions

options and costs (Santilli and Vogenberg 2015). Healthcare organizations are discovering that patient satisfaction is linked to how well it understands and is prepared to address the changing cost-conscious behaviors of its consumers.

Lesson 2: Systemic Structure Is Not Readily Visible

Systemic structure is not readily visible unless a conscious effort is made to find it. Just because managers do not see what is below the organizational waterline does not mean that a systemic structure is not present in the organization. For example, a newly hired manager at an academic medical center was assigned to facilitate an improvement project for a patient care unit. If the project proved successful, the intent was to expand the intervention organization-wide. Despite positive results—as measured by improved efficiencies and increased patient and staff satisfaction—the project was not implemented beyond the original pilot site. When the manager began to explore possible reasons the project was not replicated on other units, he discovered that over the years numerous project teams had designed and implemented successful pilot projects aimed at improving specific problems. However, few of these projects had actually been integrated into the ongoing activities of the organization (i.e., institutionalized).

On further investigation, he uncovered the following systemic structures operating in this organization. First, all improvements in the organization were called "pilots." The expectation was that a trial would be conducted for a specified period, results would be presented to the administrative team, and the administrative team would then authorize the project to continue or not. The problem was that this process occurred independently from the budgeting process. When the "special pools" of dollars to fund pilot initiatives were gone, no mechanisms were in place to reallocate funds either in or among departments to support institutionalizing successful improvements or innovations.

The label of "pilot" also brought with it other short-term perceptions related to support, staffing, and budgets. Because of these hidden, but real, relationships among the variables required to support change, this academic medical center demonstrated a constant stream of successful improvement pilot efforts, yet sustained improvement in the overall organizational performance never occurred.

Lesson 3: Information Is Essential to Identifying Systemic Structure

A *pattern* is defined as "something that happens in a regular and repeated way" (Merriam-Webster 2016). This definition implies that identifying or recognizing a pattern requires more than one observation. In the staffing example, the discussion among the RT manager and nurse manager colleagues about issues in their respective areas provided an opportunity to observe the behavior of many employees across multiple units. Only when these observations were combined did the organizational pattern become evident.

The need for multiple observations or data points has implications for how managers determine reporting relationships, how they interact and communicate, and how they present performance data. The traditional vertical organizational structure, which compartmentalizes groups in rigid reporting lines, reduces the opportunity to interact across departments and disciplines and minimizes managers' ability to identify organizational patterns.

Communication methods based on "telling" rather than "sharing" information also reduces opportunities to identify organizational patterns by limiting two-way communication and the "fresh eyes" often needed to interpret and link events. Reporting data by single periods only (e.g., monthly departmental financial reports) reduces managers' ability to identify patterns over time in their own departments. In addition, reporting aggregated organizational data reduces managers' opportunity to identify patterns across smaller units of analysis in the organization.

Strategies that can promote pattern identification and prompt investigation into underlying structures include

- organizational structures and cultures that encourage interaction among levels and units,
- open and free flow of information, and
- performance data displayed graphically and plotted over time to make data trends more visible.

Lesson 4: Successful Change Requires Going Below the Waterline

To implement successful and lasting change efforts, managers must go below the organizational waterline. The iceberg metaphor explains why the potential of many change or improvement efforts is not fully realized. If changes are targeted at the event or pattern levels (i.e., what we do) rather than at the systemic structure level (i.e., what causes the system to behave the way it does), the effect will be only temporary. Because structure influences behavior, the only way to truly change behavior in the system is to identify, target, and change the underlying structures.

Many ideas have been proposed on how to improve organizational systems; however, a common challenge for managers and care providers alike is how to actually implement these ideas. Organizational culture may be thought of as an underlying systemic structure. The influence of the healthcare organization's culture on the ability to convert continuous quality improvement concepts into effective implementation has been described in the healthcare research literature (Glickman et al. 2007). Health services researchers have found that cultural characteristics such as effective governance and management of human capital and supportive dynamics are essential structural elements of quality improvement in healthcare organizations (Jiang et al. 2009; Mannion, Davies, and Marshall 2005; Tsai et al. 2015). These types of studies have helped inform policy changes that target underlying structures at the national level.

Going Below the Waterline

The captain of a ship sailing in the North Atlantic uses radar, sonar, and a bow watch (a sailor posted at the front of the ship to look out for danger) to alert him to underwater ice. Likewise, managers may also use strategies that alert them to underlying systemic structures. Following are three strategies managers may use:

1. Understanding history
2. Being aware of mental models
3. Integrating double-loop learning into management philosophy and approach

Understanding History

History is a powerful underlying structure. A healthcare manager's current work may be influenced by her department's history, the organization's history, a professional group's history, the community's history, or the sector's history. For example, in one organization, the sudden death of a well-respected department manager had a long-lasting impact on the department staff. The new incumbent manager was faced not only with getting settled in a new role and a new department but also with addressing the staff's grief. For new employees, the lack of shared history with the deceased manager was a source of polarization between the "before" and "after" staff and interfered with the entire staff's ability to achieve a high level of teamwork.

As another example, a physical therapist at a rehabilitation center that had recently been purchased by a for-profit organization carefully explained the organization's history to a patient's family. The previous owners and managers of the center were proud of their heritage of religious service and quality. The family members inquired whether their loved one would still get what she needed at this for-profit facility, and the physical therapist informed the family that though the organization's ownership had changed, the staff still identified with the center's historical values.

In the book *The Social Transformation of American Medicine*, Paul Starr (1982) describes the evolution of the US medical profession and physicians' roles from the eighteenth through the twentieth centuries. Although one may agree or disagree with Starr's conclusions, this book explains how the history of physicians, hospitals, and insurance companies shaped the healthcare field of today, and as such the book provides an explanation of the current state of the US healthcare system. Understanding the circumstances surrounding the *Flexner Report*, which was published in 1910 and describes the state of medical education at the time, can provide insights into why medical schools are structured the way they are and into the role of academic medical centers in US healthcare (Starr 1982).

The simplest strategies that managers may use to understand history are to ask, listen, and read. In addition, large-group "visioning" meetings have incorporated structured discussions about history (Weisbord and Janoff 2010). Managers, especially those assuming a new role, may gain valuable insights by facilitating similar discussions with staff in their own departments. The following guidelines may help:

- Ask the group to identify significant events during defined periods. Events in the department, organization, community, clinical specialty or profession, or industry may be identified.
- List the events by periods of time (e.g., in five- or ten-year increments, depending on the group).
- Look for patterns in the listed events.

For example, one group of nurses in the postpartum area identified this event in its history discussion: At 5:00 am every day, the charge nurse would announce over the unit's intercom system, "Patients who have not had a bowel movement yet, please put on your nurse call light." The group burst into laughter, and one nurse observed, "Glad those 'good old days' are gone!" This simple observation helped the group let go of its resistance to a proposed change on the unit as it realized that it had experienced numerous changes over the years, most of which had direct benefit to the patients.

A manager in a laboratory was intrigued about the type of events identified during a history discussion with staff. Most of the identified events focused on current events from the news, and few events focused on laboratory technology or the department, as he had anticipated. The manager realized that because the demographic composition of his department had been changing over the years (the technologists were aged 50 years or older, the technical assistants and phlebotomists were aged 30 years or younger), the two distinct demographics had little in common but current events. This realization helped to explain why previous team-building sessions had been only moderately successful and prompted the manager to establish common ground for his employees through a shared vision for the department. This manager also became more attentive to age diversity; succession planning; and the needs of differing demographic groups, particularly in his approaches to recruitment and hiring (Kelly 1999).

Being Aware of Mental Models

cognitive psychology
the branch of psychology "concerned with mental processes (as perception, thinking, learning, and memory) especially with respect to the internal events occurring between sensory stimulation and the overt expression of behavior" (Merriam-Webster 2016)

schema
a "mental codification of experience that includes a particular organized way of perceiving cognitively and responding to a complex situation or set of stimuli" (Merriam-Webster 2016)

mental model
a deeply ingrained way of thinking that influences how a person sees and understands the world as well as how that person acts

The field of **cognitive psychology** is the branch of psychology "concerned with mental processes (as perception, thinking, learning, and memory) especially with respect to the internal events occurring between sensory stimulation and the overt expression of behavior" (Merriam-Webster 2016). In the field, the term **schema** refers to a "mental codification of experience that includes a particular organized way of perceiving cognitively and responding to a complex situation or set of stimuli" (Merriam-Webster 2016). In the management domain, the related term **mental model** is often used interchangeably with "paradigm" and "assumption." Although these terms are technically slightly different, they all refer to a deeply ingrained way of thinking that influences how a person sees and understands the world and how that person acts. When someone declares an unquestionable status or condition, a mental model is usually being expressed; words such as "always" and "never" are clues that mental models are being expressed. Mental models may be so strong they override the facts at hand. For example, at a quality manager workshop, one hospital manager stated her mental model as follows: "Physicians would never spend time at a workshop like this." However, sitting beside her for the duration of the workshop were two pediatricians and a family practitioner!

What this manager did not realize was that her own mental model was interfering with her ability to design appropriate strategies to engage physicians in improvement efforts in her organization. As a result of her mental model, she found numerous reasons physicians would not participate, and she was blinded to strategies to encourage physician participation. To promote learning and improvement in organizations, managers, care providers, and other employees in the organization must "look inward . . . to reflect critically on their own behavior, identify ways they often inadvertently contribute to the organization's problems, and then change how they act" (Argyris 1991). Without an understanding of our own mental models, we run the risk of unknowingly undermining our attempts to progress along the quality continuum.

For example, the mental model of "clinical guidelines are used to control physician behavior" encourages organizations to adopt top-down mandates for "cookbook medicine." Alternatively, the mental model "using evidence-based clinical guidelines to standardize steps of care can actually save physician time on routine interventions so that more time can be spent on the unique needs of the patient" encourages organizations to support and foster clinician involvement in evaluating, selecting, adapting, and implementing clinical guidelines. The mental model of "data are necessary to name, blame, and shame" encourages managers to use data to justify punitive actions directed at employees. The mental model of "knowledge is power" encourages managers to guard data tightly and to distribute them only on a "need-to-know" basis. Alternatively, the mental model of "data are the foundation of performance improvement" encourages organizations to put in place data collection, analysis, and dissemination systems that make information easily accessible. Once mental models and their subsequent actions are understood, managers may purposely choose to operate from mental models that help rather than hinder in achieving desired performance results.

Differing mental models may also be a source of conflict in an organization. A manager's view or perspective on organizations themselves will shape her management strategies, actions, and style. Two contrasting views of organizations are the rational model and the political model (Shortell 2000). A manager who views the organization through a rational model expects decision making to be logical, orderly, and focused on maximizing outcomes. Such a manager can be extremely frustrated when an administrative team, operating from a political perspective, encourages decision making that involves lots of give and take among competing interests. From the manager's point of view, the decision-making processes in this politically driven organization serve the interest of the players involved but do not result in optimal patient outcomes or cost-effective approaches. On the other hand, the members of the administrative team perceive this manager's emphasis on outcomes as interfering with the delicate political alliances they had worked hard to establish. The lack of understanding of each other's mental models creates ongoing conflict between the manager and the administrative team: The manager thought the team did not care about results, and the team thought the manager was compromising relationships with important stakeholders. Without an awareness of each other's mental models, the conflict between the manager and the administrators continued to grow until the manager finally left the organization.

Had both parties made their mental models explicit—through discussion, definition of organizational operating principles, or orientation of new managers to the culture of decision making—their conflict may have been avoided, or at least some common understanding may have been established. Instead, the results were conflict, tension, and, eventually, manager turnover.

Integrating Double-Loop Learning

A technique used to bring attention to mental models is double-loop learning. Exhibit 4.3 illustrates the difference between single-loop and double-loop learning. In single-loop learning, if one is not satisfied with the results or consequences of the actions, the actions are changed; however, the new actions are still driven by the same assumptions. In **double-loop learning**, if one is not satisfied with the results or consequences, underlying assumptions are examined, clarified, communicated, or reframed. Only then is subsequent action, based on lessons revealed, taken (Argyris 1991; Tagg 2007).

double-loop learning
a type of learning in which, if one is not satisfied with the results or consequences, before taking further action, underlying assumptions are examined, clarified, communicated, or reframed based on what the assumptions reveal. Only then is subsequent action, on the basis of lessons revealed, taken (Argyris 1991; Tagg 2007).

EXHIBIT 4.3
Single-Loop and
Double-Loop
Learning

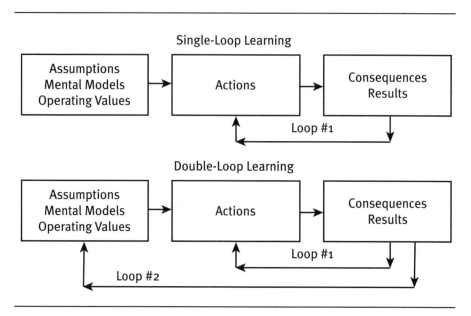

Source: Adapted from Tagg (2007).

In one large hospital, a nursing supervisor complained to the manager of environmental services that when asked, the housekeeper refused to move a piece of equipment to prepare a room for a patient admission. The supervisor accused the housekeeper of being uncooperative and an obstacle to patient care. The supervisor operated from a professional mind-set and believed the housekeeper should be able to determine when touching medical equipment is allowable. However, because of language, cultural, and educational differences among staff in entry-level positions, the environmental services staff were trained to strictly adhere to the department's standard policies and procedures, which stipulated that medical equipment must never be disturbed. The housekeeper was operating from one set of assumptions (i.e., following the rules), while the nursing supervisor was operating from a conflicting set of assumptions (i.e., doing whatever needs to be done to care for a patient). Although both parties were trying to do their jobs the best way they knew, their opposing assumptions led to conflict and antagonism.

This situation of "accidental adversaries" may be unintentionally created when underlying assumptions are not known. The numerous roles, backgrounds, personalities, levels of education, and other diverse characteristics of the healthcare workforce necessitate managerial use of double-loop learning to promote teamwork and quality in a given scope of responsibility. In the workplace, however, managers often spend more time trying to mend adversarial relationships than preventing them. Managers may minimize accidentally adversarial interactions by

- clarifying operating principles,
- helping staff members understand and communicate their own assumptions,
- helping staff ask for clarification and explanations of others' behavior, and
- explicitly describing their (the managers') own expectations for individual employees and for teams.

Double-loop learning is not appropriate for all situations in a health services organization. For example, an emergency resuscitation is not the time to question why a cardiac arrest code is carried out in a certain manner. Double-loop learning is a technique that should be part of initiatives requiring innovative solutions or improved levels of performance. Managers and care teams should be comfortable asking questions such as, "Why do we do things the way we do? Is there a better way to get the job done? Are my own mental models helping or hurting me and our group's effectiveness?"

For an improvement team, double-loop learning may take the form of discussions that question "whether operating norms are appropriate—then inventing new norms as needed" (Pierce 2000, 15). Double-loop learning has resulted in several innovative solutions, such as rapid response teams for emergency situations (Barwise et al. 2016) and the Broselow pediatric emergency tape used to predict a child's actual body weight to determine acceptable doses of emergency medications (Meguerdichian and Clapper 2012). Managers may consider assigning a team member to be the devil's advocate and present an opposing view to ensure that assumptions are tested and challenged; otherwise, the challenger may be viewed as a barrier to the team process.

Summary

Organizations may be compared to an iceberg, where events and patterns in the organization are above the waterline and system structures are below the waterline. Systemic structure refers to interrelationships among elements, components, and variables that make up the system and not to interpersonal relationships among people. Understanding systemic structure and how to identify it assists managers with solving problems by altering system behavior. Otherwise, managers risk treating symptoms of a problem and seeing the problem return over time.

Exercise 4.1
Objective: To explore "below the waterline" factors that can impede quality improvements in healthcare organizations. Managers must recognize whether

these factors exist in their work setting and determine how best to overcome these barriers when initiating operational improvements.

Instructions: Read the following article:

Berwick, D. 2003. "Improvement, Trust, and the Healthcare Workforce." *Quality & Safety in Health Care* 12 (supplement 1): i2–i6. www.ncbi.nlm.nih .gov/pmc/articles/PMC1765768/pdf/v012p000i2.pdf.

In this article, Dr. Berwick describes several historical and present-day "below the waterline" factors that inhibit healthcare quality improvement. For example, he observes that improvement is limited when the workforce is not encouraged to actively participate in reinventing the system.

- Identify three factors described by Dr. Berwick that are the most difficult for healthcare organizations to overcome and explain why.
- For the three factors you select, describe actions that managers can take to eliminate or minimize the factor so it no longer inhibits operations improvement.

Companion Readings

Hovlid, E., O. Buke, K. Haug, A. B. Aslaksen, and C. von Plessen. 2012. "Sustainability of Healthcare Improvement: What Can We Learn from Learning Theory?" *BMC Health Services Research* 12: 235. Published August 3. www.biomedcentral .com/1472-6963/12/235.

Lencioni, P. 2006. *Silos, Politics and Turf Wars: A Leadership Fable About Destroying the Barriers That Turn Colleagues into Competitors.* San Francisco: Jossey-Bass.

McComb, S., and V. Simpson. 2014. "The Concept of Shared Mental Models in Healthcare Collaboration." *Journal of Advanced Nursing* 70 (7): 1479–88.

Trbovich, P. 2014. "Five Ways to Incorporate Systems Thinking into Healthcare Organizations." *Biomedical Instrumentation & Technology: Connecting the Dots* 48 (s2): 31–36.

Web Resources

The Institute for Systemic Leadership: www.systemicleadershipinstitute.org
Pegasus Communications: https://thesystemsthinker.com

References

Argyris, C. 1991. "Teaching Smart People How to Learn." *Harvard Business Review* 69 (3): 99–110.

Barwise, A., C. Thongprayoon, O. Gajic, J. Jensen, V. Herasevich, and B. W. Pickering. 2016. "Delayed Rapid Response Team Activation Is Associated with Increased Hospital Mortality, Morbidity, and Length of Stay in a Tertiary Care Institution." *Critical Care Medicine* 44 (1): 54–63.

Glickman, S. W., K. A. Baggett, C. G. Krubert, E. D. Peterson, and K. A. Schulman. 2007. "Promoting Quality: The Health-Care Organization from a Management Perspective." *International Journal of Quality Health Care* 19 (6): 341–48.

Hanna, D. P. 1988. *Designing Organizations for High Performance*. Reading, MA: Addison Wesley Publishing Company.

Innovation Associates. 1995. *Systems Thinking: A Language for Learning and Action*. Participant manual, version 95.4.1. Waltham, MA: Innovation Associates.

Jiang, H. J., C. Lockee, K. Bass, and I. Fraser. 2009. "Board Oversight of Quality: Any Differences in Process of Care and Mortality?" *Journal of Healthcare Management* 54 (1): 15–29.

Kelly, D. L. 1999. "Systems Thinking: A Tool for Organizational Diagnosis in Healthcare." In *Making It Happen: Stories from Inside the New Workplace*, no editor, 89–98. Waltham, MA: Pegasus Communications.

Mannion, R., H. T. Davies, and M. N. Marshall. 2005. "Cultural Characteristics of 'High' and 'Low' Performing Hospitals." *Journal of Health Organization and Management* 19 (6): 431–39.

Meguerdichian, M. J., and T. C. Clapper. 2012. "The Broselow Tape as an Effective Medication Dosing Instrument: A Review of the Literature." *Journal of Pediatric Nursing* 27 (4): 416–20.

Merriam-Webster. 2016. *Online Dictionary*. Retrieved June 17. www.merriam-webster .com/dictionary.

Pierce, J. C. 2000. "The Paradox of Physicians and Administrators in Healthcare Organizations." *Healthcare Management Review* 25 (1): 7–28.

Santilli, J., and F. R. Vogenberg. 2015. "Key Strategic Trends That Impact Healthcare Decision-Making and Stakeholder Roles in the New Marketplace." *American Health & Drug Benefits* 8 (1): 15–20.

Senge, P. M. 2006. *The Fifth Discipline: The Art and Practice of the Learning Organization*, 2nd ed. New York: Doubleday Currency.

Shortell, S. M. 2000. *Healthcare Management*, 4th ed. Clifton Park, NY: Delmar Learning.

Shortell, S. M., and A. D. Kaluzny. 2006. *Health Care Management: Organization Design and Behavior*, 5th ed. Albany, NY: Delmar Thomson Learning.

Starr, P. 1982. *The Social Transformation of American Medicine: The Rise of a Sovereign Profession and the Making of a Vast Industry.* Reading, MA: Perseus Books Group.

Tagg, J. 2007. "Double-Loop Learning in Higher Education." *Change* 9 (4): 36–41.

Tsai, T. C., A. K. Jha, A. A. Gawande, R. S. Huckman, N. Bloom, and R. Sadun. 2015. "Hospital Board and Management Practices Are Strongly Related to Hospital Performance on Clinical Quality Metrics." *Health Affairs* 34 (8): 1304–11.

Weisbord, M. R., and S. Janoff. 2010. *Future Search: Getting the Whole System in the Room for Vision, Commitment and Action,* 3rd ed. San Francisco: Berret-Koehler Publishers.

VISUALIZING SYSTEM RELATIONSHIPS

Learning Objectives

After completing this chapter, you should be able to

- recognize the benefit of viewing system components when managing quality,
- explain how parts of the health services delivery system are interconnected,
- contrast four different models for illustrating system relationships, and
- describe the management implications of different system relationship models.

Just as a road map provides a picture of how places are connected in a geographic area, models can provide a picture for managers of how elements may be connected in and between systems. These models are valuable managerial tools for revealing and providing insight about systemic structure. Similar to one's preference for an electronic map over a paper map, managers may prefer one model over another depending on their work settings, backgrounds, and individual preferences. Numerous models provide healthcare managers with a picture of the organizational system in which they work to help them recognize, understand, and anticipate how the parts of the systems are related and interact to form the whole.

The most basic system may be characterized by three elements: input(s), a conversion process, and output(s). These elements are demonstrated visually in this simple diagram:

$$\text{Input(s)} \rightarrow \text{Conversion process} \rightarrow \text{Output(s)}$$

In a health services organization, examples of inputs are patients, personnel, supplies, equipment, facilities, and capital. Examples of conversion processes are diagnostic processes, clinical treatments, operational activities, and business management functions. Examples of outputs are a patient's health status and an organization's business performance.

Often, quality efforts focus on managing the inputs and conversion process that make up the system. The healthcare field regulates the quality of personnel inputs by various means, including licensure requirements, continuing education, and performance appraisals. Clinical trials and US Food and Drug Administration approval are two examples of ways to control the quality of technology inputs such as drug therapies. Clinical guidelines, process improvement, and standardization help maintain high standards for conversion processes. Controlling the quality of the inputs and conversion processes is intended to improve the quality of the outputs, such as patient clinical and functional status, satisfaction with services, cost-effectiveness, employee behaviors, and organizational culture.

Adding a feedback loop creates a more dynamic process—one that leads to a more mature quality management approach. Feedback about the quality of the outputs guides efforts to improve the quality of the inputs and the conversion processes (see exhibit 5.1). Continuous feedback promotes continuous improvement. The Donabedian (1980) categories of medical quality measures and their relationship (structure → process → outcomes) support this continuous improvement model.

In chapter 3, systems thinking is defined as "a view of reality that emphasizes the relationships and interactions of each part of the system to all the other parts" (McLaughlin and Olson 2012, 39). A systems thinking approach to quality management involves improving the quality of the parts and understanding *and* improving the quality of the relationships between the parts. This systems thinking approach requires managers to view health services organizations in a systems context. Four models are presented in this chapter to help managers better understand system relationships: the interconnected systems model, the three core process model, the Baldrige Performance Excellence Program framework, and the socioecological framework.

EXHIBIT 5.1
Quality
Management
System

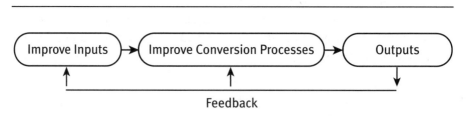

Source: Adapted from Tagg (2007).

Interconnected Systems Model

Ferlie and Shortell (2001) offer a systems view of healthcare that illustrates the interconnected clinical delivery system: the environment, the organization, the microsystem, and the patient (exhibit 5.2). The environment (e.g., government regulations, accreditation policies) has a significant impact on the delivery system. The organization's infrastructure influences how patient care is delivered. The infrastructure is shaped in part by external stakeholders, such as the federal government's push for adoption of electronic health records (EHRs). Ensuring the workforce has the right equipment and skills to properly care for patients are important elements of the infrastructure. The **patient care microsystem**, in this model, is "the level of healthcare delivery that includes providers, technology, and treatment processes" (McLaughlin and Olson 2012, 9).

patient care microsystem
"the level of healthcare delivery that includes providers, technology, and treatment processes" (McLaughlin and Olson 2012, 9)

Lessons for Healthcare Managers

The interconnected systems model is the only approach that clearly shows the patient at the center of the health system. The manner in which each layer of the system interacts with the others has a direct impact on the patient. Improving the effectiveness of clinical care requires process changes at the patient care microsystem level and in the infrastructure. For example, implementation of evidence-based treatment guidelines can help ensure patients receive appropriate treatments at the correct time. Making this goal a reality often requires changes in the organizational infrastructure. Tools such as computerized physician order

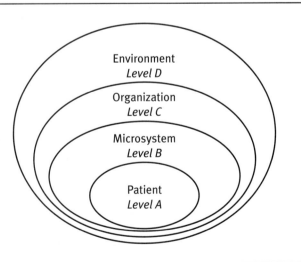

EXHIBIT 5.2
Interconnected Systems View of Healthcare

Source: Reprinted from Ransom, Joshi, and Nash (2005). Based on Ferlie and Shortell (2001).

entry and treatment plans, together with electronic prompts or alerts built into the EHR, help remind providers of the guidelines at the point of care.

The subsystems in the interconnected systems often have feedback mechanisms that reinforce or balance system performance. Exhibit 5.3 illustrates how a change in the environment level ripples throughout the other three levels of the system.

Three Core Process Model

The three core process model shown in exhibit 5.4 represents a "horizontal" view of a health services delivery organization. All processes in the organization (represented by the arrows) should operate in an aligned fashion toward improving performance. The model starts on the right of the exhibit by defining desired results using a balanced set of outcomes: the patient's clinical outcomes, functional status, satisfaction, and cost of services.

In the three core process model, the many processes that take place in a health services organization are grouped into three core categories: (1) clinical, medical, and technical processes; (2) operational or patient-flow processes; and (3) administrative processes.

Clinical, medical, and technical processes are the fundamental reasons individuals seek the assistance of a health services organization—that is, to take care of some need that involves diagnosis, treatment, prevention, or palliative care. Physicians and nonphysicians provide these services. The processes may be medical, such as surgery; mental health related, such as counseling or therapy; connected to daily care, such as nursing care after a stroke; or required by special treatments, such as obtaining oxygen or other durable medical equipment for the home.

EXHIBIT 5.3
Linkages in the
Interconnected
Clinical Delivery
System:
Chemotherapy

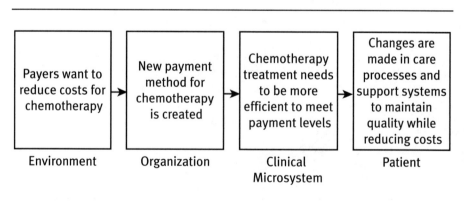

| Environment | Organization | Clinical Microsystem | Patient |

Source: Reprinted from McLaughlin and Olson (2012, 12). Used with permission.

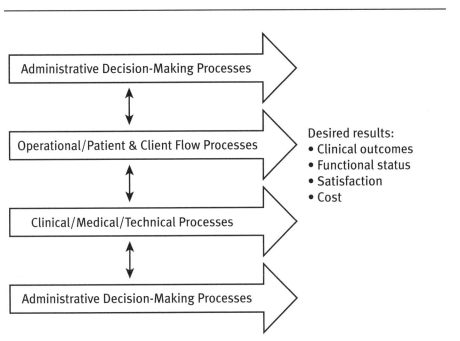

EXHIBIT 5.4
Three Core
Process Model

Operational or patient-flow processes enable an individual to access the clinical, medical, and technical processes. This category includes processes such as registering patients, scheduling activities, and coordinating services. Administrative decision-making processes occupy two positions in the exhibit, above and below the other two core processes. In this way, the model illustrates how administrative processes influence the overall organization. These processes include decision making, communication, resource allocation, and performance evaluation. The arrows linking the three core processes reflect the interdependence of the processes.

Lessons for Healthcare Managers

The three core process model teaches managers several lessons. First, the interdependent relationships between the three core processes suggest that improvement in any one of these processes has the potential to increase the value of the service provided. However, the *concurrent* targeting of these core processes provides a synergy that can accelerate the achievement of improved outcomes. "An efficient clinical process supported by an inefficient operational process, or vice versa, is still an inefficient process. . . . In addition, if . . . changes are made independent of clinician involvement, the likelihood of implementation is reduced. It is therefore necessary to have decision-making processes that actively engage clinicians in change efforts" (Kelly et al. 1997, 127–28).

For example, in one ambulatory surgery unit, the patient postoperative length of stay—the time the patient leaves the operating room to the time the patient is discharged—was found to be longer than in other, similar ambulatory surgery units. An improvement effort aimed at ameliorating the discharge process was undertaken in hopes of reducing the length of stay. As the improvement effort progressed, the team realized that anesthesia practices were affecting its ability to achieve better results. If patients were being heavily sedated in the operating room and were slow to wake up as a result, the gains from improving the discharge process could not be fully realized. Likewise, if the physicians implemented a new clinical protocol for anesthesia and pain management but patients still had to wait for the nurses to discharge them, gains from improving the anesthesia process could not be fully realized. Recognizing the interdependence of these two processes and targeting the discharge process *and* the anesthesia protocol for improvement allowed the benefits of both improvement efforts to be achieved. Furthermore, if the administrative processes did not permit employees to be scheduled away from clinical duties so they could be involved in the quality efforts, neither of the improvements could take place.

Second, the three core process model helps promote a patient-focused orientation by recognizing the need for aligning processes and improvement efforts toward the needs of the patient. The conceptual view of operations and administration observes how the patient (or client) moves through the entire system to access a clinical process. For example, a seemingly simple supervisory decision such as scheduling lunch breaks took on new meaning for one emergency department (ED) when the decision was viewed with patient flow in mind. Although scheduling staff lunch breaks at noon seemed reasonable, this practice created unnecessary patient delays and bottlenecks in the patient care processes because patient visits typically increased during the hours of 11:00 am to 1:00 pm. After ED management observed the situation from the patient-flow perspective, the break policy was revised so staff breaks occurred before and after—rather than during—busy patient times.

Third, the model reinforces the different yet necessary and interdependent contributions each core process and each provider (or implementer) of those processes provide to patient care and organizational outcomes. This way, collaboration among the entire care team can be promoted.

Fourth, when the administrative role is viewed as a process rather than a function or a structure, the tools used to improve other types of processes may also be applied to administrative processes. If one of the desired outcomes is patient satisfaction, the administrative decision-making processes must include mechanisms to regularly collect, analyze, report, and evaluate patient satisfaction data and to communicate these results throughout the organization.

Baldrige Performance Excellence Program Framework

The healthcare criteria of the Baldrige Performance Excellence Program (BPEP) provide a well-established systems approach for improving organizational effectiveness. Charleston (WV) Area Medical Center Health System found the criteria provided "an overarching framework for the system. . . . CEO Dave Ramsey reported that . . . 'Baldrige added ways to achieve quality in our support of the community, our working relationship with vendors, our relationship with the medical staff, medical researchers and the workforce, pretty much everything'" (Asplund 2016). For readers who desire a more in-depth explanation, information about these criteria and examples of how health services organizations address the criteria can be found on the program's website (www.nist.gov/baldrige).

Exhibit 5.5 illustrates the essential elements in the Baldrige framework and the links between these elements. The following passage explains how to read and interpret the exhibit (BPEP 2015, 1):

> The Organizational Profile sets the context for your organization. It serves as the background for all you do. The performance system consists of the six categories in the center of the exhibit. These categories define your processes and the results you

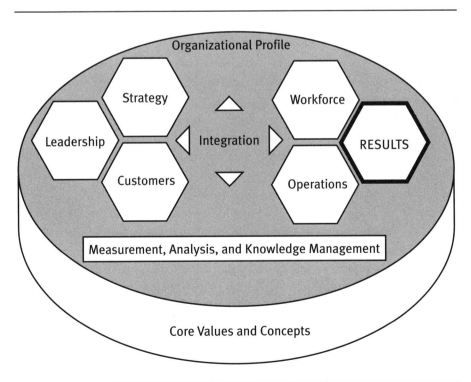

EXHIBIT 5.5
Organizational Profile: Baldrige Performance Excellence Program Framework for Health Care

Source: Reprinted from Baldrige Performance Excellence Program (BPEP) (2015).

achieve. Performance excellence requires strong Leadership and is demonstrated through outstanding Results. Those categories are highlighted in the exhibit. The word "integration" at the center shows that all the elements of the system are interrelated.

The leadership triad (Leadership, Strategy, and Customers) emphasizes the importance of a leadership focus on strategy and customers. The results triad (Workforce, Operations, and Results) includes your workforce-focused processes, your key operational processes, and the performance results they yield. All actions lead to results—a composite of health care and process, customer-focused, workforce-focused, leadership, and governance, and financial and market results.

The system foundation (Measurement, Analysis, and Knowledge Management) is critical to effective management and to a fact-based, knowledge-driven, agile system for improving performance and competitiveness. The basis of the Health Care Criteria is a set of Core Values and Concepts that are embedded in high-performance organizations.

The center horizontal arrowheads show the critical linkage between the leadership triad and the results triad and the central relationship between the Leadership and Results categories. The center vertical arrowheads point to and from the system foundation, which provides information on and feedback to key processes and the organizational environment.

Lessons for Healthcare Managers

Managers may take several lessons from the Baldrige systems model. First, the model describes the essential elements of organizational effectiveness (represented by the seven boxes in the model) and how they are related. The model recognizes the unique circumstances in which different organizations operate and encourages managers to base decisions, strategies, and interventions on their unique organizational profiles. The overarching nature of the organizational profile promotes ongoing consideration of external influences, such as environmental, regulatory, or market demands.

When viewed in light of the Baldrige model, one can see that the traditional principles of total quality (customer focus, continuous improvement, teamwork), described in chapter 1, touch on some, but not all, of the required elements (customer focus, operations focus, and workforce focus). The Baldrige model visually illustrates that a systems approach to quality management in a healthcare organization requires managers to focus on more than just the three principles of total quality. Achieving organizational effectiveness also requires a focus on the external environment, leadership, strategic planning, measurement, analysis and knowledge management, and on how the workforce members contribute individually and collectively to achieving the desired organizational performance results.

Managers who use this model understand the importance of alignment in the organization. This alignment means that the activities in each box in the model are directed toward achieving the same results and that organizational and management choices are consistent with the organization's mission, vision, values, strategic direction, and patient and stakeholder requirements. Without alignment, improvement efforts can be less effective. For example, one health services organization offers comprehensive quality improvement training for its managers. Each manager is expected to design and carry out an improvement effort as a requirement of the training, so each selects a topic on which to focus his improvement project. Although each manager demonstrates improvement in the chosen area, the collective improvements of all the training participants may not contribute to the overall organizational objectives. This observation is illustrated by one manager who devoted much time and effort to improving a service area that was eliminated by the organization the following year. Another healthcare organization offering a similar type of training engaged senior leaders to help select improvement topics that would not only provide benefit within the managers' scope of responsibility but also contribute to the overall organizational strategy.

The Baldrige model also illustrates the link between management and human resource needs. Before implementing a process improvement, managers ask themselves, "What needs to happen to ensure the staff will succeed at implementing the new process?" As a result, when a new process is initially implemented, managers support employees as they learn the new process or their new roles. Adapting to something new takes time, and by anticipating slight disruptions during the transition period, the manager is better prepared to accommodate whatever short-term budget or productivity variances might occur. An understanding of the framework that helps managers realize their role in process improvement also includes ensuring that employees have the information, training, and tools they need to successfully implement improvements in the work setting.

Finally, the Baldrige model illustrates essential linkages in the system. For every key leadership, management, and daily work process of the organization, the Baldrige criteria ask four questions (BPEP 2015):

1. Do you have a systematic approach, tools, and tactics?
2. Is your approach deployed to the people who need to use it?
3. Do you evaluate and improve the approach periodically?
4. Does this particular approach integrate into and align with other organizational approaches in other areas?

Integration of the leadership and results elements, represented by the arrows, is a vital component of an effective organizational system. For example, one health services manager realized the connection between the leadership triad and the results triad was one-way only. Communication flowed in one direction only with little opportunity for the managers and other staff to provide feedback for consideration in decision making at the organizational level. This realization helped to explain her perceived disconnect between organization-wide initiatives and her department's local circumstances and needs.

Socioecological Framework

The socioecological framework represents a transdisciplinary systems perspective on promoting health and wellness that uses and reflects theory from multiple fields, including medicine, public health, and behavioral and social sciences. Social ecology scholar Daniel Stokols (2000, 27) further describes the underpinnings of the framework:

> The healthfulness of a situation and the well-being of its participants are assumed to be influenced by multiple facets of both the physical environment (e.g., geography, architecture, and technology) and the social environment (e.g., culture, economics, and politics). Moreover, the health status of individuals and groups is influenced not only by environmental factors but also by a variety of personal attributes, including genetic heritage, psychological dispositions, and behavioral patterns. Thus, efforts to promote human well-being should be based on an understanding of the interplay among the diverse environmental, biological, or behavioral factors.

Key to this framework is the recognition of "the complexity of human environments" and the emphasis on multilevel, interrelated influences and multilevel, interrelated interventions influencing health and wellness (Stokols 2000). These multiple levels may be thought of as nested systems within systems, starting with the individual and expanding to include "interpersonal, organization, community, society, supranational" (Kok et al. 2008, 438). Peter Reed illustrates the multiple and interrelated levels of influences (determinants) and interventions in exhibit 5.6. Reading the exhibit top to bottom illustrates the four levels of determinants of health behavior: individual, organization, community, and population (Reed 2001). Reading the exhibit left to right illustrates that for each of these levels of determinants, specific interventions may be implemented and their effects evaluated. For example, the model may be used to better understand smoking behavior.

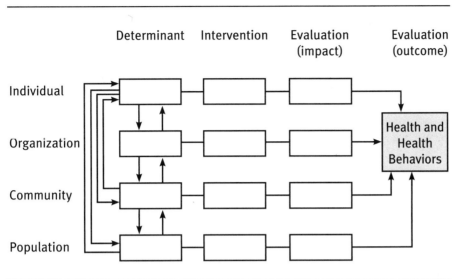

EXHIBIT 5.6

Socioecological Framework

Source: This illustration reprinted with permission by Peter Reed, MPH, JoAnne Earp, ScD, and the instructors of HBHE 131, *Introduction to Social Behavior in Public Health*, Department of Health Behavior and Health Education, University of North Carolina at Chapel Hill, School of Public Health, 2001.

Individual determinants of smoking behavior include a person's knowledge of associated health risks and the smoking behavior of family and friends. Individual interventions to reduce smoking behaviors may include smoking cessation classes and pharmacotherapy (e.g., nicotine patches). The impact is measured by whether the person stops smoking or does not start in the first place.

Organizational determinants of smoking behavior include policies regarding smoking in the workplace and the availability of smoking cessation classes as an employee health benefit. Prohibiting smoking, offering limited access to on-site smoking areas, and reimbursing employees for smoking cessation classes are interventions targeted at the organizational level. The proportion of employees who smoke and the "quit rate" are common organizational evaluation measures.

Community determinants of smoking behavior include social norms and beliefs. For example, smoking may be linked to social status and acceptance. Because of the history of tobacco farming in the southeastern United States, smoking has also been associated with the community's economic livelihood and therefore viewed more favorably. Redefining social norms and recruiting nontobacco economic opportunities would be considered community-level interventions. Impact may be measured in terms of community smoking rates.

Population determinants of smoking behavior include regulations regarding smoking in public places. No-smoking airline flights, no-smoking buildings, or a "sin tax" on cigarettes are examples of population-level interventions. The effect may be measured by compliance with regulations and population smoking rates.

In exhibit 5.6, the arrows between the levels indicate the interconnectedness of the determinants, interventions, and impact at all levels. While a level-specific intervention may be effective, recognizing the relationships between the levels creates a synergy to enhance desired outcomes. Using the example on smoking, one can understand the limited impact of enrolling a person in a smoking cessation class when he is surrounded by smokers in the family, in the workplace, and in public venues.

Lessons for Healthcare Managers

The major lesson from this framework for healthcare managers is that it provides a more expansive view of the nature of health and wellness in general and of health services specifically. In doing so, the model offers a larger context in which to understand interventions designed to improve the quality and safety of services provided by health services organizations and, in turn, to understand complementary and competing interventions within and between levels. This knowledge is particularly important to partners in accountable care organizations that share medical and financial responsibilities for providing coordinated care to a population of patients (Gold 2015).

In 2001, the Institute of Medicine recommended that "the changes needed to realize a substantial improvement in health care involve the health care system as a whole" (20). This recommendation implies understanding not only how organizations work as systems but also how the multiple players and layers involved in the health services sector are interrelated.

Summary

Systemic structures may not be readily visible. System models are valuable managerial tools to help managers identify the elements and connections between those elements in their organizations and the environments in which they operate. Exhibit 5.7 summarizes lessons from the four system models discussed in this chapter. Managers are encouraged to identify, integrate, and continuously apply lessons from each of these models to further develop their skills in understanding systemic structures.

Interconnected Systems Model	Three Core Process Model	Baldrige Performance Excellence Program Framework	Socioecological Framework
Places the patient at the center of healthcare delivery	Encourages concurrent improvement of interdependent processes	Shows how the components of organizational effectiveness are related	Broadens and expands the manager's view
Fosters feedback mechanisms that reinforce or balance system performance	Aligns processes around patient/client/ customer needs	Recognizes the context in which the organization operates	Addresses community and policy influences on health outcomes
Encourages awareness of linkages between major elements affecting patient care	Values all provider/employee groups	Promotes alignment of all organizational activities, including performance measurement	Illustrates the interrelationships among multiple levels involved in improving health outcomes
Illustrates the ripple effect of changes in the environment	Views administrative role as a process rather than a function	Illustrates essential links in the system	Encourages inter-related, multilevel interventions

EXHIBIT 5.7
Systems
Models:
Lessons for
Managers

Exercise 5.1

Objective: To practice identifying activities that represent essential elements in the Baldrige Performance Excellence Program (BPEP) framework.

Instructions: Think about your healthcare services work area or area of interest. Identify two activities a manager in this area does to advance organizational excellence in each of the following Baldrige framework categories:

- Strategy
- Customers
- Workforce
- Operations

Examples of what healthcare recipients of the Baldrige National Quality Award have done in these areas can be found online at www.nist.gov/baldrige.

Companion Readings

Baldrige Performance Excellence Program (BPEP). 2015. *2015–2016 Baldrige Excellence Framework: A Systems Approach to Improving Your Organization's Performance (Health Care).* Gaithersburg, MD: US Department of Commerce, National Institute of Standards and Technology.

Centers for Disease Control and Prevention. 2015. "Social Ecological Model for the Colorectal Cancer Control Program." Reviewed October 27. www.cdc.gov/cancer/crccp/sem.htm.

———. 2015. "Social Ecological Model for Violence Prevention." Reviewed March 25. www.cdc.gov/violenceprevention/overview/social-ecologicalmodel.html.

Health Administration Press. 2015. "The Baldrige Journey: In Pursuit of Excellence" (entire issue). *Frontiers* 32 (1). www.nist.gov/baldrige/enter/upload/ACHE-FrontiersThe-Baldrige-Journey.pdf.

Ruderman, M. 2013. "The Ecological Model in Public Health." The Women's and Children's Health Policy Center. Published June. www.jhsph.edu/research/centers-and-institutes/womens-and-childrens-health-policy-center/eco-model/eco-model.html.

Web Resource

Baldrige Performance Excellence Program Healthcare and National Quality Award Winners: http://patapsco.nist.gov/Award_Recipients/index.cfm

References

Asplund, J. 2016. "Prestigious Award Program Offers Hospitals a Framework for Bolstering Quality." *H&HN.* Published February 26. www.hhnmag.com/articles/6968-malcolm-baldrige-award-providing-a-framework-for-quality.

Baldrige Performance Excellence Program (BPEP). 2015. *2015–2016 Baldrige Excellence Framework: A Systems Approach to Improving Your Organization's Performance (Health Care).* Gaithersburg, MD: US Department of Commerce, National Institute of Standards and Technology.

Donabedian, A. 1980. *The Definition of Quality and Approaches to Its Assessment.* Vol. 1 of *Explorations in Quality Assessment and Monitoring.* Chicago: Health Administration Press.

Ferlie, E., and S. M. Shortell. 2001. "Improving the Quality of Healthcare in the United Kingdom and the United States: A Framework for Change." *Milbank Quarterly* 79 (2): 281–316.

Gold, J. 2015. "Accountable Care Organizations, Explained." *Kaiser Health News.* Published September 14. http://khn.org/news/aco-accountable-care-organization-faq.

Institute of Medicine. 2001. *Crossing the Quality Chasm: A New Health System for the 21st Century.* Washington, DC: National Academies Press.

Kelly, D. L., S. L. Pestotnik, M. C. Coons, and J. W. Lelis. 1997. "Reengineering a Surgical Service Line: Focusing on Core Process Improvement." *American Journal of Medical Quality* 12 (2): 120–29.

Kok, G., N. H. Gottlieb, M. Commers, and C. Smerecnik. 2008. "The Ecological Approach in Health Promotion Programs: A Decade Later." *American Journal of Health Promotion* 22 (6): 437–42.

McLaughlin, D. B., and J. R. Olson. 2012. *Healthcare Operations Management*, 2nd ed. Chicago: Health Administration Press.

Ransom, S. B., M. S. Joshi, and D. B. Nash (eds.). 2005. *The Healthcare Quality Book: Vision, Strategy, and Tools.* Chicago: Health Administration Press.

Reed, P. 2001. "Introduction to Social Behavior in Public Health." Course lecture at the Department of Health Behavior and Health Education, School of Public Health, University of North Carolina at Chapel Hill.

Stokols, D. 2000. "The Social Ecological Paradigm of Wellness Promotion." In *Promoting Human Wellness: New Frontiers for Research, Practice and Policy*, edited by M. D. Jamner and D. Stokols, 21–37. Los Angeles and Berkeley, CA: University of California Press.

Tagg, J. 2007. "Double-Loop Learning in Higher Education." *Change* 9 (4): 36–41.

SETTING THE STAGE FOR SUCCESS

ESTABLISHING SYSTEM DIRECTION

Learning Objectives

After completing this chapter, you should be able to

- link the role of mission, vision, and context to organizational results;
- appreciate how the purpose principle can aid managers in problem solving;
- distinguish the relationships between purpose, desired results, measures of results, interventions, and improvement goals; and
- compare the concepts of mental model and context as they are used in organizations.

The quality department at Hospital A defines its mission as "help departments improve their quality measures and meet requirements of oversight groups." The hospital has consistently passed accreditation surveys by The Joint Commission and has demonstrated improvements in quality measures required by The Joint Commission and the Centers for Medicare & Medicaid Services (CMS). Yet, physicians at Hospital A consistently complain to the CEO about bottlenecks in scheduling X-ray examinations for their patients and delays in receiving results for just about any diagnostic test.

The quality department at Hospital B defines its mission as "provide technical and consultative support to departments, managers, and teams to help them improve value to their customers." Hospital B also consistently passes accreditation surveys by The Joint Commission and demonstrates improvements in quality measures required by The Joint Commission and CMS. However, Hospital B has improved cycle times in numerous clinical diagnostic processes, reduced its overall operational costs, and improved employee satisfaction and retention.

Organizations operating from the mature end of the quality continuum know that a mission is much more than a catchy slogan or a poster on the wall. The **mission** defines the system's identity. The mission statement is used to explain and communicate why the organization or department exists, what the department is organized to do, or what a group is trying to achieve. A clear and shared understanding of the system's identity is essential

mission
statement that defines the system's identity

for sustainability and to successfully adapt to changing external demands in its operating environment. In this book, the identity or reason for being is referred to as **purpose**.

purpose
an identity or
reason for being

The quality department in Hospital A defined itself in terms of a narrow purpose ("help," "meet") and a singular goal ("improve"). The department was looking to attain specific results in accordance with defined performance measures. Hospital A succeeded in achieving these results, but it was not successful in achieving an overall quality organization. In Hospital B, the quality department defined itself in a broader way that permitted flexibility in how it defined its goals, focus, and interventions. For example, departmental goals could include "improve care delivered to those patient populations addressed by the measures." A focus on improving the hospital's overall admission and discharge processes could improve several aspects of patient care that are required by CMS. The hospital could do better at identifying patients at risk for pneumonia so pneumococcal and influenza immunizations can be given before discharge (a CMS-required activity) and could also improve the patient's experience as she transitions from the acute care setting to another level of care (CMS 2013, 2014).

Managers should consciously and consistently question purpose at all levels of the organization—that is, the purpose of individual activities, roles, processes, departments, programs, and the organization overall. At the system level, purpose defines the system. A clear understanding of purpose guides managers in establishing direction for improvements, helps them know they are working on the right problems, and increases the likelihood that quality efforts will achieve intended results. Without a clear understanding of purpose, managers run the risk of wasting time and resources by working on the wrong problem or improving something that should not exist in the first place. This chapter explores the concept of purpose and its importance for managers. Companion concepts of vision and context are also discussed.

Purpose

Donabedian's causal relationship of quality-of-care measures was described in chapter 1 as Structure → Process → Outcome (Donabedian 1980). However, when designing or redesigning interventions to improve results, the sequence is conceptually reversed: A clear understanding of purpose should guide the way organizations define desired outcomes. The purpose and desired outcomes should guide the manner in which processes are designed to support achieving that purpose, and the structure (how people are organized, roles are defined, and tools and technology are selected) should be guided by the requirements of the process. This sequence may be thought of as follows:

Purpose/Desired outcomes → Process → Structure

When using this conceptual sequence, understanding and clarifying purpose serve important roles in setting direction by defining why an entity exists. Discussions of purpose also ensure that the right problem is addressed, common ground is fostered, and breakthrough ideas and solutions are promoted.

Setting Direction

A student's purpose or identity shapes his selection of classes. A student with an identity of musician may take music theory and instrument classes, whereas a medical student may choose anatomy and physiology classes. Similarly, the identity of an organization or a department shapes its management's choices of goals, priorities, resource allocation, and improvement targets.

A hospital-based laboratory performed tests for the inpatient and outpatient populations of the tertiary care hospital in which it was located and for smaller hospitals and physicians' offices in the area. The manager and medical director, faced with the need to redesign the laboratory's operations, set a departmental goal to redesign the processes and the work area to improve efficiency and better meet customer needs. To accomplish this objective, they created a redesign team.

One of the first topics the redesign team discussed was the laboratory's purpose. Initially, the team described the laboratory's purpose as providing customer service. For a hospital that had formally adopted a total quality philosophy several years before, the team's focus on customer service indicated that it had integrated this total quality principle into its way of operating. However, to provide customer service was not a reason to exist; customer service was a part of what the laboratory provided but was not its sole function.

The improvement facilitator and the manager invited panels of internal customers to talk with the team about its expectations and experiences as customers of this laboratory's service. The common theme heard from each customer, whether a nurse in the emergency department or a physician in a doctor's office, was that they depended on the information the laboratory gave them to make patient care decisions. In its efforts to provide quality service, the laboratory had lost sight of the reason it existed: to provide information. The team realized that quality service was a desired characteristic in how it delivered the information.

As the team continued to discuss the laboratory's purpose, it also realized it provided customers with three distinct types of information. The first type of information was clinical patient data in the form of test results. Within this "product line" were numerous types of results from many types of specimens, from blood for analyzing cholesterol levels to tissue for analyzing a cancerous tumor. Over the years, however, the laboratory's role had evolved in response to changing reimbursement schemes, new technology, and published research on clinical treatments and interventions. As a result, the laboratory provided its customers with two additional product lines: (1) evidence on how to use and interpret newly available tests and testing methods and (2) information related to technical and regulatory requirements, which became important as tests moved away from the laboratory to point-of-care techniques carried out by nurses or physicians.

Clarifying its purpose became an empowering realization for the laboratory staff. Each of the three product lines of information was necessary to provide laboratory services to all of its customers; however, only one—clinical laboratory results—was a potential source of measurable revenue or expense for this department. The other two product lines were solely a source of expense for the department. Equipped with a clear definition of purpose and arguing from a systems point of view, the laboratory manager and medical director were able to negotiate budgetary expectations with their administrator. They were able to articulate that the laboratory may be incurring expenses that ultimately benefited the quality of patient care in other departments and reduced the cost of the patient's total hospital experience. The budget discussions changed focus from reducing laboratory expenses to measuring and preserving the laboratory's essential role in providing overall high-quality laboratory services to all patients within its service domain, not simply for work carried out within the boundaries of the laboratory's walls (Kelly 1998).

Addressing the Right Problem

The manager in an ambulatory surgery unit was faced with the problem of frequent patient delays, which led to patient complaints and higher costs. The manager assembled a team to address the goal of improving patient flow to improve clinical outcomes, patient satisfaction, and cost-effectiveness (Kelly et al. 1997).

In one of the first improvement team meetings, the improvement facilitator asked team members to identify the major phases of care that make up the entire process of care for a patient experiencing ambulatory surgery. The team identified five phases that an ambulatory surgery patient goes through:

1. Preadmission phase: care occurring somewhere other than in the ambulatory surgery unit
2. Preoperative phase: care occurring in the ambulatory surgery unit before the patient goes to the operating room
3. Intraoperative phase: actual operation taking place in the operating room

4. Postoperative phase: care supporting patient recovery and taking place in the recovery room or the ambulatory surgery unit

5. Postadmission phase: care occurring after the patient is discharged from the ambulatory surgery unit (which may include a follow-up phone call by a nurse or follow-up care in the physician's office)

The facilitator then asked the team to select an area that, if improved, could have the biggest impact on improving patient flow and reducing delays. The team chose the preadmission phase because this process was "upstream" to all of the others. If delays or breakdowns occurred during this phase of care, the rest of the process would also be delayed.

Next, the facilitator led a discussion about the purpose of the preadmission phase of care. Immediately, the team replied, "To prepare the patient for surgery; to make sure the patient is ready." As the purpose discussion continued, the team had a breakthrough when it realized that, although the preadmission phase of care helped to prepare the patient, its primary purpose was to prepare the *ambulatory surgery unit* to receive and care for the patient in the most effective and efficient manner. If this preparation occurred, the patient was more likely to progress through the other phases of care without unnecessary delays or surprises. This realization of purpose, along with an understanding of the interconnectedness of operational and clinical processes, played an important role in redesigning the patient-flow process.

Previous efforts to improve other surgery-related processes, such as the patient preregistration process, achieved just that—an improved preregistration process. An understanding of the purpose of the preadmission phase of care led the surgery team to look at registration occurring before admission in a different way. The team identified an entire package of information required before a patient's admission that would help prepare the care providers and the facility to most efficiently provide the outpatient surgery. This package included registration information (e.g., patient demographics, insurance data) and patient education materials such as clinical preparation of the patient (e.g., laboratory results, special orders, patient history), surgery scheduling, and information about the surgical procedure so that any special equipment or supplies could be arranged in advance. A preadmission information-gathering process was then designed to help assemble this package during a patient encounter at the physician's office and to ensure the package arrived at the hospital in advance of the patient's admission. A phone call to the patient the day before surgery confirmed last-minute details and provided the patient with an opportunity to ask any additional questions. In this way, the facility and care providers were better prepared to receive the patient, provide individualized care, anticipate and prevent delays or cancellations as a result of miscommunication or lack of information, and decrease the preoperative length of stay (Kelly et al. 1997).

While this approach to ambulatory surgery is commonplace today, the example is included here to offer insight regarding the role of purpose (explicitly or intuitively) in shaping the contemporary standard of care.

Fostering Common Ground

Without a clear understanding of what has to be accomplished, discussions on alternative solutions to a problem often lead to an impasse. Selecting one approach over another is hindered because people often bring to the discussion their own intense ownership of a particular solution, intervention, or idea. Discussing purpose can be a less threatening way to begin a discussion about a problem. Rather than highlighting differences among possible options and inviting comments on their perceived merit or shortcomings, discussing purpose helps to create a common ground from which to focus people with divergent opinions and views.

For example, consider two executives living in Seattle scheduled to present a lecture together at a professional conference in Chicago. The executives' presentation is on Monday at 11:00 am. They must be back in Seattle by Wednesday at noon for a board of directors meeting. They are considering various travel options. The purpose is to get from Seattle to Chicago. They find numerous means of travel that will achieve this purpose. They may drive, take a train, or fly. They further refine the purpose to get from Seattle to Chicago and back to meet the Monday and Wednesday obligations. If one wants to drive and one wants to fly, this refined purpose now leaves only one option: to fly. Next, they must decide on airlines, routes, and so on. Rather than argue over the options, they add decision criteria to guide their decision: They would like to fly nonstop within a specified price range and time of day. They find two flights on different airlines. Because they are frequent fliers on the same airlines, they easily choose the flight on their preferred airline. Even if the two executives start with different ideas about their travel, clarifying their purpose and adding decision criteria naturally lead them to a common decision.

Understanding purpose to foster common ground may be extended to the use of clinical decision support in health services organizations. Information systems are used for a variety of purposes: storing, retrieving, and streamlining and automating access to data. Many information systems began as accounting systems. As more clinical applications are being developed and demands for electronic health records and computerized physician order entry increase, questioning the purpose of these systems is important to ensure that the purpose, applications, uses, and outcomes are all aligned.

Reviewing early efforts in designing electronic clinical-decision support tools provides insights into the role of purpose in enhancing successful implementation of new technology. The clinical epidemiology and medical informatics team at LDS Hospital in Salt Lake City, Utah, has used computerized systems to improve patient care for more than 30 years. In 1998, an article in the *New England Journal of Medicine* described the development of LDS Hospital's computer-assisted management program for antibiotics and other anti-infective agents (Evans et al. 1998). This is how the LDS Hospital team defined the purpose of clinical information systems: "The project was designed to augment physicians' judgment, not to replace it. The computer was simply a tool that offered data on individual patients, decision logic, and prescribing information to physicians in a useful and non-threatening way" (Garibaldi 1998).

The purpose of the clinical information system was to support decision making, and this intent in turn promoted cooperation between information specialists and clinicians. A clear description of the purpose can create common ground for diverse members of a group, contribute to their ability to focus on a common goal, and enlist buy-in to enhance successful implementation of initiatives to improve patient outcomes.

Promoting Breakthrough Ideas and Solutions

Lessons from the public health domain offer examples of innovative solutions within the context of understanding purpose. Three types of prevention exist (Merrill and Timmreck 2006, 16–17):

1. **Primary prevention** is preventing a disease or disorder before it happens.
2. **Secondary prevention** is "aimed at health screening and detection activities [to] block the progression of disease."
3. **Tertiary prevention** "blocks the progression of a disability, condition, or disorder to keep it from advancing and requiring excessive care."

Consider the historical treatment of infectious diseases. Victims of smallpox were quarantined to prevent the disease from spreading. A more effective solution emerged when the scientific thinking about infectious disease changed from containing the disease to strengthening a person's defenses against a disease. This powerful redefinition of purpose ultimately led to the development of vaccines. The magnitude of the innovation has been described this way: "Indeed, if you asked a public health professional to draw up a top-ten list of the achievements of the past century, he or she would be hard pressed not to rank immunization first. Millions of lives have been saved and microbes

primary prevention the effort to prevent a disease or disorder before it happens (Merrill and Timmreck 2006, 16)

secondary prevention activities "aimed at health screening and detection activities [to] block the progression of disease" (Merrill and Timmreck 2006, 17)

tertiary prevention intervention that "blocks the progression of a disability, condition, or disorder to keep it from advancing and requiring excessive care" (Merrill and Timmreck 2006, 17)

stopped in their tracks before they could have a chance to wreak havoc. In short, the vaccine represents the single greatest promise of biomedicine: disease prevention" (Stern and Markel 2005, 611–12).

The Purpose Principle

Managers must develop the habit of asking themselves, "What are we really trying to achieve? On the basis of changes in the environment, technology, or customer requirements, what is our purpose? Does our current method of operating serve that purpose, or are there more effective alternatives?" When the purpose is clear, new solutions usually become clear as well.

purpose principle
a tool to aid managers in identifying the right purpose to address

The **purpose principle** is a tool to aid managers in this process. It comes from the concept of breakthrough thinking (Nadler and Hibino 1994), an approach to problem solving developed from the study of effective leaders and problem solvers from various industries and disciplines. The tool was popularized in 2009 by Kevin Doherty in a self-help book titled *The Purpose Principle: 11 Strategies to Help You Experience Ultimate Freedom in Your Health, Wealth, and Love Life*.

Nadler and Hibino (1994, 1) found that "when confronted with a problem, successful people tend to question why they should spend their time and effort solving the problem at all," and that effective problem solvers "always placed every problem into a larger context . . . to understand the relationship between what effective action on the problem was supposed to achieve and the purposes of the larger setting of which the original problem was a part." By questioning purpose and enlarging the boundaries from which they examined the problem, effective problem solvers are able to purposely and systematically choose the right problem and, in turn, the best solution.

Discussions of purpose encourage accompanying mental models regarding the problem and solution to be brought into the open. Purpose may be considered a systemic structure and the purpose principle a tool that promotes double-loop learning by challenging assumptions about the nature of a problem. By encouraging the viewing of the problem and solution from the larger context of the entire system, the purpose principle also promotes an understanding of the connections between the problem at hand and other elements or components of the system.

From Concept to Practice

A series of questions can help managers to examine and clarify purpose. The first question should be, "What am I trying to accomplish?" Sometimes, the response to this question results in a directional statement (e.g., improve, reduce). It is important to remember that action verbs describe a purpose (e.g., provide, build), while directional verbs describe a goal. To focus on the purpose rather than a goal, ask next, "What is this process, intervention, or department designed to accomplish?"

The purpose principle continues with a series of questions to identify and understand how the problem is related to the larger context in which it exists. Think of an onion. The effort of expanding the purpose is like starting from the inside of an onion and adding on the layers to construct a whole onion rather than peeling the onion, which is typically how the onion metaphor is presented. In this way, the larger purposes may be identified—and more layers are added to the onion. When the original purpose has been expanded several times, then another question should be asked: "What larger purpose might eliminate the need to achieve this smaller purpose?" (Nadler and Hibino 1994, 154).

Example 1

Here is an example to illustrate how the purpose principle might be used. The CEO of a large, tertiary care hospital closely follows his hospital's quality performance and compares his organization's performance with that of the other hospitals in the community, in the state, and across the nation using the Medicare Hospital Compare website (www.medicare.gov/hospitalcompare). Over the past several years, his hospital has shown steady improvement in some of the measures related to congestive heart failure (CHF), community-acquired pneumonia (CAP), and acute myocardial infarction (AMI). However, the percentile rankings are disappointing, as other hospitals are also steadily improving in these three areas. He wonders why some of the CAP measurement results are still well below the performance results for both AMI and CHF and why the hospital shows three different results in the smoking cessation measure (the one measure common to all three conditions). He also wonders why the hospital is not doing as well in performance measurement areas recently added by CMS. The CEO ponders a series of purpose questions to redefine the organization's quality goals.

- *What is the purpose of what I am trying to accomplish?*

  To improve my hospital's performance in the CMS quality measures.

- *What is the process I am investigating? (Note: Defining the process/ activities helps to shift one's response from the directional verb "improve" to an action verb representing the purpose.)*

  Measuring and reporting performance measures on selected diseases as required by CMS.

- *Have I further expanded the purpose? What is the purpose of measuring and reporting performance?*

  To provide feedback about how we are doing as an organization. In our case, this feedback could suggest that

  - we provide quality care, and my organization does not document what we do very well;
  - we have many different ways of doing the same thing; and
  - because the CMS performance measures are evidence-based (i.e., the actions being evaluated are shown by scientific studies to improve the quality of outcomes for that disease), our clinical protocols may not be based on the most current evidence; come to think of it, I wonder if we have clinical protocols?

- *Have I further expanded the purpose? What is the purpose of performance feedback?*

  In a complex organization, to provide information about the behavior of the system. Based on feedback, I am beginning to realize that the organization is operating like a lot of little systems. Individual physicians are making their own decisions, and individual departments are involved in their own improvement efforts. No coordinated focus on improving care for patients with specific diseases or conditions exists currently.

- *Have I further expanded the purpose? What is the purpose of providing information about the behavior of the system?*

  To better understand the system. If we do not understand the system, we will not be able to improve it. If we do not change the behavior of the system, we are only treating symptoms of the problem. We need to be able to change to function more cooperatively as a system.

- *For the patients, what is the purpose of reporting quality measurement data?*

  To give patients information that allows them to choose providers. However, employers and insurance companies will likely use the information more than the patients will.

- *For clinical staff, what is the purpose?*

  To fulfill bureaucratic demands. Staff members see reporting quality measurement data as just "one more thing to do" or as a hassle. They may not realize that these measures actually reflect evidence-based practice or that performance on these indicators may eventually determine reimbursement.

- *What larger purpose may eliminate the need to achieve this smaller purpose altogether?*

  Going back to the "old days," when all these groups, like CMS and The Joint Commission, were not telling us what to do to the extent they are today.

- *What is the right purpose for me to be working on? Describe how this purpose differs or does not differ from my original purpose.*

  CMS performance measures may be used to promote improvement for the organization *overall*, which is different from what I was originally trying to achieve: to improve my hospital's performance on the CMS measures. If I look at the measurement results as feedback about our system, I realize my purpose is to listen to the feedback to better understand the system.

- *Review my responses to the previous questions. Given my understanding of purpose, what quality goals will I now set?*
  - Coordinate and align improvement efforts throughout the organization.
  - Evaluate and improve the process for identifying stakeholder requirements and integrating them into how we conduct business.
  - Identify and improve system processes, such as patient discharge and teaching; update current evidence and incorporate it into how we treat patients; and collect performance data for analysis and review.

Example 2

Here is another example of how the purpose principle might be used. The administrator for a large, multispecialty, ambulatory medical practice has implemented a new quality management system for the entire organization.

When the office manager for one of the obstetrics and gynecology practices is given the first "clinic report card," the data for obstetrics patients show the practice has performed well in the area of pregnancy-associated complications. However, the practice has performed poorly in the areas of patient satisfaction. In particular, patients are not satisfied with their level of involvement in their own care and their preparation for labor, delivery, breast-feeding, and care of their newborns.

The manager knows staff members are committed to quality patient care and are hard workers. Out of curiosity, the manager asks one of the obstetricians, "What is the purpose of prenatal care and the prenatal office visits?" The physician replies, "To identify signs of problems with the mother or the fetus and to intervene early to prevent problems from getting worse." The manager then asks the physician what kinds of problems could potentially occur, to which he replies, "Conditions like toxemia in the mother or growth retardation in the fetus."

The manager initially identifies the problem as patient dissatisfaction with prenatal care, the process to be improved as prenatal care, and the purpose of the prenatal visits (as described by the physician) as early identification of and intervention with problems with the mother and the fetus or baby. The manager then asks a series of purpose questions:

- *What am I trying to accomplish?*

  To improve the clinic's report card results in the area of patient satisfaction with prenatal care.

- *Have I expanded the purpose of addressing this problem? What is the purpose of the clinic's report card?*

  To monitor patient satisfaction with the care they receive in our clinic.

- *Have I further expanded the purpose? What is the purpose of monitoring patient satisfaction with the care received in our clinic?*

  To keep existing patients and to attract new patients to our clinic.

- *Have I further expanded the purpose? What is the purpose of keeping existing patients and attracting new patients to our clinic?*

  To stay in business and pay the bills.

- *For physicians, what is the purpose of prenatal care?*

  To identify signs of problems with the mother or the fetus and to intervene early to prevent problems from getting worse.

- *For patients, what is the purpose of prenatal care?*

  To have a healthy pregnancy and a healthy baby; to learn about prenatal classes and other parenting resources.

- *For the insurance companies, what is the purpose of prenatal care?*

  To prevent complications that result in extended hospitalization of the mother or the baby and to keep overall healthcare costs down.

- *What larger purpose would eliminate the need to achieve these smaller purposes altogether?*

  If women did not get pregnant or have babies.

- *What is the right purpose for me to be working on? How does this purpose differ or not differ from my original purpose?*

  By answering these questions, it becomes apparent that the physicians, the office manager, the patients, and the insurance companies have different yet overlapping purposes. The purpose principle may be used to align all of these parties around a common purpose. A more comprehensive purpose for prenatal care that addresses all of the stakeholder requirements and purposes would be more effective.

  For example: The purpose of the clinic's prenatal services is to assess, monitor, and manage the physiological and psychosocial needs of families during the childbearing process.

By questioning, identifying, and documenting different purposes, the manager or team may select the most appropriate level of purpose—the purpose that best enables them to solve the right problem and that is within their means (e.g., resources, scope of authority). At first, the questions may be difficult to answer and may appear to be redundant. However, with practice, the ability to answer the questions will improve and the repetition will encourage a deeper level of thinking about the problem.

Improving System Performances: Corollaries to Purpose

Once the purpose is defined, the activities to achieve that purpose can be identified according to the different stakeholders. Clarifying corollaries to the purpose may be helpful to ensure the various stakeholders or discussion participants can see their ideas are addressed.

For the obstetrics and gynecology clinic described previously, examples of such corollaries include the following:

- The desired results are healthy clinical outcomes, satisfied patients, and cost-effective services.
- The clinic will measure how successful it is in achieving the desired results with data such as: maternal and infant complications, early diagnosis, patient satisfaction, and payer satisfaction.
- The service mix, processes, and interventions used to accomplish the purpose may then be strategically determined, designed, and improved.
- The goals for performance improvement efforts are to validate the purposes of the key stakeholders identified earlier; refine the clinic's purpose for prenatal care services on the basis of any new information obtained; evaluate current practices to determine the extent to which the clinic is accomplishing its purpose; define a service mix that is consistent with the purpose; prioritize those services needing improvement; and design, redesign, and implement improved processes that meet all stakeholder requirements and accomplish the new definition of purpose.

The results of this example may seem intuitive or obvious, but without the discussion of purpose, the clinic manager may set goals to improve the aesthetics surrounding care, rather than the actual care processes themselves.

Vision

vision
ideal future state

In the examples, the desired results may also be considered the ideal future state or **vision** for the practice. Vision plays a role in leadership (Kouzes and Posner 2012), personal effectiveness (Covey 2004), organizational effectiveness (Senge 2006), art (Fritz 1989), and even survival (Frankl 1962).

An organizational vision and mission go hand in hand. Mission represents the organization's identity or purpose. The vision represents this identity in its ideal future state. Exhibit 6.1 summarizes the differences between mission and vision statements.

Visions may be found at a variety of levels within health services. For example, the Healthy People initiative, coordinated by the Office of Disease

	Focus	Example
Mission Statement	Who we are, what we do	Working in partnership to promote and improve health, wellness, safety, and quality of life in San Bernardino County
Vision Statement	Where we are going	Healthy people in vibrant communities

EXHIBIT 6.1
Mission and Vision Statement Differences: San Bernardino County Department of Public Health

Source: Data from San Bernardino County Department of Public Health (2014, 12).

Prevention and Health Promotion within the US Department of Health and Human Services (2010), offers an overall vision for the nation's health: "A society in which all people live long, healthy lives." This vision provides a common direction for diverse groups that share an interest in improving health and healthcare in the United States so that they may individualize their own community visions within the larger national context. As shown in exhibit 6.2, the Healthy People 2020 vision is complemented by the corollaries to purpose described previously. The future desired state (results) is represented in the vision and overarching goals; the purpose of the Healthy People 2020 initiative is represented by the mission; the services, processes, and categories of interventions used to accomplish the purpose are identified accordingly in the defined priority topic areas; the improvement goals are represented by the objectives within these topics; and the measures of success are represented by the health indicators within four major categories.

Organizations often have an overall vision for the future. Managers may also use the concept of vision in a variety of ways and at various levels within the organization. Managers may have visions for their careers, for their own professional contribution to good-quality healthcare, or for their ideal departments or service areas. Managers may ask a team to describe its ideal vision for a particular work process or process of care. In creating a vision, describing ideal characteristics rather than ideal interventions allows flexibility in how the vision will be accomplished while fostering adaptability to changing internal and external conditions. For example, questions physicians may pose when creating a vision for their own office practice may include the following:

If my practice were recognized as one of the best in the country,

- What would patients and families say about the care they received?
- What would patients and families say about their interactions with me? With my office staff?

EXHIBIT 6.2

Healthy People
2020

Vision and Overarching Goals of Healthy People 2020

A society in which all people live long, healthy lives.

- Attain high-quality, longer lives free of preventable disease, disability, injury, and premature death
- Achieve health equity, eliminate disparities, and improve the health of all groups
- Create social and physical environments that promote good health for all
- Promote quality of life, healthy development, and healthy behaviors across all life stages

Mission of Healthy People 2020

- Identify nationwide health improvement priorities
- Increase public awareness and understanding of the determinants of health, disease, and disability and the opportunities for progress
- Provide measurable objectives and goals that are applicable at the national, state, and local levels
- Engage multiple sectors to take actions to strengthen policies and improve practices that are driven by the best available evidence and knowledge
- Identify critical research, evaluation, and data collection needs

Topics

Examples of topics and an example of recommended intervention

- Adolescent health: therapeutic foster care
- Cancer: screen for breast, cervical, and colorectal cancer
- Environmental safety: test older homes for presence of lead paint
- Heart disease and stroke: Work site nutrition and physical activity programs
- Immunizations and infectious diseases: targeted vaccinations
- Mental health and mental disorders: screening for depression in adults
- Nutrition and weight status: screening for obesity in children and adolescents
- Substance abuse: community interventions to reduce alcohol-impaired driving

Objectives

Examples of objectives

- Reduce the annual number of new cases of diagnosed diabetes in the population
- Increase the proportion of persons with health insurance
- Reduce infections caused by key pathogens transmitted commonly through food
- Increase the proportion of women with a family history of breast and/or ovarian cancer who receive genetic counseling
- Reduce the number of new AIDS cases among adolescents and adults
- Increase access to trauma care in the United States

Categories of Measures

- General health status
- Determinants of health
- Health-related disparities

Source: Data from US Department of Health and Human Services, Office of Disease Prevention and Health Promotion (2010).

- What would my colleagues around the country say about my practice?
- What processes in my office would colleagues most want to emulate?

In addition, physicians may want to consider these questions:

- How do I and my office staff feel after a day's work?
- If a prominent journal or newspaper were writing about my office practice, what would the article say?

When creating a vision, one should not be limited by what is possible or what is not possible. By defining characteristics of the ideal future rather than ideal interventions, a manager may balance describing an ideal future with present constraints. When asked about their ideal unit or office, healthcare workers often respond with, "We would have that new computer system" or "We would totally remodel the office." However, financial constraints may not allow for these expenditures, which make constructing the vision an exercise in futility rather than a chance to describe a future ideal state. Rather than "We would have that new computer system," the ideal answer might be, "We have streamlined, user-friendly documentation and communication mechanisms in place to provide needed information for safe care, efficient internal office operations, and patient education." Rather than "We would totally remodel the office," the ideal answer might be, "Patients will find a clean, accessible, comfortable, and relaxing office environment that respects their privacy and confidentiality."

By defining characteristics of the ideal future rather than ideal interventions, opportunities for finding creative and flexible ways of achieving the vision while working within the constraints of the situation may be enhanced.

Context

As stated in chapter 4, a mental model is a deeply ingrained way of thinking that influences how a person sees and understands the world and how a person acts. **Context** is a concept closely related to mental models and is defined as "the unquestioning assumptions through which all experience is filtered" (Davis 1982, 64). In this book, the phrase *mental models* refers to an individual's assumptions, and the term *context* refers to organizational assumptions that guide how the organization defines itself and how it operates.

context
"the unquestioning assumptions through which all experience is filtered" (Davis 1982, 64)

The following two examples illustrate the subtle difference between mental models and context. Here is the first illustration (Goss, Pascale, and Athos 1998, 88–89):

> Consider this analogy. You inherit your grandmother's house. Unknown to you is one peculiarity: all the light fixtures have bulbs that give off a blue rather than yellow light. You find that you don't like the feel of the rooms and spend a lot of time and money repainting walls, reupholstering furniture, and replacing carpets. You never seem to get it quite right, but nonetheless, you rationalize that at least it is improving with each thing you do. Then one day you notice the blue light bulbs and change them. Suddenly, all that you fixed is broken.
>
> Context is like the color of the light, not the objects in the room. Context colors everything in the corporation. More accurately, the context alters what we see, usually without our being aware of it.

An external community focus may represent one operating context for a health services organization, while an internal organizational focus may represent a different operating context. A focus on improving the quality of health services delivered may represent one operating context, while a focus on improving health of the community is another. Management decisions about resource allocation, prevention, or continuum-of-care issues differ depending on the context or assumptions about the organization's focus or role in the community.

Consider this second illustration of context (Davis 1982, 64), which suggests a corollary to the concept: content.

> Most parents have dreams for their children. Some want their children to be doctors, some musicians, and all want them to be healthy, wealthy, and wise. These are parents raising their children by focusing on content. Following in a father's footsteps, or in the footsteps father never had and therefore wants for his son, [is a] well-known example of this approach. Other parents, however, raise their children by focusing on context. In Helen Keller's famous phrase, their dream is, "be all you can be." The orientation here is to "parent" the context and let the child discover the content.

As stated in the illustration, managers may also find themselves facing the dichotomy of which to manage: context or content. One may think of the distinctions between context and content as they are illustrated by a circle. The boundary of the circle is the context; the inside of the circle is the content (Davis 1982). Historically, health services managers have been promoted on the basis of their content expertise: an excellent pharmacist becomes the manager of the entire pharmacy department; an excellent engineer becomes the manager of the facilities maintenance department; or an excellent clinician becomes a department, division, or unit manager. These managerial roles generally include direct supervision of the people and the work.

Today, the organizations, environments, processes, and technologies in the health services sector are so complex that managers cannot be experts on both managing and on the content of the work that needs to be managed. Managers' roles will increasingly move away from managing content to managing context. This shift means employees with fundamental knowledge of the work itself will carry out and improve their work processes, while managers will ensure that employees have the appropriate tools, information, knowledge, and competency to effectively do their jobs and deliver quality services and products.

Managing context also suggests managing the boundaries of the system, which may be a unit, a department, an office practice, a service line, or an entire organization. Boundaries may be defined in terms of scope of work, decision-making authority, expectations, and accountability. The manager may set or reset the boundaries on the basis of environmental conditions and other organizational considerations. In a department with a high ratio of experienced employees, the manager may expand the boundary so that staff members are more autonomous in their decision making. However, in a department composed of a young or inexperienced staff, the manager may tighten the boundaries of decision making until the employees gain knowledge, ability, and confidence in their own decision-making skills.

Managing the boundaries of the system also suggests that managers define their own areas of responsibility, as well as the interfaces that occur at the boundaries. As healthcare organizations become more complex and teams are increasingly used to accomplish the organization's work, the supervisory role also shifts to one of "boundary manager" (Fisher 2000). This change means rather than supervising individuals, the supervisor helps teams interact with each other to coordinate work, communicate information, or resolve problems. Likewise, effectively managing context requires an awareness and understanding of the interfaces with other systems within and outside of the organization. For example, to maintain quality outcomes for patients while also reducing hospital lengths of stay, managers must proactively work with nursing homes to understand and improve the interface between acute care and nursing home care.

The best way to become aware of context and draw the appropriate boundary for the system is by asking the right questions (Davis 1982). For managers, the key to asking the right questions is being willing to challenge current assumptions. When current assumptions are not being challenged, answers to the questions will simply be restatements of what is already known and the questioning process will not help the manager understand and explore what is beyond the current boundary of knowledge or awareness.

The importance of challenging assumptions (e.g., double-loop learning) may be seen in the ambulatory surgery improvement example in chapter 4. The prevailing assumption at the time was to use restructuring to reduce costs—specifically, to reduce the number of registered nurse (RN) positions by eliminating RNs or replacing them with unlicensed personnel (Gordon 2005). In the ambulatory surgery example, "because the outcome of cost savings and value had been defined at the onset of the project in terms of length of stay and total consumption of resources, not just in terms of staffing mix, cost savings [were] realized despite a predominantly RN staff" (Kelly et al. 1997, 126). By questioning the assumption that restructuring was the only solution and replacing it with a principles-driven change process, this team was able to improve throughput, reduce costs, maintain clinical outcomes, and improve patient satisfaction while retaining RNs in their care delivery model. This approach was "quite different from the trend of decreasing professional staff and increasing mix of unlicensed support personnel" (Kelly et al. 1997, 128).

Summary

Understanding the role of mission, vision, and context as underlying structures is essential for managers to adapt and improve continuously in the presence of complexity and uncertainty. The mission or purpose describes the identity of the organization—the reason it exists. Within this identity, the vision (the ideal future state) and context are defined.

The purpose principle aids in clarifying, defining, or validating purpose. The relationship between vision and context is illustrated with the example of a young child putting together a puzzle. The child empties the puzzle pieces from the box and props up the box to see a picture of what the puzzle is supposed to look like when it is completed. He then sorts the pieces: one group contains pieces with a straight edge or a corner shape, and one group contains the odd shapes. When asked why, the child replies, "To make the outside first." Once the outer edge of the puzzle is assembled, he goes about fitting in the rest of the pieces, knowing that each piece will eventually have its own place in the picture.

The manager's role in establishing vision may be thought of as making sure everyone in the organization has the ability to see the entire picture—that is, what the puzzle will look like when it is completed. The manager's role in setting the boundaries or context of the system may be thought of as putting together the outer edge of the puzzle. The images or shapes of the individual pieces may be thought of as the content, which is what goes on or what is done within the organization. Although there is much ambiguity at first about where the individual pieces should go, enough information is available to continue the task of building the puzzle, or, in the manager's case, moving toward the vision of the future.

Exercise 6.1

Objective: To think about and clarify professional purpose.

Instructions:

- Write your own professional purpose or mission.
- Practice the purpose principle by writing your responses to the following questions as they relate to your professional purpose:
  a. What am I trying to accomplish?
  b. What is the process(es) or activity(ies) involved in the response to a? (Be sure to use an active, not directional, verb.)
  c. What is the purpose of the response to b?
  d. What is the purpose of the response to c?
  e. What is the purpose of the response to d?
  f. What is my purpose according to my patients, clients, or customers?
  g. What larger purpose may eliminate the need to achieve this smaller purpose altogether?
  h. What is the right purpose for me to be working on? Describe how this purpose differs or does not differ from my original purpose.

Companion Readings

Compton-Phillips, A., and U. R. Kotagal. 2016. "'Being the Best at Getting Better'— Creating a Culture of Change." *NEJM Catalyst.* Published June 1. http:// catalyst.nejm.org/being-the-best-at-getting-better-creating-a-culture-of-change.

Ingersoll, G., P. A. Witzel, and T. C. Smith. 2005. "Using Organizational Mission, Vision, and Values to Guide Professional Practice Model Development and Measurement of Nurse Performance." *Journal of Nursing Administration* 35 (2): 86–93.

Johns Hopkins Medicine. 2016. "Johns Hopkins Medicine Strategic Plan." Accessed November 8. www.hopkinsmedicine.org/strategic_plan/patient_and_family_ centered_care.html.

Nadler, G., and W. J. Chandon. 2004. "Introducing the Smart Question Approach: Moving Beyond Problem-Solving to Creating Solutions." In *Smart Questions: Learn to Ask the Right Questions for Powerful Results,* 1–41. San Francisco: Jossey-Bass.

Shuman, J., and J. Twombly. 2010. "Collaborative Networks Are the Organization: An Innovation in Organization Design and Management." *Vikalpa: The Journal for Decision Makers* 35 (1): 1–13.

Web Resources

American Hospital Association, Great Boards: www.greatboards.org
National Center for Healthcare Leadership: www.nchl.org

References

Centers for Medicare & Medicaid Services (CMS). 2014. "HCAHPS: Patients' Perceptions of Care Survey." Last modified September 25. www.cms.gov/Medicare/Quality-Initiatives-Patient-Assessment-instruments/Hospital QualityInits/HospitalHCAHPS.html.

————. 2013. "Conditions for Coverage & Conditions for Participation." Last modified November 6. www.cms.gov/CFCsAndCoPs.

Covey, S. 2004. *The Seven Habits of Highly Effective People: Powerful Lessons in Personal Change.* New York: Free Press.

Davis, S. M. 1982. "Transforming Organizations: The Key to Strategy Is Context." *Organizational Dynamics* 10 (3): 64–80.

Donabedian, A. 1980. *Explorations in Quality Assessment and Monitoring.* Vol. 1 in *The Definition of Quality and Approaches to Its Assessment.* Chicago: Health Administration Press.

Evans, R. S., S. L. Pestotnik, D. C. Classen, T. P. Clemmer, L. K. Weaver, J. F. Orme, J. F. Lloyd, and J. P. Burke. 1998. "A Computer-Assisted Management Program for Antibiotics and Other Antiinfective Agents." *New England Journal of Medicine* 338 (4): 232–38.

Fisher, K. 2000. *Leading Self-Directed Work Teams: A Guide to Developing New Team Leadership Skills.* New York: McGraw-Hill.

Frankl, V. E. 1962. *Man's Search for Meaning: An Introduction to Logotherapy.* Boston: Beacon Press.

Fritz, R. 1989. *The Path of Least Resistance: Learning to Become the Creative Force in Your Own Life.* New York: Ballantine.

Garibaldi, R. A. 1998. "Computers and the Quality of Care—A Clinician's Perspective." *New England Journal of Medicine* 338 (4): 259–60.

Gordon, S. 2005. *Nursing Against the Odds: How Health Care Cost Cutting, Media Stereotypes, and Medical Hubris Undermine Nurses and Patient Care.* Ithaca, NY: ILR Press.

Goss, T., R. Pascale, and A. Athos. 1998. "The Reinvention Roller Coaster: Risking the Present for a Powerful Future." In *Harvard Business Review on Change,* 83–112. Boston: Harvard Business School Press.

Kelly, D. L. 1998. "Reframing Beliefs About Work and Change Processes in Redesigning Laboratory Services." *The Joint Commission Journal on Quality Improvement* 24 (9): 154–67.

Kelly, D. L., S. L. Pestotnik, M. C. Coons, and J. W. Lelis. 1997. "Reengineering a Surgical Service Line: Focusing on Core Process Improvement." *American Journal of Medical Quality* 12 (2): 120–29.

Kouzes, J. M., and B. Z. Posner. 2012. *The Leadership Challenge: How to Make Extraordinary Things Happen in Organizations*, 5th ed. New York: John Wiley & Sons.

Merrill, R. M., and T. C. Timmreck. 2006. *Introduction to Epidemiology*, 4th ed. Sudbury, MA: Jones & Bartlett Publishers.

Nadler, G., and S. Hibino. 1994. *Breakthrough Thinking: The Seven Principles of Creative Problem Solving*. Rocklin, CA: Prima Publishing.

San Bernardino County Department of Public Health. 2014. *Strategic Plan 2015–2020*. Accessed October 18, 2016. www.sbcounty.gov/uploads/dph/publichealth/documents/2015-SBC-DPH-Strategic-Plan.pdf.

Senge, P. M. 2006. *The Fifth Discipline: The Art and Practice of the Learning Organization*. New York: Doubleday Currency.

Stern, A. M., and H. Markel. 2005. "The History of Vaccines and Immunization: Familiar Patterns, New Challenges." *Health Affairs* 24 (3): 611–21.

US Department of Health and Human Services, Office of Disease Prevention and Health Promotion. 2010. *Healthy People 2020*. Published November. www.healthy people.gov/sites/default/files/HP2020_brochure_with_LHI_508_FNL.pdf.

SETTING IMPROVEMENT GOALS IN COMPLEX SYSTEMS

Learning Objectives

After completing this chapter, you should be able to

- appreciate the impact of establishing goals in complex systems,
- identify various mental models about goals,
- recognize the linkage between goal statements and attainment of desired improvements, and
- judge the advantages and disadvantages of different types of goal statements.

Patient A presents to his primary care provider as overweight and suffering from high blood pressure. The treatment goals the provider sets for the patient are to lose weight and to take the prescribed blood pressure medicine. The patient begins dieting and taking his blood pressure medicine. Within six months, Patient A has lost 30 pounds and shows improved blood pressure. However, at Patient A's annual checkup several months later, his provider is dismayed to find that he has gained back the 30 pounds.

Patient B is also overweight and suffering from high blood pressure when she sees her primary care provider. The treatment goals the provider sets for the patient are to integrate a balanced diet and regular exercise into her daily lifestyle and to reduce blood pressure through lifestyle change and medication. Within six months, Patient B has also lost 30 pounds and shows improved blood pressure. At her next annual physical, Patient B has kept off the 30 pounds and informs her provider that she feels much better as she has been walking three days a week and eating healthier food.

The seemingly subtle difference in how the treatment goals were set for these two patients actually represents the relationship between the goals and the subsequent results that are obtained.

Goals serve a variety of purposes for individuals throughout the realm of health services. Clinical providers use goals when establishing plans of care in all settings. For example, goals may be set for managing a patient's respiratory status in an intensive care unit, targeting functional activity in the rehabilitation setting, planning a patient's discharge from a hospital, and promoting comfort and end-of-life care in palliative and hospice services. Managers use goals when conducting employee performance appraisals to determine how well employees are fulfilling their job responsibilities, target areas for improvement, and guide rewards and incentives. Project managers use goals when implementing administrative and clinical information systems. Goals inform every step of the project management process and are the bases for time lines focused on capital purchases, information system programming needs, user training, and installation. Academic educators use goals (also referred to as *learning objectives*) when teaching health services professionals. Health educators use goals when designing health prevention and promotion programs targeting smoking, obesity, and hypertension. Program managers and researchers use goals when writing grant proposals.

Goals are also used for a variety of purposes in organizations (Scott 2003). Strategic goals provide direction for decision making. An organizational goal to increase market share in obstetrics influences management decisions about prioritizing capital expenditures for remodeling patient care units in the hospital. Organizational goals, such as being the first-choice medical provider in the community, may motivate employees and other stakeholders. A goal to become a center of excellence for cardiovascular care can foster employee pride and loyalty, serve as a recruitment strategy for physicians and other clinical providers, and bring prestige in the community. A goal to be the "premier center for cancer research" can legitimize investment in research infrastructure at an academic medical center, which in turn leads to research funding from external groups.

An organization's effectiveness in setting and aligning goals gives clues about its path along the quality continuum. Scoring criteria for the Baldrige Performance Excellence Program (BPEP) offer a systems view on the quality continuum, which includes the role of goals. This continuum is illustrated in exhibit 7.1 (BPEP 2015, 34).

EXHIBIT 7.1
Goals and
the Quality
Continuum

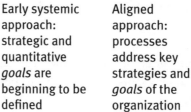

| Reaching to problems: strategic and operational *goals* are poorly defined | Early systemic approach: strategic and quantitative *goals* are beginning to be defined | Aligned approach: processes address key strategies and *goals* of the organization | Integrated approach: processes and measures track progress on key strategic and operational *goals* |

Less mature ─────────────────────────────────▶ More mature

Source: Reprinted BPEP (2015, 34).

When one realizes how pervasively goals are used by individuals and organizations in both clinical and nonclinical settings, one may begin to appreciate the widespread impact of effective goal-setting skills on organizational performance. The importance of setting effective goals may be further appreciated when one realizes that all subsequent actions follow and are influenced by how the initial goal is set.

Relationship Between Goals and Results

The ability to set goals effectively is a requisite skill for managers at all levels of an organization. The following example of two hospitals facing similar challenges illustrates how goals set by leadership influence subsequent actions and the results of those actions.

The Hospital Consumer Assessment of Healthcare Providers and Systems (HCAHPS) reports for Hospital A and Hospital B show that both perform below the national average for hospitals of a similar size and type. Senior leaders at each hospital decide to focus on improving customer service and patient satisfaction as an organizational priority. To address the problem of low patient satisfaction scores, the senior management team at Hospital A sets the following goal: improve customer service.

To achieve this goal, Hospital A hires a customer service specialist and institutes mandatory customer service training for all employees. The nurse managers in the hospital are faced with a dilemma. Their departmental education budgets are limited, and their staff members are already subject to mandatory education in areas such as infection control and fire safety. One more mandatory educational requirement will deplete the education dollars and eliminate the managers' resources for funding continuing education to maintain the staff's clinical competence.

Hospital B uses a different approach to address the problem of low patient satisfaction scores. Because the source of the problem was not evident to Hospital B's administrators, they first try to gain a better understanding of why the problem is occurring. The senior management team at Hospital B sets the following partial or intermediate goal: understand why patients are not satisfied with their hospital experience. This goal guides further study of the hospital's satisfaction data, which show that patients are least satisfied with the communication with nurses and feel rushed to leave the hospital without being fully prepared to do so. The organization conducts an investigation to learn why communication and discharge planning are not occurring effectively. The analysis reveals that, although staffing seems adequate on a day-to-day basis, the hospital's reliance on temporary staff and traveling nurses has increased significantly over the past year. Although the temporary staff and traveling nurses are experienced in their technical duties, their lack of familiarity with the hospital's specific procedures and resources increasingly leads to communication breakdowns within and among departments. The organizational analysis highlights this common problem for the departments responsible for patient registration, billing, and housekeeping and in the nursing, respiratory therapy, and pharmacy departments. On the basis of this information, senior leaders at Hospital B prioritize the contributing factors and develop specific goals to address the top priority factors. They revise their goals as follows: (1) increase the proportion of staff who are permanent employees, (2) improve the discharge planning process, (3) reallocate resources spent on temporary staff to fund the aforementioned improvements, and (4) monitor the impact of staffing and process improvements on patient satisfaction.

Which hospital's goals are most likely to improve patients' satisfaction with their hospital experience? A vague goal offering little direction, such as Hospital A's goal to "improve customer service," often results in the problem-solving approach called **repair service behavior**. Organizations or individuals are using repair service behavior when they solve a "problem" they know how to solve, whether or not it is the problem they need to solve (Dörner 1996). An example of repair service behavior is when a novice gardener responds to the problem of withering leaves on a new plant by watering more instead of repotting and fertilizing the plant, which is what the plant needs. Examples of repair service behavior in health services organizations can include creating new positions, conducting training, writing a new policy, or requesting more funds.

repair service behavior
a type of problem solving where organizations or individuals solve a problem they know how to solve, regardless of whether it is the problem they need to solve (Dörner 1996)

Hospital A knew how to create new positions and conduct training. However, it did not know how to identify the underlying cause of a widespread organizational problem. This example also illustrates how a poorly conceived goal (e.g., improve customer service) may cause unintended consequences or create more problems in other areas of the organization. In this case, the mandatory customer service training took resources away from technical education, which could ultimately reduce the overall clinical competency of the nursing staff.

In contrast, Hospital B's response illustrates the senior leaders' understanding of how goal setting should be approached in complex systems such as healthcare organizations (Dörner 1996, 63–64):

- When working with a complex, dynamic system, first develop at least a provisional picture of the partial goals to achieve; those partial goals will clarify what needs to be done when.
- In complex situations, almost always avoid focusing on just one element and pursuing only one goal; instead, pursue several goals at once.

By approaching the problem using a partial goal (understand why patients are not satisfied with their hospital experience), Hospital B defined the underlying problems and then developed a clear, multidimensional statement to guide the improvement interventions. Hospital B avoided an intervention that may not have solved the problem and was able to avoid the repair service behavior often associated with an unclear goal.

Although it is a requisite skill for managers, goal setting is an area where managers err. Several of the errors defined in *Management Mistakes in Healthcare* (Hofmann 2005, 11) are related to faulty goal setting in an organization's management or administrative domain. These errors include

- inadequate preparation of or by decision maker(s),
- political pressure,
- a flawed decision-making process, and
- ignorance of legitimate alternatives.

By improving their goal-setting skills, managers promote positive movement along the quality continuum.

Setting Improvement Goals in Complex Systems

Just as experience can influence how one defines quality, one's experience can influence one's mental models about setting goals. In some contexts, the SMART approach (a mnemonic for specific, measureable, achievable, realistic or relevant, time sensitive) to setting goals is recommended. In some contexts, the accepted approach to goal setting is based on the definition of a goal as (Gitlin and Lyons 2008, 89)

> a clear and concise statement that represents what will be accomplished as a result of the program. It is a global or broad statement describing the overarching purpose(s) of the project or what will be achieved by conducting the proposed program. . . . In turn, each goal has a specific set of objectives. An objective is a statement about a specific outcome of a program that can be evaluated and measured. Thus, an objective must be written in such a way as to reflect a qualitative or quantitative measurement strategy.

This section is not intended to replace these and other approaches to planning. Rather, this section provides an alternative mental model regarding goals in the context of complex systems. Questioning goals in the context of complex systems can better enable managers to purposely and systematically choose goals that will help improve organizational performance and achieve desired results.

Use Intermediate Goals to Better Understand the Problem

Vague, general, or unclear goals may lead to repair service behavior. However, phrasing a partial goal in general terms is useful to set the overall direction (as illustrated in the example of Hospital B). Specific goals can be established once decision makers gain new information and clarity about the problem. For example, a surgical services manager may use general goals to set the overall direction for his department over the next several years. These goals may be to improve clinical outcomes, improve patient satisfaction, improve cost-effectiveness, and integrate services across multiple sites. Each year, during the annual planning process, specific short-term or intermediate goals may also be established. The goal in Year 1 may be to implement a standard performance measurement system across all sites. The goal in Year 2 may be to increase the percentage of first surgical cases for the day that are started on time for each of the operating rooms in the service. The goal in Year 3 may be to implement standard preoperative testing protocols to eliminate unnecessary variation in preoperative tests (Kelly et al. 1997).

In this example, a general goal is used to communicate overall direction. Because the manager also understands the concept and importance of partial goals, he is able to establish the first partial goal (develop a measurement system) to help him understand how to prioritize subsequent annual improvement goals.

Be Aware of Implicit Goals

An administrator with responsibility for a large community hospital's emergency department (ED) was challenged with delays and bottlenecks in transferring patients from the ED to inpatient beds. The administrator gave this improvement goal to the ED manager: decrease the time from decision to admit to the actual admission to 20 minutes or fewer. The improvement team organized to meet this goal found that one cause of delays was the numerous phone calls made to the receiving inpatient unit to coordinate the transfer with the nursing staff. The team decided on this intervention: If by the third phone call the nurse was not available to receive a report on the patient by phone, the patient would be taken to the assigned room by the ED technician and the report would be faxed to the inpatient unit.

The team implemented the new process and the time to transfer dropped to 20 minutes or fewer. The implicit goal *not* conveyed by the administrator was to ensure that improvements were based on safe practices. Without this implicit goal being defined, the team members became so focused on the

20-minute goal that their judgment of safe communications during handoffs was clouded. As a result, their "improvement" was in direct opposition to The Joint Commission's requirement that hospitals "improve the effectiveness of communication among caregivers" (Joint Commission 2007).

An undefined implicit goal can contribute to a situation of accidental adversaries. In this ED example, such was the case between the manager and the administrator (the ED manager thought she was meeting her boss's goal, while the administrator was dissatisfied with the team's efforts) and between the ED nurses and the inpatient nurses (each "blamed" the other for not understanding their patient flow–related issues).

In contrast, the surgical services manager in the previous example understands the concept of implicit goals. For example, the manager knows cultivating positive and collaborative relationships between physicians and administrators is essential to achieving the desired level of performance. Although not on the written list of goals, positive relationships are reinforced at every staff meeting, and a philosophy of collaboration guides the manager in designing the performance measurement system and improving first-case start times. As a result of the manager's implicit goal of building relationships in Years 1 and 2, implementing a clinical standard of care can be accomplished more smoothly in Year 3.

Refine, Revise, and Reformulate as Needed

Managers may find that setting goals is an iterative process. As new information becomes available, managers must be willing to evaluate previous goals and reformulate them as needed. For example, a nurse manager of a 30-bed inpatient rehabilitation unit was charged with improving the overall performance of her area. She realized that the goal of "improve performance" was too vague to identify specific interventions, expectations, and action plans for her staff.

The manager reformulated her original goal—"improve performance"— to more clearly establish the general direction of the improvement effort. Her new goals were to (1) promote teamwork, (2) promote continuity of care, (3) meet or exceed local and national standards of care, (4) integrate performance improvement into the daily work environment, (5) promote staff satisfaction, and (6) improve cost-effectiveness.

Understanding dynamic complexity encourages managers to reformulate goals as new information becomes available or the original situation changes. In such cases, managers should consider reformulating goals not as a sign of indecisiveness or weak managerial skills but rather as a validation of their understanding of complex dynamic systems.

Use Multiple Goals to Recognize System Relationships

The nurse manager in the previous example demonstrated another important approach for setting effective goals. Because of the interrelationships among activities, processes, and other elements in healthcare organizations, focusing on multiple interrelated goals is necessary. Although a single goal may be useful for a simple process improvement, a systems perspective suggests the need for setting multiple goals that may be carried out concurrently or sequentially to take into account the interrelationships in the system.

In this rehabilitation unit, the nurse manager assembled a team of charge nurses and rehabilitation specialists to work together intensively to help determine how to meet the unit's goals. After several meetings directed toward understanding the hospital's history, operating requirements, and environmental challenges; analyzing current processes; and identifying causes of performance gaps, the team discussed its ideal vision for the unit. The members described their ideal unit according to desired clinical outcomes, the nature of their relationships with patients and families, teamwork, and business requirements. This vision became the unit's long-term goal.

The team focused on multiple interdependent interventions to achieve its vision. Although it would not be able to implement multiple interventions all at once because of resource constraints, the team realized the importance of identifying, prioritizing, and establishing time lines to accomplish the specific goals in the general direction set by the manager. Some of the interventions (e.g., establishing a staff communication book and bulletin board) could be implemented immediately without much effort. Some of the goals (e.g., improving the way in which daily census and productivity were tracked, reported, communicated, and managed) would take some time to implement and were identified as short-term goals. Other goals (e.g., clarifying care team roles, structure, and job descriptions) required more in-depth development and implementation considerations and were identified as medium-term goals.

The team converted an implicit goal to an explicit one by adding the following long-term goal: enhance the personal accountability of all staff. Clear goals provided the direction; a performance measurement system and a simple project-tracking report enabled the manager, the team, and the unit staff to track their progress toward their goals and their progress toward becoming their ideal unit.

Types of Goal Statements

Along with setting effective goals, managers must purposefully craft a goal statement that will best help them succeed in a given situation. For example, a manager has just learned that the immunization rates for the patients in his large pediatric practice are below both the state and national averages. He is faced with the problem of substandard immunization rates. How does he now communicate improvement goals to the practice in ways that will use the approaches just described?

Some types of goal statements have been introduced through the examples presented earlier in the chapter. The different types of goals may be thought of as pairs of opposites: positive or negative, general or specific, clear or unclear, simple or multiple, and implicit or explicit (Dörner 1996). Exhibit 7.2 provides a definition for each of these types and examples of how each may be used by the manager of the pediatric practice.

Critiquing Goal Statements

Goal statements need to be effective. When faced with a problem to solve, a manager may state the goal in different ways and evaluate the pros and cons of each statement as a way to enhance his decision-making skills. The goals in exhibit 7.2 are critiqued here, listed in order of effectiveness, beginning with the most effective goal statement for the situation and ending with the least effective.

Explicit Goal. *Improve the ability to identify, deliver, and monitor pediatric preventive care services, including age-appropriate immunizations.*

Of all the sample goals, the statement for the explicit goal is the most effective for the situation because it

- is appropriate for an improvement effort, not a daily operational expectation;
- addresses the underlying work processes linked to the desired clinical outcomes;
- incorporates changes in how the clinic functions as a whole, not just the individual encounter between the caregiver and the patient;
- includes an expectation for ongoing evaluation and continuous improvement;
- sets the stage for a highly leveraged intervention (by stating the goal in terms of preventive services and not simply immunizations, the improved process will contribute to improvements in multiple results, not just a single outcome); and
- reflects an understanding of *upstream processes* that could influence results (identify preventive care services).

This goal statement actually is a combination of an explicit, a clear, a multiple, a specific, and a positive goal. As more experience is gained in setting

EXHIBIT 7.2
Examples of
Types of Goals

Definition	Type of Goal	Example
Working toward a desired condition	Positive	Achieve immunization rates that are in the top 10 percent statewide.
Making an undesirable condition go away	Negative	Reduce the number of patients with incomplete immunizations.
Few criteria	General	Improve immunization rates.
Multiple criteria	Specific	Ensure all infants in the practice receive the appropriate vaccinations at ages 1 month, 2 months, 4 months, 6 months, 12 months, 15 months, 18 months, and 24 months, according to the Centers for Disease Control and Prevention's Recommended Childhood Immunization Schedule.
Difficult to determine if the goal has been met	Unclear	Work with the office staff to improve pediatric care.
Precise criteria permitting the evaluation of whether the goal is being met	Clear	Select a team to enroll in the quality improvement collaborative offered by the State Pediatric Association from April through September. Design and implement processes to improve the clinic's compliance with the Centers for Disease Control and Prevention's Recommended Childhood Immunization Schedule. Measure overall immunization rates on a quarterly basis. Report at staff meetings.
Single goal	Simple	Give age-appropriate immunizations at each well-child appointment.
Series of sequential or concurrent goals that take into account relationships within the system	Multiple	Track patient compliance with wellchild exams. Notify and schedule patients who have missed well-child exams. Give age-appropriate immunizations during well-child exams.
Hidden	Implicit (unstated)	Improve immunization rates.
Obvious	Explicit	Improve the ability to identify, deliver, and monitor pediatric preventive care services, including age-appropriate immunizations.

Source: Adapted from Dörner (1996).

goals, one will find that the most effective goals for an improvement effort usually contain a combination of all of these characteristics.

Clear Goal. *Our clinic will select a team to enroll in the quality improvement collaborative offered by the State Pediatric Association from April through September. The team will design and implement processes to improve the clinic's compliance with the Centers for Disease Control and Prevention's Recommended Childhood Immunization Schedule. The team will measure overall immunization rates on a quarterly basis. Results will be reported at staff meetings.*

The clear goal is the next most effective goal statement for an effort to improve immunization rates in this scenario. This goal is also a combination statement, incorporating features of a clear goal, a multiple goal, a specific goal, and a positive goal. Although readers may like this goal because it is very clear, this goal statement includes the following pitfalls. First, because the focus is solely on immunizations, the opportunity to leverage this effort (i.e., the time and effort by the team) to influence a broader array of similar processes and services is lost. Although the broader scope may be implicit to the manager, the manager will likely get just what he asks for—an exclusive focus on immunizations. Second, the prescriptive nature of this goal statement may exclude opportunities for other possible and more effective solutions. By stating that results will be measured quarterly, the team may default to retrospective review and miss an opportunity to design a concurrent data collection process.

Specific Goal. *Ensure all infants in the practice receive the appropriate vaccinations at ages 1 month, 2 months, 4 months, 6 months, 12 months, 15 months, 18 months, and 24 months, according to the Centers for Disease Control and Prevention's Recommended Childhood Immunization Schedule.*

Many readers will like this goal statement because it is very specific and, at first glance, appears to be effective. However, this statement (similar to an objective as defined previously) actually describes the results or data to be measured to determine if the goal has been met. No improvement goal is included in this statement; rather, it is a restatement of targeted performance. The pitfalls of this statement include the risk of micromanaging the activities that occur at the patient encounter rather than improving the underlying work process (i.e., the focus is on the operational activities, not on an improvement process). In addition, the manager again risks "getting what he asks for" (i.e., an exclusive focus on immunizations).

Multiple Goals. *Track patient compliance with well-child exams. Notify and schedule patients who have missed well-child exams. Give age-appropriate immunizations during well-child exams.*

At first glance, this goal statement also might appear to be effective; however, it reflects a solution, not a goal. Because these statements are specific interventions to be carried out, this type of goal would be appropriate to describe new work expectations for care providers once the improved process has been designed. Differentiate between implementation goals (i.e., behavior expectations or guidelines for implementing a predetermined intervention) and goals for an improvement effort (i.e., to identify and design interventions that will lead to improved performance) to ensure that the goal statement is consistent with the purpose or intent.

Implicit (or General) Goal. *Improve immunization rates.*

The goal statement "improve immunization rates" may be considered implicit or general. Often, goals are stated in general terms, such as "improve the quality of care." Instead, try posing a question: "If I knew nothing about the problem and you gave me this goal, could you be sure that you would get the results that you desired when I was 'done'?" If the answer to this question is no, implicit goals that need to be made explicit are likely hidden in the statement. General goals may be appropriate for setting overall direction for a team, department, or organization; however, more specific direction will help ensure the success of an improvement effort.

Simple Goal. *Give age-appropriate immunizations at each well-child appointment.*

Although this goal may appear to be effective, the major pitfall of this goal statement is that it limits the nature of the improvements. For example, by stating the goal in this way, interventions will most likely be limited to the well-child appointment. Opportunities to combine sick-child visits with preventive care may not be considered, and children who miss well-child appointments may be overlooked.

Unclear Goal. *Work with the office staff to improve pediatric care.*

With an unclear goal such as this one, the goal may be met but the desired results not achieved. Because the goal is vague, efforts to meet it may improve pediatric care (e.g., care of patients with asthma) but not address the problem of immunization rates.

Negative Goal. *Reduce the number of patients with incomplete immunizations.*

Negative language leads one to focus on problems rather than solutions, which could dampen the motivation of those participating in the improvement effort.

SMART Goals and Complex Systems

Applying the concept of SMART goals to quality management in complex systems yields the following lessons.

Specific

Goals should be specific enough to give direction. However, improvement goals that are too specific may limit the opportunity for improvement. When working in complex systems, a general goal statement used as a partial or intermediate goal is appropriate if there is inadequate information about the problem.

Measurable

If improvement goals are limited to only those areas that one can measure, improvement efforts are confined by one's current abilities. As quality and improvement skills mature, so should our ability to define and measure quality. Sometimes in improvement efforts, developing the measure is part of the effort.

Achievable

If improvement goals are limited to the perception of what is achievable, the potential for innovative or breakthrough solutions is also limited. Including numeric targets at the strategic level is common practice and perhaps necessary; however, such inclusion risks placing a ceiling on the improvement effort. For example, staff may stop improvement efforts at the target of 3 percent rather than seek the innovative solution that could result in 20 percent improvement. In complex systems, monitoring the ongoing performance and variability over time is more important than focusing on a static target.

Relevant

What is perceived as relevant from one perspective may not be relevant when viewed from another perspective. Perspective and context are required to determine relevance and are a prerequisite to setting appropriate goals.

Time Sensitive

Improvement should be continuous. Having time-sensitive expectations for implementing interventions is common. However, expectations for when the interventions will yield system improvement results are difficult to define. If a goal does not address systemic causes of the problem, a time frame can set up the effort to fail, instead of promoting its success.

Corollaries to Purpose and Goals

Purpose and goals go hand in hand when viewing quality management from a systems perspective. The corollaries represented in the following questions can help managers understand the complete picture:

- What is the purpose? (Why does "it" exist?)
- What are the desired results? (How is the successful accomplishment of the purpose defined?)
- What activities are used to accomplish the purpose? (What are the processes and interventions to achieve the purpose?)
- How is the accomplishment of the purpose measured? (How does one determine how well the purpose is being accomplished?)
- What are the improvement goals? (What goals must be reached to improve the process by which the purpose is being accomplished?)

To illustrate how purpose and goals go hand in hand, consider how the two elements are related for the prenatal services at the obstetrics and gynecology clinic featured in chapter 5:

- The purpose of the clinic's prenatal services is to assess, monitor, and manage the physiological and psychosocial needs of families during the childbearing process.
- The desired results are healthy clinical outcomes, satisfied patients, and cost-effective services.
- The clinic will measure its success in achieving the desired results with the following data: maternal and infant complication rates, early diagnosis rates, patient satisfaction, payer satisfaction, and so on.
- The service mix, processes, and interventions used to accomplish the purpose are strategically determined, designed, and improved.
- The goal for improvement efforts may be to validate the purposes of the key stakeholders identified earlier; refine the clinic's purpose for prenatal care services based on any new information obtained; evaluate current practices to determine the extent to which the clinic is accomplishing its purpose; define a service mix that is consistent with the purpose; prioritize those services needing improvement; and design, redesign, and implement improved processes that meet all stakeholder requirements and accomplish the new definition of purpose. (This goal is multiple, positive, and clear and incorporates partial or intermediate goals.)

Even those experienced in quality improvement may set goals on the basis of ingrained habits and may find setting goals from a systems perspective counterintuitive. For example, an online training program in quality improvement advertises this way: "Improving Your HCAHPS Score Through Patient-Centered Care" (Institute for Healthcare Improvement 2010). An understanding of systems thinking would reframe this statement to this: "Improve your organization's ability to deliver patient-centered care as *measured* by your HCAHPS scores."

Summary

Effective goals precede effective performance. Familiar mental models concerning goals are represented in SMART goals and how goals and objectives are defined in the context of program planning. This chapter has explored mental models from the perspective of improvement in complex systems and techniques managers may use to improve their own goal-setting skills. Although no single correct or incorrect approach to setting a goal exists, managers should be aware of the advantages and pitfalls of each approach and the ways the goals are communicated. To enhance their effectiveness in setting improvement goals in the context of complex systems, managers should (Kelly 2009)

- differentiate improvement goals from operational expectations;
- clarify the differences among solutions, goals, action plans, and improvement efforts;
- address underlying work processes that lead to results;
- leverage similar processes;
- remember that setting a goal is different from measuring how effectively the goal is being met; and
- use intermediate goals and revise as new information is gathered.

Exercise 7.1
Objective: To practice linking goal statements with results.

Scenario: The quality committee at a hospital reviewed its performance measurement data for acute myocardial infarction (AMI), congestive heart failure (CHF), and pneumonia on the Medicare Hospital Compare website (www.medicare.gov/hospitalcompare). The hospital's performance scores for pneumonia and CHF were very similar to the scores attained by hospitals in the state and throughout the nation. The hospital's performance on the AMI measures was not as favorable. The results suggest that the hospital approached performance improvements in a fragmented, disease-specific manner.

Instructions: Consider how organizational goals may have contributed to some improvements in care provided to patients with CHF and pneumonia while improvements in care for patients with AMI lagged. The measures for each of these conditions can be found on the Medicare website (www.medicare.gov). On the following goals worksheet, you will find examples of goal statements the hospital could have established that would have led to the results described. Critique each goal statement and document your critique on a worksheet such as the one shown here. Remember, you are critiquing the goal statement, not the merit of the intervention represented by the goal statement.

Goals Worksheet

Goal Statement	Pros	Cons
Improve performance in all the CMS disease-specific indicators.		
Ensure all patients admitted to the ED with the diagnosis of AMI receive aspirin within ____ minutes of admission.		
Improve performance on the following AMI indicators: • Timeliness of administration of aspirin • Prescribing aspirin at discharge • Smoking cessation counseling		
Research the available clinical guidelines on care of the patients with AMI, and implement a guideline that • demonstrates a strong degree of evidence; • ensures meeting all regulatory and payer requirements; and • permits ease of documenting, retrieving, and reporting the necessary performance indicators.		
Reduce the number of patients with AMI who are discharged without smoking cessation counseling and a prescription for aspirin.		

Companion Readings

Amabile, T. M., and S. J. Kramer. 2011. *The Progress Principle: Using Small Wins to Ignite Joy, Engagement, and Creativity at Work.* Boston: Harvard Business Review Press.

American Animal Hospital Association. 2016. "Interactive Tool: Create Your Own SMART Goals." Accessed November 11. www.aaha.org/professional/resources/smart_goals.aspx.

Dörner, D. 1996. *The Logic of Failure: Recognizing and Avoiding Error in Complex Situations,* 49–70. Reading, MA: Perseus Books.

Minnesota Department of Health. 2016. "SMART and Meaningful Objectives." Accessed November 11. www.health.state.mn.us/divs/opi/qi/toolbox/objectives.html.

Pope, J., E. Padula, and D. Wallace-Dooley. 2015. "Improving Ourselves for the Sake of Others: Our Baldrige Journey." *Frontiers of Health Services Management* 32 (1): 3–16.

Ransom, S. B., and E. R. Ransom. 2014. "Implementing Quality as the Core Organizational Strategy." In *The Healthcare Quality Book: Vision, Strategy, and Tools,* 3rd ed., edited by M. S. Joshi, E. R. Ransom, D. B. Nash, and S. B. Ransom, 393–421. Chicago: Health Administration Press.

Toussaint, J. S. 2016. "How Health Care Systems Can Effectively Manage Process." *NEJM Catalyst.* Published June 20. http://catalyst.nejm.org/how-health-systems-can-effectively-manage-process.

Web Resources

Goal Setting Basics: www.goalsettingbasics.com
Mind Tools: www.mindtools.com

References

Baldrige Performance Excellence Program (BPEP). 2015. *2015–2016 Baldrige Excellence Framework: A Systems Approach to Improving Your Organization's Performance (Health Care).* Gaithersburg, MD: US Department of Commerce, National Institute of Standards and Technology.

Dörner, D. 1996. *The Logic of Failure: Recognizing and Avoiding Error in Complex Situations.* Reading, MA: Perseus Books.

Gitlin, L. N., and K. J. Lyons. 2008. *Successful Grant Writing: Strategies for Health and Human Service Professionals.* New York: Springer Publishing Company.

Hofmann, P. B. 2005. "Acknowledging and Examining Management Mistakes." In *Management Mistakes in Healthcare: Identification, Correction and Prevention,* edited by P. B. Hofmann and F. Perry, 3–27. Cambridge, UK: Cambridge University Press.

Institute for Healthcare Improvement. 2010. "Expedition: Improving Your HCAHPS Score Through Patient-Centered Care." Published February 2. www.ihi.org/education/webtraining/expeditions/hcahps/Pages/default.aspx.

Joint Commission. 2007. *Comprehensive Accreditation Manual for Hospitals.* Oak Brook, IL: Joint Commission Resources.

Kelly, D. 2009. "Creating and Leading Error-Free Management Systems." Seminar presented by the American College of Healthcare Executives, Atlanta, GA, September 16–17.

Kelly, D. L., S. L. Pestotnik, M. C. Coons, and J. W. Lelis. 1997. "Reengineering a Surgical Service Line: Focusing on Core Process Improvement." *American Journal of Medical Quality* 12 (2): 120–29.

Scott, R. A. 2003. *Organizations: Rational, Natural, and Open Systems,* 5th ed. Upper Saddle River, NJ: Prentice Hall.

FOSTERING A CULTURE OF COLLABORATION AND TEAMWORK

Learning Objectives

After completing this chapter, you should be able to

- describe why a supportive culture, collaboration, and teamwork are essential to quality health services delivery;
- recognize mental models about teams and the manager's role in team effectiveness;
- describe the importance of purposeful team design on organizational results; and
- identify evidence-based strategies for improving collaboration and teamwork.

During a hospital improvement project aimed at reducing door-to-balloon times for patients presenting to the emergency department (ED) for treatment of a heart attack, a cardiac clinical nurse specialist involved in the project commented (Webster et al. 2008, 175):

> We spent months just team building and dealing with all of the personality problems and the vying for control . . . that was necessary because it was an interdisciplinary thing. It wasn't something we were trying to change within one service. We were asking the emergency department, the cath lab, and cardiology services—everyone— to sit down around the table and agree about what they were going to do. Some of it meant that spans of control had to be given up, and that didn't set well.

Another hospital involved in a similar project greatly reduced door-to-balloon time delays caused by ED inefficiencies, yet problems still existed in other areas. For example, the transport department lacked adequate protocols for moving patients from the ED to the catheterization laboratory, and on-call catheterization teams had inconsistent response times. An interventional cardiologist at this hospital commented (Webster et al. 2008, 172):

> A year and a half into the project, we hit a major brick wall. Our team was doing as much as we could, but we did not have the authority to break down the barriers that were coming from this . . . inertia. It all came to a head when the emergency department was getting very good at this. They could get the patient cleared and diagnosed in 20 to 30 minutes, and then the patient would sit in the emergency department.

The comments from these project participants illustrate how functional and professional silos in healthcare organizations can make it challenging to enact quality improvements that require cooperation among different disciplines and departments. No facility "is immune from the silo syndrome in which barriers develop among the organization's many parts" (Rosen 2010, 1). Silos in healthcare organizations can be vertical or horizontal. "Individual departments can have high barriers between them or senior leadership can be completely isolated from lower management levels" (Kotter 2011, 1). To keep the silo syndrome from disrupting quality improvement effects, healthcare leaders and managers must adopt an organization-wide collaborative culture that rewards teamwork.

The ability to create effective teams and encourage horizontal and vertical collaboration is an essential management skill. The published literature already offers managers a wealth of information about these topics, so this chapter does not review or summarize that information. This chapter does, however, explore some issues related to organizational culture and collaboration and teamwork strategies associated with specific quality management concepts described in this book.

Creating a Supportive Culture

A newly hired hospital chief medical officer (CMO) was finding it difficult to gain support for reducing the number of days patients remained in the hospital. The prevailing culture in the organization supported maintaining the status quo. There was pushback from nursing staff members who expressed concerns that cost cutting was taking precedence over quality of care. Physicians felt continuity of care may be disrupted for patients if discharged too soon to posthospital care facilities where a different physician would be caring for them. Therapists and technicians did not want to start working weekend shifts just so patients could be discharged a day or two earlier. To gain support and encourage collaboration among the various stakeholders to make changes, the CMO had to revise the objective. The CMO refocused his message on the fact that hospitals can be a dangerous place for sick people.

The longer a patient stays in the hospital unnecessarily, the greater the risk of a new infection or injury. This message, which appealed to the personal values of all stakeholders, helped to change the culture and bring people together to strategize ways to safely discharge patients sooner. Ultimately, the average hospital length of stay fell by 45 percent with no negative impact on readmission rates or patient outcomes.

Unknown to the CMO, he had employed one of the leadership levers that Edmondson (2016, 57) identified as an effective tactic for encouraging team collaboration: "Appeal to personal values, invite input on the vision and celebrate change." By using a motivation lever, the CMO was able to channel the energy of a diverse group of stakeholders to achieve a worthwhile improvement goal. According to Edmondson (2016), the three other leadership levers that managers can use to encourage cross discipline teamwork are (1) promoting psychological safety, (2) enabling knowledge sharing, and (3) encouraging collaborative iteration.

The culture of a healthcare organization greatly affects the ability of its managers to achieve collaboration among functional and professional silos. To understand how organizational culture influences collaboration and teamwork, the question of what culture is must be answered. Edgar Schein (1984, 3), the MIT professor whom many consider to be the father of organizational culture research, defines culture as follows:

Organizational culture is the pattern of basic assumptions that a given group has invented, discovered, or developed in learning to cope with its problems of external adaptation and internal integration, and that have worked well enough to be considered valid, and therefore to be taught to new members as the correct way to perceive, think, and feel in relation to those problems.	**organizational culture** a consistent, observable pattern of behavior in an organization; the way things get done

Another way to think about organizational culture is that it is a consistent, observable pattern of behavior in an organization. Basically it is the way things get done.

The newly hired hospital CMO in the scenario tried to change habits in an organization without understanding the historical patterns of behavior. Like the CMO, it may be necessary for managers to enact culture-changing strategies when faced with quality improvement challenges requiring collaboration and teamwork among various functional and professional groups. Schein (1984, 14) points out that "no single model of such change exists: managers may successfully orchestrate change through the use of a wide variety of techniques, from outright coercion at one extreme to subtle seduction . . . at the other extreme." Some culture-changing techniques are described in this chapter.

Teams in Healthcare

team
a group of people working together to achieve a common goal (Grumbach and Bodenheimer 2004)

At its most basic level, a **team** is a group of people working together to achieve a common goal (Grumbach and Bodenheimer 2004). Many types of teams are found in health services organizations. Taplin, Foster, and Shortell (2013) describe the four most common teams:

1. Work teams charged with accomplishing tasks in an ongoing manner in a specific setting (e.g., home health care team, operating room team)
2. Parallel teams formed to address specific challenges, with members typically drawn from several work teams (e.g., rapid response team, incident management team)
3. Projects teams responsible for time-limited deliverables (e.g., electronic health record implementation team, process improvement team)
4. Management teams with oversight responsibilities (e.g., quality management council, professional nursing practice committee)

The term *team* carries with it many meanings, perceptions, and approaches, depending on one's frame of reference. Just as an organization should have a shared definition of quality, managers must ensure a shared definition of team, team roles, expectations, and communication if teams are to execute their responsibilities in a safe, effective, and high-quality manner. The diversity of the health services workforce and the dynamic complexity inherent in the field require a common, shared understanding of the concept of a team and how it is operationalized in one's specific organization.

Effective teams do not just happen; they are thoughtfully and purposefully designed. The following sequence of questions should be asked any time a manager is considering a team approach on any level, whether for a work team, parallel team, project team, or a management team:

1. What is the purpose of the team (e.g., activity, process, function)?
2. What is the ideal, step-by-step process or approach to achieve that purpose?
3. What is the most appropriate structure to support and carry out that process? (Structure includes how people are organized to carry out the process, how roles are defined, and how the roles interact with each other.)
4. How does the team define and measure success?

Research has shown that high-functioning teams have agreed on shared goals and clear roles and responsibilities to which members are held accountable.

High-functioning teams actively work to build and maintain a respectful trusting environment, which supports effective communication among team members, patients, and other participants (Mitchell et al. 2012).

Collaboration and Teamwork

While collaboration and teamwork in healthcare are often used synonymously, they are not identical. Clements, Dault, and Priest (2007) identified interprofessional collaboration as a process that can take place whether or not health professionals consider themselves to be part of a team. For example, following an automobile accident, an injured patient may receive care from an emergency physician, an orthopedic surgeon, a primary care physician, several nurses, a physical therapist, and a dentist. While these various providers might collaborate with one another, it is unlikely they view themselves as a functioning team. On the other hand, effective teamwork rarely happens where there is no collaboration (Oandasan et al. 2006).

To provide the best possible care for patients throughout the healthcare continuum, collaborative teamwork is needed. A **collaborative team** is a group with "health care professionals assuming complementary roles and cooperatively working together, sharing responsibility for problem-solving and making decisions to formulate and carry out plans for patient care" (O'Daniel and Rosenstein 2008, 2-272).

collaborative team "health care pro-fessionals assuming complementary roles and coop-eratively working together, sharing responsibility for problem-solving and making deci-sions to formulate and carry out plans for patient care" (O'Daniel and Rosenstein 2008, 2-272)

As illustrated by the automobile accident, various healthcare professionals often offer their expertise and divide up responsibilities for improving a patient's health. Ideally, an interdisciplinary rather than multidisciplinary approach is used. In a multidisciplinary approach, each professional is responsible only for setting and achieving patient care goals related to his own discipline. In an interdisciplinary approach, common patient care goals are jointly defined by the professionals (ideally with patient input), and everyone works cooperatively to achieve these goals. An interdisciplinary, rather than multidisciplinary approach, has also proven to be successful at improving operational performance (Bender et al. 2015).

Mental Models Affecting Team Design

The manager's mental models and the organization's context influence how teams are defined, designed, and employed in an organization. Historically, when a physician entered the hospital unit, nurses offered their chairs to the physician because the nurses held lower positions in the organizational and professional hierarchies governing power, status, and authority. Remnants of this tradition (e.g., deferring to someone higher in the hierarchy, issuing orders to someone lower in the hierarchy) may still be seen in how health services organizations approach teams and teamwork—or the lack thereof. In simulation-based study, researchers found that most anesthesiology residents complied with an attending physician's order to transfuse blood to a patient, even though the patient had explicitly refused transfusions for religious reasons (Bould et al. 2015).

A case that received a lot of media attention involved the death of Betsy Lehman, a health reporter for the *Boston Globe* who was treated for breast cancer in 1994 at Dana Farber Cancer Center (Altman 1995). While participating in a clinical trial in which higher-than-normal doses of chemotherapy were administered, a clerical error caused her to receive much more than the dose recommended for the trial. The nurses saw the error but did not speak up because they presumed the doctors knew what they were doing and the drug doses were correct. While this event happened many years ago, mental models about authority still influence communication in team settings and, in turn, affect the quality of clinical outcomes.

Academic centers are steeped in traditions based on multiple and parallel hierarchies. For example, novel ideas from junior or nontenured faculty may be dismissed simply because of their position in the hierarchy rather than the merit of the idea. In the academic medical center, the CEO and the administrative team occupy the top positions in the management hierarchy, and frontline supervisors occupy the bottom. The department chairs are at the top of the medical staff hierarchy, and the interns or medical students are at the bottom. Physicians, followed by nurses, are at the top of the professional hierarchy, whereas other professionals (e.g., social workers, pharmacists, occupational therapists) all hold intermediate places lower in the hierarchy. Physicians and nurses hold the top spots in the jobs hierarchy, and the hourly manual laborers (e.g., environmental services workers, food service workers) are designated to the lower spots. Although each group performs its respective duties in a competent manner, the hierarchies foster a fragmented approach to patient care. For example, physician teams typically make their morning patient rounds while nurses are occupied with the change-of-shift report. As a result, the nurses and physicians caring for the same patients rarely talk to each other during the course of day-to-day patient care.

This fragmented approach to patient care reinforces different concepts of teamwork among physicians and other members of the healthcare team. Dr. Tina Brashers, the lead physician for the interprofessional education program at the University of Virginia, notes that nurses are "likely to define good teamwork as a relationship in which everyone's input counts," whereas doctors have a different teamwork experience. She calls it the "'poof factor': doctors type into the computer and POOF, the order happens, with no input from nursing needed and little knowledge of nurses' importance to patient care" (Brown 2013). There is no better method to build a common understanding of one another's contribution than to visit people in their own environment or location—"this kind of 'management by walking around' is a powerful approach" (Ledlow and Coppola 2014, 116).

A hospital with a traditional team-design mental model may enact many quality improvement team projects. However, its improvement teams tend to have an exclusive makeup (e.g., physician teams, nurse teams). Departments such as the laboratory often attempt to create improvement teams with a mix of different providers but find it difficult to cross the rigid boundaries of the professional and job hierarchies in the organization. Finding only a few examples of improvement projects that involve teamwork across and in the hierarchies is common.

One tactic for overcoming the traditional mental model surrounding team design in healthcare organizations is to adopt a clinical microsystems mental model. Nelson and colleagues (2007) have studied high-performing, frontline clinical teams in various healthcare settings and offer insights into success factors for designing a clinical microsystem to enhance quality outcomes and patient safety. According to Nelson and colleagues (2007, 14), high-performing microsystems are characterized by

> constancy of purpose, investment in improvement, alignment of role and training for efficiency and staff satisfaction, interdependence of care team to meet patient needs, integration of information and technology into work flows, ongoing measurement of outcomes, supportiveness of the larger organization, and connection to the community to enhance care delivery and extend influence.

On closer examination, one sees that these characteristics result from intentional role and team design.

Mental Models About Work Team Differences

Most managers and employees prefer agreement and harmony, yet diverse perspectives supply the essential elements of creative tension that often result in innovations and improvements. Tucker and Edmondson (2003) found in different situations the "ideal" employee from the manager's perspective was not the employee most likely to influence innovations and improvement (see exhibit 8.1).

Diverse perspectives can create fertile ground for accidental adversaries, conflict, and team breakdowns. Managers are challenged to find tools and

EXHIBIT 8.1
"Ideal" Employee
Behaviors
Versus Employee
Behaviors
That Promote
Learning

When the Employee Faces:	"Ideal Employee" Behaviors	Employee Behaviors Conducive to Organizational Learning
Missing materials or information	Adjusts to shortcomings in materials and supplies without bothering managers or others.	*Noisy Complainer*: Remedies immediate situation but also lets the manager and supply department know when the system has failed.
Others' errors	Seamlessly corrects for errors of others—without confronting the person about their error.	*Nosy Troublemaker*: Lets others know when they have made a mistake with the intent of creating learning, not blame.
Own errors and problems	Creates an impression of never making mistakes.	*Self-Aware Error-Maker*: Lets manager and others know when they have made a mistake so that others can learn from their error. Communicates openness to hearing about their errors discovered by others.
Subtle opportunities for improving the system	Committed to the current way of doing business— understands the "way things work" around here.	*Disruptive Questioner who won't let well enough alone*: Questions why do we do things this way? Is there a better way of providing the service to the patient?

Source: Reprinted from Tucker and Edmondson (2003). Used with permission.

approaches that enable them to take advantage of differing perspectives while maintaining effective interpersonal relationships in teams and employee groups.

Numerous frameworks are available to help managers understand and appreciate individuals and their differences. Although the taxonomy may vary, each framework defines groups on the basis of common patterns. Studies of large numbers of individuals have resulted in the identification of patterns in their preferences, predispositions, temperaments, learning styles, and strengths. These patterns have been organized and labeled according to various frameworks, including the Myers-Briggs Type Indicator, the Keirsey Temperament Sorter, Human Dynamics, and the StrengthsFinder. Specific descriptions of these frameworks are not provided in this book, but readers are encouraged to further explore them; see the web resources for this chapter.

When these different frameworks are studied as a group, patterns begin to emerge. First, the frameworks recognize that individuals bring differences with them to the workplace. The frameworks identify, categorize, and explain those differences and provide a concrete and systematic means of recognizing, describing, and understanding the differences. The frameworks also provide a common language and approach for managers and teams in the organization to understand, appreciate, and address differences in the workplace in a positive way. When two of these frameworks—the Myers-Briggs Type Indicator and Human Dynamics—are studied together, some global, crosscutting dichotomies between personality types may be seen. These include the following dualities: internal and external, practical and creative, data oriented and relationship oriented, concrete and conceptual, linear and lateral, and spontaneous and structured. Managers should begin to look for how they, as well as their employees and teams, express these global dichotomies, as the dualities influence preferences regarding leadership, communication, learning, and client interactions. Managing the interface of these dichotomies, rather than avoiding or falling victim to them, will enable managers to enhance the effectiveness of operational working teams and improvement project teams.

The manager's responsibility is to select the desired lens (i.e., manage the context) through which individuals in the organization and the organization as a whole will view their work and workplace. A lens that views differences as complementary talents may result in synergy and success, while a lens that views differences as opposing perspectives may result in conflict, breakdown, and mediocrity.

For example, as client volumes increased, a department grew from 5 employees to 20 almost overnight. When there were only 5 employees, the department functioned like a close-knit family. Yet when new employees came on board, they found themselves thrown into the work with little time to assimilate into the culture and style of the team. For the first time, the department appointed a supervisor to oversee the team, and not long after that the complaints started: "The supervisor never follows through on anything"; "a certain employee is not carrying her load"; or "the supervisor is all talk and no action." This department inadvertently set up an accidentally adversarial situation between the supervisor and the staff. Accidental adversaries, which result from differences in styles, learning preferences, and personality types, can be a common and unrecognized source of conflict in all kinds of teams.

When the employees in this department took the Myers-Briggs Type Indicator test, the results were illuminating. Of the 20 department employees, 18 were *sensing* types. They prefer the concrete, real, factual, structured, and tangible here and now; they become impatient with the abstract and mistrust intuition. Two of the employees, including the supervisor, were *intuitive* types. They preferred possibilities, theories, invention, and the new; they enjoyed discussions characterized by spontaneous leaps of intuition, and they tended to leave out or neglect details (Myers, Kirby, and Myers 1998). In this department, the supervisor inherently functioned in a manner that was opposite to the rest of the department's way of functioning. As a result, misunderstandings, misperceptions, and communication breakdowns became common.

When these differences were understood, the department could put into place specific processes and systems (which were not necessary when there were only a few employees) to minimize the potential breakdowns. For example, a standing agenda at staff meetings helped the supervisor stay on task and avoid getting sidetracked. A bulletin board, e-mail messages, and a shared network drive were used to ensure that current and complete information about departmental issues was available to everyone. A human resources performance measurement system was put into place to provide a factual base for evaluating individual productivity and workload.

By understanding and implementing processes designed to meet the differing information and communication needs of the sensing and intuitive types, the department was able to avert further conflict and misunderstanding and focus employees' energy on productive work rather than on perceived supervisory deficiencies.

Tools for Effective Teams

In any type of team, the manager's responsibility is to ensure it has the resources, tools, and leadership support to be successful (Kelly and Short 2006). This section describes some of the ways managers can fulfill this responsibility to meet quality management goals.

Human Resources Tools

Managers today must be keenly aware of the way human resources issues affect their ability to support collaborative teamwork and also promote quality patient outcomes and cost-effectiveness. Achieving these objectives requires appropriate human resources to be executed effectively. Consider the impact of nurse staffing on patient outcomes. A growing body of evidence links physician, nurse, and pharmacist staffing with patient outcomes in the hospital setting (Clarke 2007; Carayon and Gurses 2008; Clarke and Donaldson 2008; Horn and Jacobi 2006; Lopez et al. 2009; West et al. 2014). For example, levels and types of nurse staffing in hospitals have been linked with mortality rates, medication errors, wound infections, hospital lengths of stay, urinary tract infections, and pneumonia (Clarke 2007). Based on such studies, in 2004, the importance of nurse staffing to hospital patient outcomes was recognized by the National Quality Forum (2004) in its published report *National Voluntary Consensus*

Standards for Nursing-Sensitive Care: An Initial Performance Measure Set.
More recently, the Centers for Medicare & Medicaid Services (2016) added
publicly reported quality measures for skilled nursing facilities that include
several staffing measures:

- Number of registered nurse hours each resident gets per day
- Total number of licensed staff (registered nurses, licensed practical
  nurses, licensed vocational nurses) hours per resident per day
- Number of certified nursing assistant hours per resident per day
- Number of physical therapist staff hours per resident per day

Consider the impact of human resources on the finances of an
organization. Employee turnover can be costly. Filling a vacant position for a
registered nurse can cost an acute care hospital from $82,000 to $88,000 (Jones
2008), and organizational turnover costs have been estimated between 3.4
percent and 5.8 percent of the annual operating budget at one large academic
medical center (Waldman et al. 2010). In environments of scarce resources,
managers may view expenses associated with preventable staff turnover as
quality waste. McHugh and colleagues' (2010) *Using Workforce Practices to
Drive Quality Improvement: A Guide for Hospitals* provides managers with a
summary of best human resources practices.

Collaborative Team Tools

Many required and recommended patient safety initiatives are accompanied
by operational tools to promote teamwork. For example, the World Health
Organization (WHO) Surgical Safety Checklist is shown in exhibit 8.2. Built
into this tool are recommendations for the specific team members required
for the three verification steps.

Managers today may draw from a growing number of evidence-based tools
that promote team effectiveness and enhance communication in and between
teams to aid in institutionalizing desired team behaviors. Shared understanding
of important information can be exchanged during team interactions such as
huddles and debriefings (Hunt 2010). A huddle or information update is a
short meeting to discuss and reinforce essential information such as team roles, a
patient's clinical status, patient care goals and barriers, and issues affecting team
operations. This short meeting often occurs at shift change but can occur any
time when necessary. A debriefing is a team meeting that occurs after an event
(such as a patient fall) to discuss what happened and why and to incorporate
lessons learned into an updated patient care plan.

Successful communication is vital to collaborative teamwork. Whenever
team members are exchanging information, the communications should

EXHIBIT 8.2
WHO Surgical
Safety Checklist

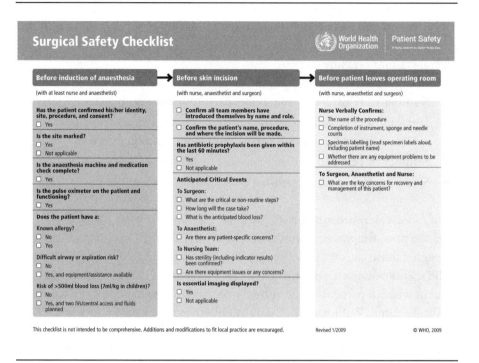

be complete, clear, brief, and timely (Hunt 2010). Strategies to improve communication and information exchange include the following:

- Situation, Background, Assessment, and Recommendation (SBAR) is a standard method to communicate information about a patient's condition. An example of a situation in which SBAR should be used is when a hospital nurse is phoning a physician to update her on a patient's condition and receive new orders for care (Haig, Sutton, and Whittington 2006).

- Call-out is used to communicate critical information during an emergent event (Agency for Healthcare Research and Quality [AHRQ] 2016). This communication technique might be used when a patient has a cardiac arrest and the nurse "calls out" what medication he is giving to the patient.

- Check-back or repeat-back can be used to verify and validate that information has been accurately exchanged between the sender and receiver. "This method of communication . . . requires the receiver to repeat the message back to the sender to validate that the appropriate message was received" (Center for Chemical Process Safety 2016). An example of this communication technique is when the laboratory calls a critical laboratory result to a physician's office and the medical assistant repeats all the information back to verify that it is correct.

- Standardized handoffs allow for the exchange of necessary information during transitions in care (Arora and Johnson 2006). An example of such an exchange would be the report from the emergency department to the medical floor where the patient is being admitted.

- TeamSTEPPS is a training program that facilities can use to provide healthcare workers with the necessary collaborative teamwork strategies and tools to improve performance (AHRQ 2016). A link to these training materials is in the web resources box at the end of this chapter.

Summary

The importance of the manager's role in team design cannot be overestimated. Shared team expectations and role definitions, along with defined communication processes, are necessary to promote effective collaborative teamwork and prevent breakdowns. Mental models about authority, hierarchy, talents, and differences in the workplace can influence the design and execution of teamwork. Managers should examine their mental models and incorporate an understanding of mental models that define the context of the work environment and should design the structure in which teams operate.

Exercise 8.1
Objectives:

- To practice identifying management behaviors that demonstrate collaborative teamwork and continuous improvement.
- To explore how collaborative teamwork and continuous improvement influence the patient experience.

Instructions:

- Read the case study, which is drawn from *The New Pioneers: The Men and Women Who Are Transforming the Workplace and Marketplace* (1999) by former *Wall Street Journal* columnist Thomas Petzinger Jr.
- Describe several examples of how management demonstrated the principle of continuous improvement in the case study.
- Describe several examples of how management demonstrated the principle of teamwork in the case study.

- Describe how your responses to the two previous instructions contributed to the quality of the patient's experience (service quality) and the quality of the clinical service (content quality).

Case Study: The following section is reprinted with slight changes with the permission of Simon & Schuster Adult Publishing Group from *The New Pioneers: The Men and Women Who Are Transforming the Workplace and Marketplace* by Thomas Petzinger Jr. Copyright © 1999 by Thomas Petzinger Jr.

While many companies are getting better at customer service, one industry has gotten a lot worse lately. That industry is medicine. The onslaught of managed care has commoditized what was once the most delicate relationship in all of commerce, that of doctor and patient. Accounting for the payment of services has overwhelmed the rendering of the services themselves. Yet a few islands of people have thrown off their Newtonian blinders and recognized that putting the customer first can redound to the benefit of the provider as well. With so many competing claims on every dollar, every process, and every hour of time and attention, the interests of the customer—the patient—serve as a common ground for making the entire system more efficient.

One hospital is such a place: a 520-bed teaching hospital and so-called trauma-one center with a stellar clinical reputation. Within the hospital, an outpatient surgery clinic was opened long ago, in which an ever-larger percentage of procedures were being conducted. And although the surgical staff was acclaimed, management recognized that the overall patient experience left something to be desired.

The main problem was delay. The surgery line was jam-packed as early as 5:30 every morning. Some patients spent the entire day lurching from check-in to pre-op to anesthesia to surgery to recovery to post-op, with too much of the time spent simply waiting. As much as some people may wish to convalesce at length as admitted hospital patients, no one wants to turn a four-hour outpatient experience into a nine-hour ordeal. If the hospital wanted to maintain (much less extend) its position in the marketplace, it had to figure out how to get patients through faster without degrading clinical results.

The job of facilitating the planning process went to an internal quality consultant who had worked for 15 years as a registered nurse, mostly in neonatal intensive care, before earning her MBA and fulfilling this new organizational role. In her years in intensive care, she was often perplexed by the priorities that families exhibited in the most dire medical situations. "I'm working like crazy to save a baby, but the parents get upset because the grandparents didn't get to see the baby!" she recalls. In time she could see that medicine was only part of healthcare. "Healthcare providers hold people's lives in their hands at a very vulnerable time," she says. "Healthcare is about a personal encounter."

Most of the people on the business side of healthcare have little intellectual grasp and less emotional grasp of this concept. Indeed, after moving to the business side herself, she became convinced that some of the most intractable problems of the industry could be solved only by people who, like her, combined far-flung disciplines. "Innovation will come from people who have crossed the boundaries from other disciplines," she says—from business to medicine, from medicine to law, and so on.

The facilitator insisted on involving the maximum number of nurses—people who knew the whole patient as well as the individual surgeries they variously received. The new administrator over the area requested that the members of the improvement committee visit as many other hospitals as possible within their large hospital system to explore which outpatient surgical practices could be employed at their own site. And throughout the study process, the administrator continually harped on the "vision statement" of the initiative, which put as its first priority "to provide a patient/family focused quality culture."

This new administrator in the surgery service, a nurse herself, was a powerful force in leading the improvement effort. Under the previous leadership, the policy for change was simply "give the surgeons whatever they want," as she put it. The administrator acknowledged that the surgeon must call the shots on procedures—but not necessarily on process. In that respect she, too, insisted on using the patient as the point of departure. "If you're guided by only one phrase—what is best for the patient—you will always come up with the right answer," the administrator insists. (Hearing the administrator and facilitator say this over and over began to remind me of the best editors I have worked for. When in doubt, they would often say, do only what's right for the reader. Everything else will fall into place.)

Studying the surgery line from the patients' point of view was disturbingly illuminating. Surgeons showing up late for the first round of surgeries at 7:30 am threw off the schedule for the entire day. The various hospital departments—admitting, financing, lab, surgery—all conducted their own separate interaction with the patient on each of their individual schedules. A poor physical layout, including a long corridor separating the operating rooms from pre-op, compounded the inefficiencies. Once a patient was called to surgery, he spent 40 minutes waiting for an orderly to arrive with a wheelchair or gurney. And, because this was an outpatient surgery center located inside a hospital, the anesthesiologists were accustomed to administering heavy sedation, often slowing the patient's recovery from otherwise minor surgery and further clogging the entire line. The operation was a success, but the patient was pissed.

In talking to patients, the researchers discovered a subtext in the complaints about delays: resentment over the loss of personal control. Patients spent the day in God-awful gauze gowns, stripped of their underwear, their backsides exposed to the world. Partly this reflected a medical culture that considered the procedure, not the patient, as the customer. As the administrator put it to me, "If you're naked on a stretcher on your back, you're pretty subservient." Family members, meanwhile, had to roam the hospital in search of change so they could coax a cup of coffee from a vending machine. She marveled at the arrogance of it. "You're spending $3,000 on a loved one, but you'd better bring correct change."

Fortunately, this administrator had the political standing to push through big changes, and although the staff surgeons effectively had veto power, most were too busy to get deeply involved in the improvement process. Because few patients enjoy getting stuck with needles, the nurses created a process for capturing the blood from the insertion of each patient's intravenous needle and sending it to the lab for whatever tests were necessary. This cut down not only on discomfort, but on time, money, and scheduling complexity. The unremitting bureaucratic questions and paperwork were all replaced with a single registration packet that patients picked up in their doctors' offices and completed days before ever setting foot in the hospital; last-minute administrative details were attended to in a single phone call the day before surgery. The nurses set up a check-in system for the coats and valuables of patients and family members, which eliminated the need for every family to encamp with their belongings in a pre-op room for the entire day. A family-friendly waiting area was created, stocked with free snacks and drinks. There would be no more desperate searches for correct change. That was only the beginning. Patients had always resented having to purchase their post-op medications from the hospital pharmacy; simply freeing them to use their neighborhood drugstore got them out of the surgery line sooner, further relieving the congestion. Also in the interest of saving time, the nurses made a heretical proposal to allow healthy outpatients to walk into surgery under their own power, accompanied by their family members, rather than waiting 40 minutes for a wheelchair or gurney. That idea got the attention of the surgeons, who after years of paying ghastly malpractice premiums vowed that the administrator, not they, would suffer the personal liability on that one. The risk-management department went "eek" at the idea. Yet as the improvement committee pointed out, the hospital permitted outpatients to traverse any other distance in the building by foot. Why should the march into surgery be any different?

In a similar vein, the nurses suggested allowing patients to wear underwear beneath their hospital gowns. The administrators could scarcely believe their ears: "Show me one place in the literature where patients wear underwear to surgery!" one top administrator demanded. (The nurses noted that restricting change to what had been attempted elsewhere would automatically eliminate the possibility of any breakthrough in performance.) And why stop at underwear, the nurses asked. The hospital was conducting more and more outpatient cataract operations; why not let these patients wear their clothes into surgery? "Contamination!" the purists cried. But clothing is no dirtier than the skin beneath it, the nurses answered. This change eliminated a major post-op bottleneck caused by elderly patients who could not dress themselves or tie their shoes with their heads clouded by anesthesia and their depth perception altered by the removal of their cataracts.

As the changes took effect, the nurses observed another unintended effect. Patients were actually reducing their recovery times! People were no longer looking at ceiling tiles on their way into surgery like characters in an episode of *Dr. Kildare*. They went into surgery feeling better and came out of it feeling better. In case after case they were ready to leave the joint faster; this in turn freed up more space for other patients. Because they had studied practices at a number of stand-alone clinics, the nurses even suggested to the physicians that the outpatients would be better off with less anesthesia, hastening their recoveries, speeding their exit, and freeing up still more capacity.

Within a year, the volume at the outpatient surgery unit had surged 50 percent with no increase in square footage and no increase in staff. Customer-service surveys were positive and costs were under control. And it dawned on the facilitator that the nurses' intuitive conviction that the patient should come first benefited the surgery line itself at every single step. Everyone and everything connected to the process—surgeon, staff, insurers, time, cost, and quality—seemed to come out ahead when the patients' interests came first.

What was really happening, of course, was that the change teams simply put common sense first. In a complex process of many players, the interest of the patient was the one unifying characteristic—the best baseline for calibration—because the patient was the only person touched by every step.

Companion Readings

Boutros, A., and V. S. Lee. 2016. "Measuring the Intangible: Teams and Teamwork." *NEJM Catalyst.* Published June 2. http://catalyst.nejm.org/videos/measuring-the-intangible-teams-and-teamwork.

Edmondson, A. C., and E. H. Schein. 2012. *Teaming: How Organizations Learn, Innovate, and Compete in the Knowledge Economy.* San Francisco: Jossey-Bass.

Health Research & Educational Trust and Agency for Healthcare Research and Quality. 2010. *Using Workforce Practices to Drive Quality Improvement: A Guide for Hospitals.* Published June. www.hret.org/workforce/resources/workforce-guide.pdf.

Health Research & Educational Trust, Hospitals in Pursuit of Excellence, and the American Hospital Association. 2016. *Improving Patient Safety Culture Through*

Teamwork and Communication: TeamSTEPPS. Accessed November 11. www .hpoe.org/resources/hpoehretaha-guides/2598.

Lenderman, H., H. Reffett, J. Moran, and M. Beaudry. 2014. "Selecting Quality Improvement Team Members." Public Health Foundation. Published May 19. www.phf.org/resourcestools/Documents/Team_Member_Selection_Tool.pdf.

Meyers-Briggs Foundation. 2016. "MBTI Basics." Accessed November. www.myers briggs.org/my-mbti-personality-type/mbti-basics.

Mitchell, P., M. Wynia, R. Golden, B. McNellis, S. Okun, C. E. Webb, V. Rohrbach, and I. Von Kohorn. 2012. "Core Principles and Values of Effective Team-Based Healthcare." Institute of Medicine. Published October. www.nationalahec.org/pdfs/vsrt-team-based-care-principles-values.pdf.

Reid, J. 2013. "Speaking Up: A Professional Imperative." *Journal of Perioperative Practice* 23 (5): 114–18.

Salas, E., S. A. Almeida, M. Salisbury, H. King, E. H. Lazzara, R. Lyons, K. A. Wilson, P. A. Almeida, and R. McQuillan. 2009. "What Are the Critical Success Factors for Team Training in Health Care?" *The Joint Commission Journal on Quality and Patient Safety* 35 (8): 398–405.

Thomas, E. J. 2011. "Improving Teamwork in Healthcare: Current Approaches and the Path Forward." *BMJ Quality and Safety* 20 (8): 647–50.

Warner, S. 2013. "Bridge the Silos: Nursing, Imaging and the Laboratory Work Independently and Collaborate When Needed to Care for Patients." *ADVANCE* Healthcare Network for Laboratory. Published November 20. http://laboratory-manager.advanceweb.com/Features/Articles/Bridge-the-Silos.aspx.

Web Resources

Team Strategies and Tools to Enhance Performance and Patient Safety (TeamSTEPPS): www.teamstepssportal.org

Frameworks About Talents and Differences

Gallup StrengthsFinder 2.0: http://strengths.gallup.com/110659/Homepage.aspx

Human Dynamics International: www.humandynamics.com

Keirsey: http://keirsey.com/default.aspx

References

Agency for Healthcare Research and Quality (AHRQ). 2016. "TeamSTEPPS®: Strategies and Tools to Enhance Performance and Patient Safety." Reviewed May. www.ahrq.gov/professionals/education/curriculum-tools/teamstepps/index.html.

Altman, L. K. 1995. "Big Doses of Chemotherapy Drug Killed Patient, Hurt 2d." *New York Times*, March 24, A18.

Arora, V., and J. Johnson. 2006. "A Model for Building a Standardized Hand-off Protocol." *The Joint Commission Journal on Quality and Patient Safety* 32 (11): 646–55.

Bender, J. S., T. O. Nicolescu, S. G. Hollingsworth, K. Murer, K. R. Wallace, and W. J. Ertl. 2015. "Improving Operating Room Efficiency via an Interprofessional Approach." *Journal of the American College of Surgeons* 220 (6): 1070–76.

Bould, M. D., S. Sutherland, D. T. Sydor, V. Naik, and Z. Friedman. 2015. "Residents' Reluctance to Challenge Negative Hierarchy in the Operating Room: A Qualitative Study." *Canadian Journal of Anaesthesia* 62 (6): 576–86.

Brown, T. 2013. "Healing the Hospital Hierarchy." *New York Times*. Published March 16. http://opinionator.blogs.nytimes.com/2013/03/16/healing-the-hospital-hierarchy.

Carayon, P., and A. P. Gurses. 2008. "Nursing Workload and Patient Safety—A Human Factors Engineering Perspective." In *Patient Safety and Quality: An Evidence-Based Handbook for Nurses*, edited by R. G. Hughes. Agency for Healthcare Research and Policy. Published April. www.ncbi.nlm.nih.gov/books/NBK2657.

Center for Chemical Process Safety. 2016. "Repeat-Back." Retrieved July 30. www.aiche.org/ccps/resources/glossary/process-safety-glossary/repeat-back.

Centers for Medicare & Medicaid Services. 2016. "Staffing Charts." Retrieved July 20. www.medicare.gov/NursingHomeCompare/Data/Staffing.html.

Clarke, S. P. 2007. "Nurse Staffing in Acute Care Settings: Research Perspectives and Practical Applications." *The Joint Commission Journal on Quality and Patient Safety* 33 (11s): 30–44.

Clarke, S. P., and N. E. Donaldson. 2008. "Nurse Staffing and Patient Care Quality and Safety." In *Patient Safety and Quality: An Evidence-Based Handbook for Nurses*, edited by R. G. Hughes. Agency for Healthcare Research and Policy. Published April. www.ncbi.nlm.nih.gov/books/ NBK2676.

Clements, D., M. Dault, and A. Priest. 2007. "Effective Teamwork in Healthcare: Research and Reality." *HealthcarePapers* 7 (SP): 26–34.

Edmondson, A. C. 2016. "Wicked Problem Solvers: Lessons from Successful Cross-Industry Teams." *Harvard Business Review* 94 (6): 53–59.

Grumbach, K., and T. Bodenheimer. 2004. "Can Primary Health Care Teams Improve Primary Care Practice?" *Journal of the American Medical Association* 29 (10): 1246–51.

Haig, K. M., S. Sutton, and J. Whittington. 2006. "SBAR: A Shared Mental Model for Improving Communication Between Clinicians." *The Joint Commission Journal on Quality and Patient Safety* 32 (3): 167–75.

Horn, E., and J. Jacobi. 2006. "The Critical Care Clinical Pharmacist: Evolution of an Essential Team Member." *Critical Care Medicine* 34 (3S): S46–S51.

Hunt, C. M. 2010. "Patient Safety Is Enhanced by Teamwork." *PA Patient Safety Advisory* 7 (Suppl 2): 14–16. Published June 16. http://patientsafetyauthority. org/ADVISORIES/AdvisoryLibrary/2010/jun16_7(suppl2)/Pages/14.aspx.

Jones, C. B. 2008. "Revisiting Turnover Costs: Adjusting for Inflation." *Journal of Nursing Administration* 38 (1): 11–18.

Kelly, D. L., and N. Short. 2006. "Exploring Assumptions About Teams." *The Joint Commission Journal on Quality and Patient Safety* 32 (2): 109–12.

Kotter, J. 2011. "Breaking Down Silos: A Q&A with John Kotter." Published May 13. www.lifescienceleader.com/doc/breaking-down-silos-a-q-a-with-john-kotter-0001.

Ledlow, G. R., and M. N. Coppola. 2014. *Leadership for Health Professionals: Theory, Skills, and Applications*, 2nd ed. Burlington, MA: Jones & Bartlett Learning.

Lopez, L., L. S. Hicks, A. P. Cohen, S. McKean, and J. S. Weissman. 2009. "Hospitalists and the Quality of Care in Hospitals." *Archives of Internal Medicine* 169 (15): 1389–94.

McHugh, M., A. Garman, A. McAlearney, P. Song, and M. Harrison. 2010. *Using Workforce Practices to Drive Quality Improvement: A Guide for Hospitals.* Chicago: Health Research & Educational Trust.

Mitchell, P., M. Wynia, R. Golden, B. McNellis, S. Okun, C. E. Webb, V. Rohrbach, and I. Von Kohorn. 2012. *Core Principles and Values of Effective Team-Based Health Care.* Institute of Medicine. Published October. www.nationalahec.org/ pdfs/vsrt-team-based-care-principles-values.pdf.

Myers, I. B., L. K. Kirby, and K. D. Myers. 1998. *Introduction to Type: A Guide to Understanding Your Results on the Myers-Briggs Type Indicator*, 6th ed. Palo Alto, CA: Consulting Psychologists Press.

National Quality Forum. 2004. *National Voluntary Consensus Standards for Nursing-Sensitive Care: An Initial Performance Measure Set.* Published October. www.qualityforum.org/Publications/2004/10/National_Voluntary_ Consensus_Standards_for_Nursing-Sensitive_Care__An_Initial_Performance_ Measure_Set.aspx.

Nelson, E. C., P. B. Batalden, T. P. Hubor, J. K. Johnson, M. M. Godfrey, L. A. Headrick, and J. H. Wasson. 2007. "Success Characteristics of High-Performing Microsystems." In *Quality by Design: A Clinical Microsystem Approach*, edited by E. C. Nelson, P. B. Batalden, and M. M. Godfrey, 3–33. San Francisco: Jossey-Bass.

Oandasan, I., G. R. Baker, K. Barker, C. Bosco, D. D'Amour, L. Jones, S. Kimpton, L. Lemieux-Charles, L. Naismith, L. San Martin Rodriguez, J. Tepper, and D. Way. 2006. *Teamwork in Healthcare: Promoting Effective Teamwork in Healthcare in Canada*. Canadian Health Services Research Foundation. Published June. www.hrhresourcecenter.org/node/1773.

O'Daniel, M., and A. H. Rosenstein. 2008. "Professional Communication and Team Collaboration." In *Patient Safety and Quality: An Evidence-Based Handbook for Nurses*, edited by R. G. Hughes. Agency for Healthcare Research and Policy. Published April. www.ncbi.nlm.nih.gov/books/NBK2637.

Petzinger, T., Jr. 1999. *The New Pioneers: The Men and Women Who Are Transforming the Workplace and Marketplace*. New York: Simon & Schuster Adult Publishing Group.

Rosen, E. 2010. "Smashing Silos." *Bloomberg*. Published February 5. www.bloomberg .com/news/articles/2010-02-05/smashing-silos.

Schein, E. H. 1984. "Coming to a New Awareness of Organizational Culture." *Sloan Management Review* 25 (2): 3–14.

Taplin, S. H., M. K. Foster, and S. M. Shortell. 2013. "Organizational Leadership for Building Effective Health Care Teams." *Annals of Family Medicine* 11 (3): 279–81.

Tucker, A. L., and A. C. Edmondson. 2003. "Why Hospitals Don't Learn from Failures: Organizational and Psychological Dynamics That Inhibit System Change." *California Management Review* 45 (2): 55–72.

Waldman, J. D., F. Kelly, S. Arora, and H. L. Smith. 2010. "The Shocking Cost of Turnover in Healthcare." *Healthcare Management Review* 35 (3): 206–21.

Webster, T. R., L. Curry, D. Berg, M. Radford, H. M. Krumholz, and E. H. Bradley. 2008. "Organizational Resiliency: How Top-Performing Hospitals Respond to Setbacks in Improving Quality of Cardiac Care." *Journal of Healthcare Management* 53 (3): 169–82.

West, E., D. N. Barron, D. Harrison, A. M. Rafferty, K. Rowan, and C. Sanderson. 2014. "Nurse Staffing, Medical Staffing and Mortality in Intensive Care: An Observational Study." *International Journal of Nursing Studies* 51 (5): 781–94.

World Health Organization (WHO). 2016. "WHO Surgical Safety Checklist." Retrieved July 25. www.who.int/patientsafety/safesurgery/checklist/en.

ACHIEVING QUALITY RESULTS IN COMPLEX SYSTEMS

MEASURING PROCESS AND SYSTEM PERFORMANCE

Learning Objectives

After completing this chapter, you should be able to

- describe how managers use measurement for performance management purposes,
- distinguish types of measures and comprehensive measurement sets,
- explain how performance measurement fits into the quality continuum, and
- identify sources of comparative performance data for health services organizations.

E very day we use data to make decisions and monitor our personal interests, whether we are following the progress of our favorite sports team (reviewing team rankings), determining how to dress (checking the weather report), shopping (calculating the balance on a debit or credit card), or knowing when to mow the lawn (seeing the grass is too high).

People use data to guide their own healthcare activities, too. A child's hot forehead alerts a mother to the possibility of a fever. A grandfather with diabetes measures his daily blood glucose level to regulate his insulin dosage. People exercise 30 minutes a day, five times a week, to remain fit. Care providers use data to diagnose, treat, and monitor clinical conditions and the effectiveness of interventions. Blood tests, X-rays, and vital signs all provide information to enhance the care provider's effectiveness. In each of these examples, data add value to the process. Data give us information about something we are interested in, help us choose among various options, alert us when something needs to be done, and define the boundaries of an activity.

When we follow our favorite sports team during the course of the season, we are looking at data over time for trends and progress. When we check to see what place the team is in relation to the other teams in the same division, we are comparing data points. When we realize the grass is high compared with the neighbors', we are using a benchmark to signal that we need to mow it.

If we check the weather report for the barometric pressure or chance of rain, we are using formal measures. When we use our hand to check a forehead for fever, we are measuring informally.

These measurement lessons from personal life are easily overlooked in the workplace. While immersed in data and reporting, health services managers face the risk of being "data rich and information poor" about how their unit, department, or organization is actually performing. Managers operating in various types of health service organizations and settings are charged with understanding and continuously improving services. The foundation of these responsibilities is measurement. Managers need many types of data and information to effectively manage the performance of their areas of responsibility. Data and information can "come in many forms, such as numerical, graphical, and qualitative, and from many sources, including internal processes, surveys, and social media" (Baldrige Performance Excellence Program [BPEP] 2015, 42).

This chapter offers lessons for managers that assist them with recognizing the role of measurement in performance management, differentiating types of measures, and selecting a balanced set of measures. This chapter also illustrates how performance measurement fits into the quality continuum and provides resources for managers to find comparative data.

Quality Measures and Their Uses

quality measure (or metric)
"any type of measurement used to gauge a quantifiable component of performance" (Spath 2013, 34)

quality indicators
statistical measures that give an indication of process or output quality

A **quality measure (or metric)** is "any type of measurement used to gauge a quantifiable component of performance" (Spath 2013, 34). To understand, use, and communicate quality metrics, managers must be able to differentiate between types of metrics and their respective characteristics.

A word that managers may find used synonymously with measure is "indicator." This terminology is used by groups such as the Agency for Healthcare Research and Quality (AHRQ) to describe performance measures used in health services organizations. **Quality indicators** are statistical measures that give an indication of process or output quality.

In the context of systems thinking and improving system performance, the purpose of performance management measures is to provide feedback about the system's behavior—in other words, provide understanding. Measures are used to monitor ongoing performance, provide clues about the determinants of system behavior, and offer direction for further investigation. Performance management measures help identify patterns across processes to better understand the underlying system causes or structures generating the system outcomes. Feedback about the system's behavior provides clues about systemic structure. Understanding systemic structure enables one to better manage underlying system issues affecting performance.

The performance management cycle, illustrated in exhibit 9.1, shows the role of measurement in continuous improvements in a manager's domain of responsibility (i.e., department, program, organization). The **performance management cycle** links performance standards, performance measurement, performance improvement, and reporting progress in an ongoing cycle. This perspective emphasizes the need to continuously review, evaluate, and integrate changing customer, stakeholder, and regulatory requirements. Data are part of every element of this cycle. Measurement data are used during the identification of customer or stakeholder requirements when performance standards are established. Finding performance gaps requires collection and analysis of measurement data. During the improvement process itself, measurement data can be useful in setting performance requirements, and reporting of progress is done using measurement data.

> **performance management cycle**
> ongoing cycle in which performance standards, performance measurement, performance improvement, and reporting progress are linked

Selecting Performance Measures

Customer, stakeholder, and market requirements are the foundation for and drivers of all work performed by the organization. These requirements guide process design and also define criteria against which process and organizational

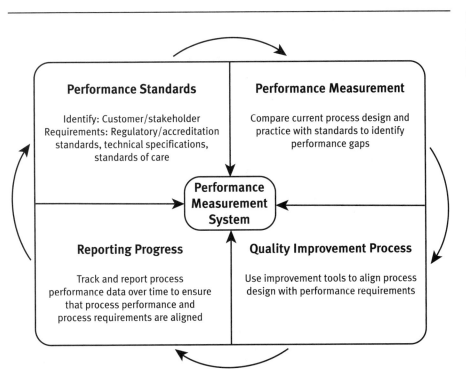

EXHIBIT 9.1
Performance Management Cycle

Performance Standards

Identify: Customer/stakeholder Requirements: Regulatory/accreditation standards, technical specifications, standards of care

Performance Measurement

Compare current process design and practice with standards to identify performance gaps

Performance Measurement System

Reporting Progress

Track and report process performance data over time to ensure that process performance and process requirements are aligned

Quality Improvement Process

Use improvement tools to align process design with performance requirements

Source: Adapted with permission from Public Health Foundation (2016).

effectiveness are judged. The BPEP (2015, 42–43) suggests the following principles be considered in the selection and use of performance measures in a healthcare organization:

> The measures or indicators you select should best represent the factors that lead to improved health care outcomes; improved patient, other customer, operational, financial, and societal performance; and healthier communities. A comprehensive yet carefully culled set of measures or indicators tied to patient/other customer and organizational performance requirements provides a clear basis for aligning all processes with your organization's goals.

Managers must purposefully select performance indicators that are linked to and aligned with their organizations' goals, business strategy, and customer and stakeholder requirements. Integrating internal and external measurement requirements may also be thought of in terms of a Venn diagram. In exhibit 9.2, one circle represents internally driven performance measures, while the other circle represents externally driven performance measures. To leverage time, effort, and resources, managers should strategically select measures that allow for the largest area of overlap between the circles. In this way, performance measures may be used for multiple purposes internally and externally.

Internally Driven Measures

The BPEP (2015, 42) provides direction on the criteria to be considered when a healthcare organization selects internally driven measures:

EXHIBIT 9.2
Leveraging
Performance
Measures

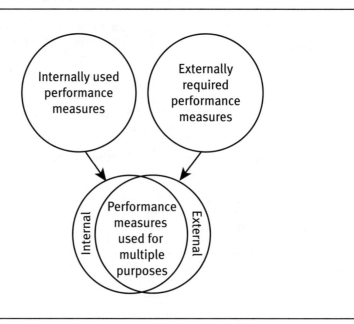

Management by fact requires you to measure and analyze your organization's performance, both inside the organization and in your competitive environment. Measurements should derive from organizational needs and strategy, and they should provide critical data and information about key processes, outputs, results, outcomes, and competitor and industry performance.

Internally driven measures are organization specific, as the measures are derived from the organization's unique strategic goals. For example, one hospital may set a goal of improving patient satisfaction, with success being measured by the ratings on surveys filled out by patients. Another hospital may set a goal to eliminate preventable patient harm, with success being measured by counting the number of hospital-acquired infections. Employee retention rates might be used by an organization to measure its success at improving teamwork, whereas another hospital might have the same goal but use attainment of the Magnet Status award from the American Nurses Credentialing Center as the measure of success.

At the departmental level, organization-wide strategic and operational goals influence the choice of internally driven measures. As an example, exhibit 9.3 shows performance measures used by a radiology service to evaluate department-specific aspects of hospitalwide goals, which were established for each of the six dimensions of quality identified in the Institute of Medicine (IOM) report *Crossing the Quality Chasm* (2001).

Quality Dimension	Performance Measures
Safe	• Number of patients who react adversely to the X-ray dye • Percentage of pregnant patients adequately protected from radiation exposure
Effective	• Average time between identification of significant (e.g., life threatening) X-ray findings and communication of these findings to the patient's doctor • Percentage of presurgery X-ray findings confirmed at the time of surgery
Patient centered	• Percentage of patients who complain about a lack of privacy in the X-ray changing rooms • Percentage of patients who report they were greeted by the receptionist on arrival in the department
Timely	• Average wait time for patients in the reception area before an exam • Percentage of outpatient X-ray results reported to the patient's doctor within 12 hours

EXHIBIT 9.3
Quality Dimensions and Performance Measures for Hospital Radiology Services

(continued)

Quality Dimension	Performance Measures
Efficient	• Percentage of X-ray exams that must be repeated because the first exam was not performed properly • Percentage of patients undergoing a screening mammogram whose information is entered into a reminder system with a target due date for the next mammogram
Equitable	• Percentage of children with clinically suspected appendicitis who undergo ultrasonography as the initial imaging modality • Number of hours each month the mobile mammography unit is available to people living in rural areas

EXHIBIT 9.3
Quality Dimensions and Performance Measures for Hospital Radiology Services (continued)

Source: Adapted from Spath (2013). Used with permission.

Externally Driven Measures

Regulatory agencies such as the Centers for Medicare & Medicaid Services (CMS) and accreditation groups such as The Joint Commission have an inordinate influence on the performance measures used in health services organizations. This influence has increased with the move toward value-based reimbursement that requires reporting of quality measurement data to payers and other external stakeholders. A list of the major national clinical care measure programs and clearinghouses for inpatient, outpatient, and emergency service measures is found in exhibit 9.4. Included in these measurement collections are more than 1,037 unique measures, some of which are required to be reported by providers to external groups (Newton et al. 2015).

In addition to the major measurement collections in exhibit 9.4, there are numerous condition- and function-specific measurement programs. For instance, the American College of Radiology (2016) sponsors measurement projects that cover topics such as lung cancer screening, computed tomography (CT) angiography, mammography, CT colonography, traumatic brain injury imaging, and general radiology quality and safety. Press Ganey (2016) supports the National Database of Nursing Quality Indicators developed by the American Nurses Association. In its 2015 assessment of its own measurement efforts, CMS analyzed more than 700 measures across 25 programs and found that only half of the measures were shared across programs, and that nearly half of the measures were developed locally by regional collaboratives such as the Integrated Healthcare Association (California), Maine Health Management Coalition, and Minnesota Community Measurement (Collaborative for Health Information Technology in Oregon 2016).

EXHIBIT 9.4
Inpatient,
Emergency,
and Outpatient
Measure
Collections of
External Groups

American Medical Association
Physician Consortium for Performance Improvement

Centers for Medicare & Medicaid Services
Accountable Care Organization Quality Measures
Children's Health Insurance Program Reauthorization Act Core Set of Measures
Health Care Quality Measures for Medicaid-Eligible Adults
Home Health Measure Set
Hospital Value-Based Purchasing
Hospital Outpatient Quality Reporting Program
Hospital Inpatient Quality Reporting Program
Meaningful Use Clinical Quality Measures (Pediatric and Adult)
Medicare-Medicaid Capitated Financial Arrangement Model
Physician Quality Reporting System—Electronic Health Record Incentive Clinical
     Quality Measures

Health Resources and Services Administration
Operation and Performance of Health Centers
Uniform Data System

The Joint Commission/CMS
Hospital Inpatient Quality Measures
Hospital Outpatient Department Measures

National Committee for Quality Assurance
Healthcare Effectiveness Data and Information Set

National Quality Forum

Source: Adapted from Newton et al. (2015).

The online National Quality Measures Clearinghouse sponsored by AHRQ is a good resource for measures of various health conditions and health service functions in different settings (see web resources at the end of this chapter).

Many payers, including CMS, require health services organizations to measure and report customer satisfaction results. The questions on these satisfaction surveys vary depending on payer specifications. A sample of the questions on the CMS nursing home satisfaction survey designed to be administered by mail to residents recently discharged after short stays (no more than 100 days) are found in exhibit 9.5.

EXHIBIT 9.5
Sample of
Questions
on the CMS
Nursing Home
Survey for
Discharged
Residents

- When you were in the nursing home, was the area around your room quiet at night?
- When you were in the nursing home, were you bothered by noise in the nursing home during the day?
- When you had visitors in the nursing home, could you find a place to visit in private?
- When you were in the nursing home, were you ever left sitting or lying in the same position so long that it hurt?
- When you were in the nursing home, could you reach the call button by yourself?
- When you were in the nursing home, was there a pitcher of water or something to drink where you could reach it by yourself?
- When you were in the nursing home, did the staff make sure you had enough personal privacy when you dressed, took a shower, or bathed?
- When you were in the nursing home, could you choose what time you went to bed?
- When you were in the nursing home, could you choose what clothes you wore?
- When you were in the nursing home, could you choose what activities you did there?
- When you were in the nursing home, were there enough organized activities for you to do on the weekends?
- Would you recommend the nursing home to others?

Source: Adapted from AHRQ (2016).

Choosing a Comprehensive Set of Measures

A manager may want to use any number of measures to evaluate performance in the area or department under her control. One approach to choosing measures is the **balanced scorecard (BSC)** introduced more than 20 years ago as a framework for organizational performance measurement. The BSC is an organization-defined set of measures that provides leaders with a concise but comprehensive view of business performance. Kaplan and Norton (2007, 174) explained,

> The balanced scorecard includes financial measures that tell the results of actions already taken. And it complements the financial measures with operational measures on customer satisfaction, internal processes, and the organization's innovation and improvement activities—operational measures that are the drivers of future financial performance.

Since its introduction 20 years ago, the BSC has progressed from a framework of performance metrics to a strategic management system (Kaplan

balanced scorecard (BSC)
an organization-defined set of measures that provides leaders with a concise but comprehensive view of business performance

and Norton 2007), and its use in healthcare organizations continues to grow and evolve (Gurd and Gao 2008). Exhibit 9.6 illustrates a simple BSC for a hospital obstetrics service. These department-specific measures are aligned with the organization's overall strategy of improving the customer's experience while delivering safe, high-quality, cost-effective services.

The **clinical value compass** may be thought of as a BSC for evaluating outcomes of a clinical process (see exhibit 9.7). The four categories that it measures (the points of the compass) are functional status and well-being of the patient (north), direct and indirect healthcare costs (south), patient and family satisfaction and perceived benefit (east), and clinical results (west) (Nelson et al. 1996). All four compass points are considered important for defining and measuring the clinical quality of care in a comprehensive manner. These four points may be used to measure, evaluate, and improve the effectiveness of a clinical process. These four points may also serve as a guide for managers when selecting metrics for measuring, evaluating, and improving the performance of their departments or organizations.

Performance management measures may also be grouped according to Donabedian's (1980) three ways to measure quality: structure measures, process measures, and outcome measures. Tools, resources, characteristics of providers, settings, and organizations are considered structure measures. Examples of structure measures are the number of hospital beds, the number of physicians on staff, and the age of the radiology equipment. Activities that occur between patients and providers—in other words, what is done to the patient—are considered process measures. Preventive care activities such as immunizations and prenatal care are examples of process measures. Changes in clinical status—in other words, what happens to the patient—are considered outcome measures. Healthcare-associated infections are examples of outcome measures.

clinical value compass
a balanced scorecard for evaluating outcomes of a clinical process that includes four categories: functional status and well-being of the patient (north), direct and indirect healthcare costs (south), patient and family satisfaction and perceived benefit (east), and clinical results (west)

Customer
- Patient and family satisfaction
- Market share
- Referral rates

Innovation and Learning
- Staff credentials and certifications
- Hours of inservice education
- Improvement teams per year

Internal
- C-section rates
- Maternal complications
- Neonatal complications
- Monitoring capacity

Financial
- Cost per delivery
- Nurse-to-patient ratio
- Supply costs
- Turnover rates

EXHIBIT 9.6
Simple Obstetrics Hospital Service Balanced Scorecard

EXHIBIT 9.7
Clinical Value
Compass

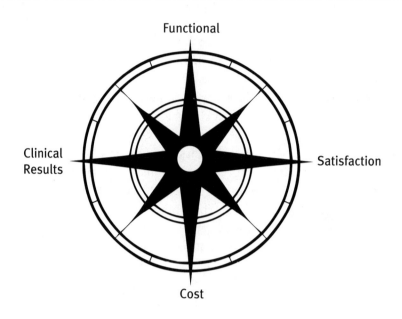

Managers may also classify measures into the categories set forth by the IOM (Hurtado, Swift, and Corrigan 2001) in *Envisioning the National Health Care Quality Report*:

- Safety refers to avoiding injuries to patients from care that is intended to help them.
- Effectiveness refers to providing services based on scientific knowledge to all who could benefit and refraining from providing services to those not likely to benefit (avoiding overuse and misuse).
- Patient centeredness refers to healthcare that establishes a partnership among practitioners, patients, and their families (when appropriate) to ensure that decisions respect patients' wants, needs, and preferences and that patients have the education and support they require to make decisions and participate in their own care.
- Timeliness refers to obtaining needed care and minimizing delays in getting that care.

A health system in the Midwest used this framework to select measures for evaluating its progress in achieving strategic goals established for each category (see exhibit 9.8).

Some healthcare organizations are using the **pillars of performance excellence** framework popularized by Quint Studer (2010). The organization-defined pillars are general categories of performance that link an organization's

pillars of performance excellence
general categories of performance that function as "the foundation for goal setting and results reporting, leadership evaluation, meeting agendas, and departmental communications" (Spaulding, Gamm, and Griffith 2010, 4)

EXHIBIT 9.8
Performance
Measures
Used in an
Anonymous
Health System

Safety Measures
1. Patient falls with injury per 1,000 patient days
2. Medication errors: total reported errors
3. Medication errors: total reported errors reaching patient
4. Medication errors: total reported errors reaching patient and causing harm
5. Clean surgical-site infection rate
6. Hospital-acquired catheter-related urinary tract infection rate
7. Hospital-acquired pressure ulcer rate
8. Rate of hospital admissions within seven days of outpatient colonoscopy

Effectiveness Measures
1. Eligible hospitalized patients: rate of smoking cessation counseling
2. Eligible hospitalized patients: rate of pneumococcal vaccine screen and administration
3. Hospital patients with pneumonia: rate of blood cultures prior to first antibiotic dose
4. Hospital patients with pneumonia: rate of oxygenation assessments within 24 hours of admission
5. Hospital patients with congestive heart failure: rate of assessment of left ventricular ejection fraction
6. Hospital patients with congestive heart failure: rate of ACE (angiotensin-converting-enzyme) inhibitor use at discharge for patients with ejection fraction less than 40 percent
7. Hospital patients with congestive heart failure: rate receiving discharge instructions regarding diet, weight, medications, appointments, and symptoms to watch for
8. Outpatient clinic: percentage of childhood immunizations completed as recommended
9. Outpatient clinic: percentage of mammogram completed as recommended
10. Outpatient clinic: percentage of pneumococcal immunizations completed as recommended
11. Outpatient clinic or primary care physicians: percentage of patients with congestive heart failure who are prescribed an ACE inhibitor if ejection fraction is less than 40 percent
12. Outpatient clinic or primary care physicians: percentage of patients with diabetes who receive recommended foot exams and microalbumin test

Patient-Centeredness Measures
1. Percentage of patients who "Would Recommend" this health system
2. Percentage of patients who rate overall quality of care as good or excellent
3. Percentage of patients who rate overall satisfaction as good or excellent

Timeliness Measures
1. Hospital patients with pneumonia: percentage of patients who receive first dose of antibiotics within eight hours of admission
2. Outpatient: average time between request for screening mammogram until appointment is available
3. Outpatient: average time between request for urgent diagnostic mammogram until appointment is available
4. Percentage of clinic obstetrics patients receiving care in first trimester
5. Percentage of clinic primary care physicians accepting new patients
6. Percentage of home health patients seen within 24 hours of referral

---

strategic plan with individual goals and work plans in each department. The pillars help keep the performance management activities in the organization balanced and aligned. Studer (2010) identified five pillars of excellence: people, service, quality, finance, and growth. "The pillars are used as the foundation for goal setting and results reporting, leadership evaluation, meeting agendas, and departmental communications" (Spaulding, Gamm, and Griffith 2010, 4). Robert Wood Johnson University Hospital Hamilton, 2004 winner of the Malcolm Baldrige National Quality Award, aligned its organizational performance around these five pillars (StuderGroup 2005).

Healthcare organizations adapting Studer's model to fit their own priorities is also common. Sharp HealthCare (2016) has seven pillars of excellence for its vision to transform the healthcare experience: quality, safety, service, people, finance, growth, and community. At University of North Carolina Health Care (2016), all entities in the system have a common set of pillars that outline the organization's priorities and key areas of focus: people, quality and service, growth, value, and innovation. The five strategy pillars used by leadership in a large multispecialty clinic in the Pacific Northwest are efficiency of care, employer of choice, transformation of care, growth, and patient experience.

Performance Measures and the Quality Continuum

Managers must recognize the difference between managing the measures and managing performance. Although a manager may successfully report the performance indicators required by internal and external stakeholders, he may still not be successfully managing his area of responsibility. For example, a hospital may be ranked above the national average on The Joint Commission's (2016b) surgical quality improvement project measure, administering timely prophylactic antibiotics, yet still be plagued with surgeries not starting on time. The same hospital may consistently document the preprocedure time-out required by The Joint Commission (2016a), yet still experience excessive overtime pay and delays in transferring patients to an inpatient bed.

Managers must see performance—not simply reporting of performance indicators—as the end result of their efforts. Measurement is essential to managing and improving organizational performance and results. An organization's use of performance management measures provides clues about their progress along the quality continuum. As illustrated in exhibit 9.9, those embarking on new or early efforts are on the far left of the continuum and are lacking data important to the mission. Those who are experienced in their efforts, shown on the far right, collect data that reflect key business requirements, demonstrate performance from key business processes, and monitor progress on strategic action plans (BPEP 2015).

The performance measurement continuum in exhibit 9.9 references comparative data. The purpose of using comparative data is to better understand one's own organization's performance in the context of how other, similar organizations and the industry in general are performing. Comparing data can lead to identifying best practices and aid in revealing systemic structure problems. In recent years, the availability of and access to comparative data in healthcare have greatly improved. Exhibit 9.10 provides data sources that managers may use in comparing performance data.

EXHIBIT 9.9
The Quality
Continuum in
Performance
Measurement

Results are not reported for any areas of importance to the accomplishment of your organization's mission.	Results are reported for a few areas of importance to the accomplishment of your organization's mission.	Results are reported for many areas of importance to the accomplishment of your organization's mission.	Organizational performance results are reported for most key patient and stakeholder, market, and process requirements.	Organizational performance results are reported for most key patient and stakeholder, market, process, and action plan requirements.	Organizational performance results fully address key patient and stakeholder, market, process, and action plan requirements.
Comparative information is not reported.	Little or no comparative information is reported.	Early stages of obtaining comparative information are evident.	Many to most trends and current performance levels have been evaluated against relevant comparisons and/or benchmarks and show areas of leadership and very good relative performance.	Many to most trends and current performance levels have been evaluated against relevant comparisons and/or benchmarks and show areas of leadership and very good relative performance.	Evidence of industry and benchmark leadership is demonstrated in many areas.
Trend data either are not reported or show mainly adverse trends.	Some trend data are reported, with some adverse trends evident.	Some trend data are reported, and a majority of the trends presented are beneficial.	Beneficial trends are evident in areas of importance to the accomplishment of your organization's mission.	Beneficial trends have been sustained over time in most areas of importance to the accomplishment of your organization's mission.	Beneficial trends have been sustained over time in all areas of importance to the accomplishment of your organization's mission.
There are no organizational performance results and/or poor results in areas reported.	A few organizational performance results are reported, and early good performance levels are evident.	Good organizational performance levels are reported for some areas of importance.	Good organizational performance levels are reported for most areas of importance.	Good to excellent organizational performance levels are reported for most areas of importance.	Excellent organizational performance levels are reported.

Early efforts ————————————————————————→ Mature efforts

Source: Adapted from BPEP (2015).

EXHIBIT 9.10
Sources of
Comparative
Data

Clinical Performance and Patient Satisfaction

Commonwealth Fund: Why Not the Best?	www.whynotthebest.org
Consumer assessment of clinicians and groups	www.cahps.ahrq.gov
HealthGrove	www.healthgrove.com
Home Health Compare	www.medicare.gov/homehealthcompare
Hospital Compare	www.hospitalcompare.hhs.gov
Nursing Home Compare	www.medicare.gov/nursinghomecompare
Physician and dialysis facility performance	https://data.medicare.gov
The Joint Commission Quality Check	www.qualitycheck.org
The Leapfrog Group	www.leapfroggroup.org

Comparative Practices

Baldrige Performance Excellence Program award recipient information	http://patapsco.nist.gov/Award_Recipients/index.cfm
CMS Innovation Center	https://innovation.cms.gov
Commonwealth Fund: Why Not the Best? case studies	www.whynotthebest.org/contents
Institute for Healthcare Improvement	www.ihi.org

Health Plans

Consumer assessment of health plans	www.cahps.ahrq.gov
HealthGrove	www.healthgrove.com
National Committee for Quality Assurance	www.ncqa.org

Population Data

AHRQ (National Healthcare Quality Report and National Healthcare Disparities Report)	www.ahrq.gov/research/findings/nhqrdr
Centers for Disease Control and Prevention (CDC): Data and Statistics	www.cdc.gov/DataStatistics
Health Resources and Services Administration Health Center data and reporting	www.bphc.hrsa.gov/datareporting
Kaiser Family Foundation State Health Facts	http://kff.org/statedata
CDC: state, tribal, local, and territorial health departments	www.cdc.gov/stltpublichealth

Utilization and Costs

Healthcare Cost and Utilization Project national and state data	www.hcup-us.ahrq.gov
Medical Expenditure Panel Survey	https://meps.ahrq.gov/mepsweb

Summary

A varied set of measures that are vertically and horizontally aligned, combined with a systematic way of analyzing and communicating information gleaned from the measures, aid managers in identifying patterns across parts of the system, provide clues about system structures, and help ensure that one area of performance is not unintentionally excelling at the expense of another. Performance indicators throughout the organization should reflect the common direction and priorities defined by the organization's mission, vision, and business strategy. A comprehensive performance management measurement system should also ensure coordination of activities to minimize the duplication of data collection efforts.

This chapter offers lessons for managers to assist them in differentiating types of measures and selecting a balanced set of measures. This chapter also illustrates the role of performance measurement along the quality continuum and provides resources for managers to find comparative data.

Exercise 9.1

Objective: To familiarize yourself with the measurement resources available on the AHRQ National Quality Measures Clearinghouse website.

Instructions: Select a healthcare service setting that you are familiar with or would like to become more familiar with. Using the search function on the National Quality Measures Clearinghouse website (www.qualitymeasures.ahrq. gov), identify measures that could be used in your chosen setting to evaluate performance in each of these quality domains: safe care, effective care, patient-centered care, timely care, efficient care, and equitable care. Identify at least one measure for each quality domain.

Companion Readings

Agency for Healthcare Research and Quality. 2016. "Toolkit for Using the AHRQ Quality Indicators." Reviewed July. www.ahrq.gov/professionals/systems/hospital/qitoolkit/index.html.

Blumenthal, D., E. Malphrus, and J. M. McGinnis (eds). 2015. *Vital Signs: Core Metrics for Health and Health Care Progress.* Washington, DC: National Academies Press.

Burstin, H., S. Leatherman, and D. Goldman. 2016. "The Evolution of Healthcare Quality Measurement in the United States." *Journal of Internal Medicine* 279 (2): 154–59.

Buying Value. 2016. "How to Build a Measure Set." Robert Wood Johnson Foundation. Accessed November 14. www.buyingvalue.org/resources/toolkit.

Farquhar, M. 2008. "AHRQ Quality Indicators." In *Patient Safety and Quality: An Evidence-Based Handbook for Nurses*, edited by R. G. Hughes. AHRQ. Published April. www.ncbi.nlm.nih.gov/books/NBK2664.

Healthy People 2020. 2016. "Leading Health Indicators." Accessed November 14. www.healthypeople.gov/2020/Leading-Health-Indicators.

Lichiello, P. 2010. *Guidebook for Performance Measurement*. Turning Point. Accessed October 12, 2016. ww.phf.org/resourcestools/documents/pmcguidebook.pdf.

Neely, A., and M. A. Najjar. 2006. "Management Learning, Not Management Control: The True Role of Performance Measurement?" *California Management Review* 48 (3): 101–14.

Web Resources

Agency for Healthcare Research and Quality

- National Quality Measures Clearinghouse: www.qualitymeasures. ahrq.gov
- Quality Indicators: www.qualityindicators.ahrq.gov

CMS QualityNet: www.qualitynet.org
National Quality Forum: www.qualityforum.org

References

Agency for Healthcare Research and Quality (AHRQ). 2016. "Get Nursing Home Surveys and Instructions." Reviewed July. www.ahrq.gov/cahps/surveys-guidance/nh/instructions/index.html.

American College of Radiology. 2016. "Performance Measures." Accessed July 10. www.acr.org/Quality-Safety/Quality-Measurement/Performance-Measures.

Baldrige Performance Excellence Program (BPEP). 2015. *2015–2016 Baldrige Excellence Framework: A Systems Approach to Improving Your Organization's Performance (Health Care)*. Gaithersburg, MD: US Department of Commerce, National Institute of Standards and Technology.

Collaborative for Health Information Technology in Oregon. 2016. "Aligning Health Measurement in Oregon." Published March 24. www.oahhs.org/sites/default/files/publications/FINAL-Aligning-Health-Measurement-in-Oregon-CHITO .pdf.

Donabedian, A. 1980. *Explorations in Quality Assessment and Monitoring.* Vol. 1 in *The Definition of Quality and Approaches to Its Assessment.* Chicago: Health Administration Press.

Gurd, B., and T. Gao. 2008. "Lives in the Balance: An Analysis of the Balanced Scorecard (BSC) in Healthcare Organizations." *International Journal of Productivity & Performance Management* 57 (1): 6–21.

Hurtado, M. H., E. K. Swift, and J. M. Corrigan (eds). 2001. *Envisioning the National Health Care Quality Report.* Washington, DC: National Academies Press.

Institute of Medicine (IOM). 2001. *Crossing the Quality Chasm: A New Health System for the 21st Century.* Washington, DC: National Academies Press.

Joint Commission. 2016a. "Hospital National Patient Safety Goals." Accessed July 7. www.jointcommission.org/hap_2016_npsgs.

———. 2016b. "Surgical Care Improvement Project (SCIP)." Accessed July 10. www.jointcommission.org/surgical_care_improvement_project.

Kaplan, R. S., and D. P. Norton. 2007. "Using the Balanced Scorecard as a Strategic Management System." *Harvard Business Review* 85 (7/8): 150–61.

Nelson, E. C., J. J. Mohr, P. B. Batalden, and S. K. Plume. 1996. "Improving Healthcare, Part 1: The Clinical Value Compass." *The Joint Commission Journal on Quality Improvement* 22 (4): 243–58.

Newton, E. H., E. A. Zazzera, G. Van Moorsel, and B. E. Sirovich. 2015. "Undermeasuring Overuse—An Examination of National Clinical Performance Measures." *Journal of the American Medical Association: Internal Medicine* 175 (10): 1709–11.

Press Ganey. 2016. "Nursing Quality (NDNQI)." Accessed July 10. www.pressganey.com/solutions/clinical-quality/nursing-quality.

Public Health Foundation. 2016. *From Silos to Systems: Using Performance Management to Improve the Public's Health.* Turning Point. Accessed October 13. www.phf.org/resourcestools/Documents/silossystems.pdf.

Sharp HealthCare. 2016. "Pillars of Excellence." Accessed July 10. www.sharp.com/about/the-sharp-experience/pillars-excellence.cfm.

Spath, P. L. 2013. *Introduction to Healthcare Quality Management,* 2nd ed. Chicago: Health Administration Press.

Spaulding, A. C., L. D. Gamm, and J. M. Griffith. 2010. "Studer Unplugged: Identifying Underlying Managerial Concepts." *Hospital Topics* 88 (1): 1–9.

Studer, Q. 2010. *Results That Last: Hardwiring Behaviors That Will Take Your Company to the Top.* New York: John Wiley & Sons.

StuderGroup. 2005. "Inside the Mind: What Leaders at High Performing Organizations Know." Accessed July 10, 2016. www.studergroup.com/hardwired-results/hardwired-results-02/what-leaders-at-high-performing-organizations-know.

University of North Carolina Health Care. 2016. "Pillars: Defined." Accessed July 10. http://news.unchealthcare.org/empnews/pillars#section-1.

USING DATA ANALYTICS TECHNIQUES TO EVALUATE PERFORMANCE

with Naveen Kumar

Learning Objectives

After completing this chapter, you should be able to

- describe basic concepts of healthcare data analytics,
- apply graphical methods for reporting measurement data,
- use descriptive analytics to understand current performance, and
- identify common pitfalls associated with reporting and analyzing measurement data.

Most managers have measurement data—often lots of data—about organizational performance. But that does not mean they always have the information they need to manage performance. Numbers by themselves are not information. The numbers must be analyzed and results evaluated to turn data into information. With the focus today on cost containment and providing value for healthcare consumers, managers cannot afford to guess or make assumptions about how well the area or department under their control is performing.

This chapter introduces basic analytical tools and a variety of techniques managers can use to analyze performance data and extract meaningful information required for decision making and improvement. A basic understanding of analytics tools and techniques is important for managers, whether they are directly involved in data analytics tasks or interacting with a team of data analysts. With a basic understanding, managers can recognize performance trends, projections, and cause-and-effect relationships that might otherwise go undetected. Information presented in this chapter is intended as a starting point for learning rudimentary analytical methods and appreciating more advanced techniques to support a variety of managerial responsibilities such as planning, reviewing performance, improving operations, managing change, and researching best practices. Readers seeking additional information will find the web resources at the end of the chapter a good place to start.

What Is Data Analytics?

Thomas Davenport and Jeanne Harris, longtime leaders in optimizing data for business decision making, describe **data analytics** as "the extensive use of data, statistical and quantitative analysis, explanatory and predictive models, and fact-based management to drive decisions and actions" (2007, 7). The National Association for Healthcare Quality (NAHQ) recognizes healthcare data analytics as one of the essential competencies for healthcare quality professionals. The competency encompasses three dimensions: (1) data management, (2) application of statistical methods, and (3) transformation of data into information (NAHQ 2015). This chapter focuses primarily on the second and third dimensions. The dimension of data management involves acquisition, validation, storage, and security, and these activities are not addressed in this chapter.

Jim Adams and Jim Klein (2011), authors of a primer on analytics in healthcare, note that analytics may be descriptive, predictive, or prescriptive. This chapter primarily covers descriptive analytics, which involves standard types of reporting that describe current situations and problems. Descriptive analytics is used to answer questions such as the following (Adams and Klein 2011):

- What is happening?
- How often and where is it happening?
- What may be causing the results?
- When should actions be taken?

This chapter also includes a brief description of predictive analytics to illustrate techniques that can be used to identify performance trends and outcomes that may occur in the future. Predictive analytics is used to answer questions such as these (Adams and Klein 2011):

- What could happen if . . . ?
- What if this pattern of performance continues?
- What action is likely to cause . . . ?

Prescriptive analytics, used to optimize clinical, financial, and other outcomes, is an advanced topic beyond the scope of this chapter. As the amount of healthcare performance data increases, analysis requires technology and software to support statistical analysis. This chapter covers some of the basic statistical or analytical tools but does not delve into the informatics components or software requirements.

Introduction to Data Analytics Techniques

"**Analysis** means extracting larger meaning from data and information to support evaluation, decision making, improvement, and innovation" (Baldrige Performance Excellence Program [BPEP] 2015, 43). By applying analytical or statistical techniques in this analysis, managers can obtain a high-level understanding of performance data. Especially when dealing with a large dataset, using various analytical tools and techniques to analyze raw data provides insights that may otherwise go unnoticed.

Statistical techniques are commonly classified into two categories: **descriptive statistics** and **inferential statistics**. Descriptive statistics deals with summarizing and describing data using concepts such as mean and standard deviation and tools such as bar graphs and histograms. Inferential statistics deals with the process of making an estimate, prediction, or decision about a population on the basis of a sample using techniques such as confidence intervals and hypothesis tests.

An important step in performance management is the collection and analysis of measurements. Descriptive statistics methods such as numerical summary measures (e.g., mean, standard deviation) and graphical representation (e.g., histogram, bar chart) can reveal interesting hidden patterns and trends in a dataset. They may also reveal relationships between attributes that can help in understanding why certain trends are occurring. In particular, gaining familiarity with the dataset using descriptive statistics methods helps a manager detect anomalies such as missing or invalid data in the dataset. In addition, familiarity with the data helps in generating new ideas on how to report or visually present the data. Detailed descriptions and applications of graphical representations and numerical summary measures are provided in later sections.

While descriptive statistics deals with summarizing and describing data, inferential statistics deals with the process of making an estimate, prediction, or decision about a population on the basis of a sample. A sample is used because studying an entire population of subjects is impractical and expensive, and gaining access to every member or subject under study may be impossible. For example, it would be difficult for a manager to identify, for study purposes, the total population of people in the hospital's market area who are suffering from diabetes. Inferential statistics techniques are typically used in market research and survey data analysis to make an inference about the entire population on the basis of the sample of data collected from surveys and market research studies. For performance management purposes, managers are most likely to start with descriptive statistics techniques to analyze data because these techniques are very simple, but powerful, to use. These techniques provide an instantaneous snapshot of the current state of the system, without the need for sophisticated knowledge of advanced statistics.

analysis
"extracting larger meaning from data and information to support evaluation, decision making, improvement, and innovation" (BPEP 2015, 43)

descriptive statistics
a catch-all term used to summarize and describe data using techniques such as mean, standard deviation, bar graph, and histogram

inferential statistics
numeric information used to make an estimate, prediction, or decision about a population on the basis of a sample using techniques such as confidence intervals and hypothesis tests

Types of Data

Understanding the type of data to be analyzed before applying any analytical techniques to the dataset is important. The type of data influences a manager's selection of the appropriate analytical methods. Exhibit 10.1 illustrates the types of data commonly used in analytical tasks.

Interval Data

quantitative data
data that can be expressed as a number or quantified

continuous data
numeric (real number) data that can be broken down into smaller and smaller subunits of measurement

discrete data
numeric (real number) data that can take on values that cannot be broken into smaller subunits of measurements

Interval data are **quantitative data** that are often the subject of analysis involving arithmetic operations. Interval data can be broadly classified into two categories: **continuous data** and **discrete data**.

Continuous data are numeric (real number) data that can take on values that can be broken down into smaller and smaller subunits of measurement. For example, a patient's body temperature can be represented as 99.9° F or 99.92° F or 99.239° F, depending on the scale or level of precision supported by the measurement device. Another example is a person's age, which could be stated in years but then broken down into months, then weeks, and so on. Arithmetic operations can be performed on interval continuous data. For example, practitioners can compute the ratio or difference between a patient's preoperative blood glucose level and the level obtained the first day after surgery. The patient's average postoperative glucose levels for an entire hospital day can be calculated.

Discrete data are also numeric; however, unlike continuous data, discrete data values cannot be broken into smaller subunits of measurements. Values that

EXHIBIT 10.1
Types of Data Commonly Used in Analytical Tasks

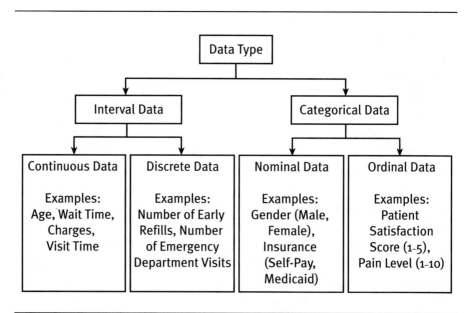

take the form of whole numbers such as number of patients admitted to the hospital each day and a person's number of children are common examples of discrete data. Representing discrete data in decimal terms is meaningless—for example, 9.2 patients admitted to the hospital each day. Similar to continuous data, arithmetic calculations can also be performed on discrete data. As an example, the number of patients seen in the emergency department (ED) on Tuesday is half the number of patients seen on Monday.

Categorical Data

Categorical data are typically **qualitative data** and are used to categorize observations. They are often collected through surveys and behavioral research methods. Categorical data can be broadly classified into two categories: nominal data and ordinal data.

Nominal data are typically used to categorize or classify attributes with no implied rank or order given to the individual values. Nominal values may be represented as text or numeric values. A common example is gender designation, with two possible values of male and female. Because nominal data values are qualitative and not quantitative in nature, performing direct arithmetic operations on them would be meaningless, and typically no one value is considered larger or better than another. However, counting the frequency of each value's occurrence is often useful to summarize a nominal variable.

Ordinal data typically have a fixed set of possible values and are used to categorize attributes, but the values assigned imply a rank or an order. Changing values of ordinal variables implies an increase or a decrease in the value of the qualitative attribute. Nursing titles of *registered nurse* and *licensed practical nurse* are examples of two ordinal data values in which one implies a higher professional rank than the other. Sometimes, assigning numeric values to text values of ordinal data makes it easier to clarify the specific order of the attributes, such as highly satisfied = 5 and highly dissatisfied = 1. Although numeric values may be assigned to ordinal data values, they are typically only used for logical comparisons and ranking purposes. They may also convey the relative weight or importance of one value compared with another. As for nominal variables, counting the frequency of each value's occurrence is often useful for summarizing an ordinal variable. However, unlike nominal variables, in certain situations it makes sense to perform arithmetic operations on ordinal data—for example, the average patient satisfaction rating for a hospital.

qualitative data any data that cannot be easily expressed as a number or quantified

nominal data text or numeric values used to categorize or classify qualitative attributes with no implied rank or order given to the individual values

ordinal data text or numeric values used to categorize or classify qualitative attributes in a fixed set of possible values with an implied rank or order given to the individual values

Applying Descriptive Statistics Techniques

Like most hospital managers, the cardiac intensive care unit manager regularly gathers lots of data (e.g., staffing and budget, patient demographics, outcomes)

for the purpose of managing performance. At the end of each month, the manager has a large volume of data that need to be reviewed and understood. The manager can use descriptive statistics for this purpose. Exhibit 10.2 illustrates the most common types of descriptive statistics used in analytical tasks.

Descriptive statistics techniques can be applied to a dataset of any size to provide a concise description or summary of the data. Managers may learn a great deal when basic descriptive statistics is used to derive meaningful information and actions from the data. This knowledge is also useful when a manager needs to guide a data analyst toward next steps, such as developing advanced predictive models, using a dataset. Descriptive statistics methods can be broadly classified into two categories: graphical and numerical. The next sections describe these two methods in detail.

Graphical Methods

Graphical methods allow for presentation of data in ways that make it easy for managers to comprehend useful information. Visual depictions of data using graphical methods can be easier to grasp and understand as compared to extensive reports and tables with textual and numerical data. Graphical methods are especially well suited for displaying raw and summary data, such as frequencies of items or events and variations of values over time. Commonly used methods for graphically displaying data are described in the next section.

EXHIBIT 10.2
Types of Descriptive Statistics Commonly Used in Analytical Tasks

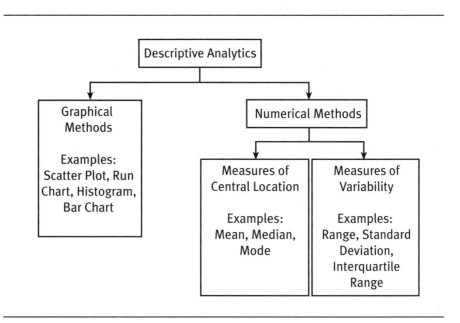

Run Chart

Consider a situation in which, for several months, the staff in an outpatient mammography center has been complaining about being too busy. The manager needs to determine whether the increase in visits is a permanent change or just a passing phenomenon. The monthly reports he receives from the finance department present the center's volume data in a spreadsheet according to this month, last month, year to date, and the same month, previous year. He uses these numeric reports to generate a **run chart** and is then able to determine the answer to his question (see exhibit 10.3).

A snowstorm of historic proportions had hit the city the previous January and shut down business for four days. The center's current volume was a reflection of the need to reschedule appointments that were cancelled as a result of the snowstorm. The appointments for the year were still on track; the monthly distribution of visits had been affected by this unusual and explainable event.

A run chart, sometimes called a *line graph*, is a graphical representation that is typically used to describe a single set of performance data, such as patient wait times in the ED, over time. Run charts are a useful graphical method of detecting any trend, pattern, or shift in a performance measure of interest over time. When data are presented on a run chart, the *x* axis (horizontal) typically represents the time (in seconds, minutes, days, months, etc.), whereas the *y* axis (vertical) displays the corresponding values of the specific performance measure.

run chart (or line graph)
a graphical representation that is primarily used to describe a single set of data over a period of time

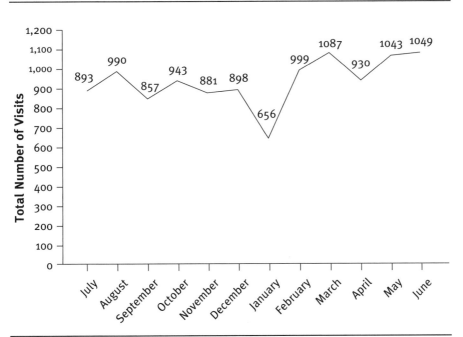

EXHIBIT 10.3
Breast Imaging Service Monthly Outpatient Visits

Note: Multiple procedures per visit are not reflected in the data.

Generally, one should plot at least 15 data points on a run chart; however, some statisticians recommend plotting at least 20 data points (Woodall 2000). Managers should also consider adding another line showing the target or goal of the corresponding performance measure of interest on a run chart, which gives them a clear picture over time of how a specific measure is faring against a target. Managers can report multiple performance measures on a single run chart; however, if the lines frequently intersect with each other as shown in exhibit 10.4, consider using more than one run chart.

Run charts are also useful graphical methods for evaluating the success of improvement efforts. Consider this example. The internal medicine clinic of a large multispecialty physician practice implemented changes in its workflow to reduce patient wait times and improve patient satisfaction. The improvements were implemented in September, and at that time the satisfaction scores were 90 percent; in October, the satisfaction scores were 83 percent. Did the effort succeed or fail? Placing the satisfaction data in a run chart over time provides the context in which the September results should be interpreted (see exhibit 10.5).

The run chart shows that patient satisfaction decreased the first month after the changes were implemented in September. This decline is not uncommon because new processes often take time to stabilize as a result of staff learning curves and adjustments. Managers must not overreact to one month's worth of data but should continue to track results over time to see the pattern of performance once the process has stabilized. This run chart demonstrates

EXHIBIT 10.4
Line Graph: Speed of Nurses' Response to Call Lights on 15 Consecutive Days

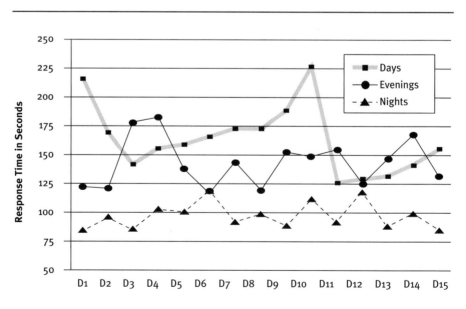

Source: Spath (2013). Used with permission.

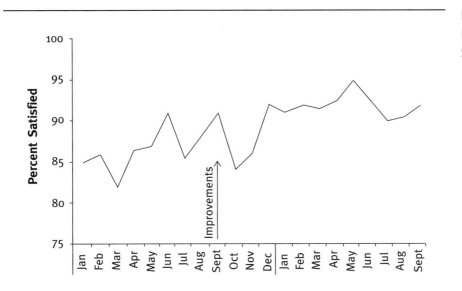

EXHIBIT 10.5
Patient
Satisfaction

that, although patient satisfaction dropped initially, in subsequent months it stabilized at a higher and consistent level.

These two examples of run charts illustrate several principles about data and complex systems (Wheeler 2000, 14, 79):

- No data have meaning apart from their context.
- Graphs reveal interesting structures present in the data.
- Graphs make data more accessible to the human mind than do tables.

Identifying patterns in lists or tables of numbers is difficult. Run charts and other graphs enable managers to see patterns more easily, which in turn can provide clues to system structures.

Bar Chart

A **bar chart** or bar graph is a graphical representation that is typically used to describe a set of categorical data, such as number of male and female patients admitted to a hospital every week. Data are presented on a bar chart; the *x* axis represents the category of variables, such as patient gender, being observed, whereas the *y* axis displays the actual performance results of each category of variables.

As an example, consider a situation in which a regional hospital system has recently implemented an electronic health record (EHR) system. A manager is interested in understanding and comparing the computer response time for accessing EHR data at four different clinics in the system. Exhibit 10.6 shows a bar graph that represents the average computer response times for a

**bar chart
(or bar graph)**
a graphical
representation that
is primarily used to
describe a single
set of categorical
data

EXHIBIT 10.6
Bar Graph:
Average
Computer
Response Times
at Four Clinics
During a Nine-
Month Period

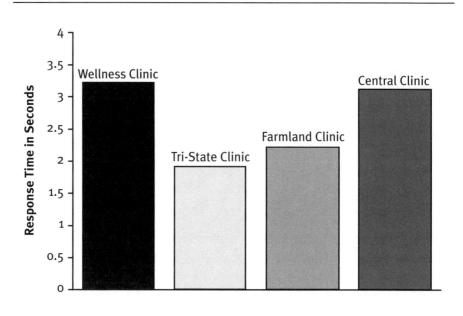

Source: Adapted from Spath (2013). Used with permission.

nine-month period at each of the clinics. The height of each bar represents the average computer response time. The clinic with the lowest average computer response time is easy to identify, and response time performance of the four clinics is easy to compare. Managers should note that the width of the bars in a bar graph is not relevant; however, it should be consistent across different categories of variables.

Histogram

histogram
a graphical representation that is primarily used to describe a single set of continuous data

A **histogram** is a graphical representation that is primarily used to describe a single set of continuous data such as patient wait times in the ED. When presenting continuous data in a histogram, the range of values from the dataset is used to create subranges, also called *bins* or *classes*, of equal sizes. The individual dataset values are then assigned to one of the bins that can be summed by their frequency or count in each bin.

For example, the wait times for the last 500 patients treated in the ED have ranged from 10 to 100 minutes. The wait time data can be reported in a histogram using eight bars that represent the number of patients whose wait times fell into each of the categories. The histogram will visually depict how many patients are in each wait time category (see exhibit 10.7).

Depending on the performance results she is considering, a manager can expect histograms to have different shapes. Recognizing the shape of the histogram created using performance measurement is important because

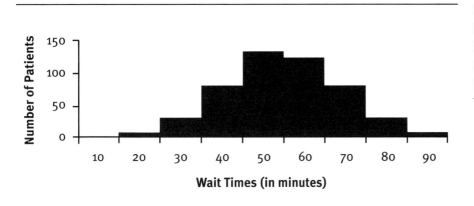

EXHIBIT 10.7
Histogram:
Emergency
Department
Patient Wait
Times

its shape reveals a pattern that may be useful for performance management purposes. See exhibit 10.8 for illustrations of common histogram shapes and what the shape can suggest to a manager reviewing the results.

Histogram Shape	Example	What the Shape Suggests
Bell-Shaped (Symmetrical)		The hospital is seeing normal variation of patient lengths of stay—a few patients with a long stay and a few with a short stay, while the majority of patients falls in the middle.
Negatively Skewed (Left Skewed)		A few hospital patients are experiencing an extremely short length of stay. These patients might have been diagnosed with some minor health-related issues and discharged quickly.
Positively Skewed (Right Skewed)		A few patients are staying in the hospital for a longer duration. These patients might be suffering from multiple conditions.

EXHIBIT 10.8
Common
Histogram
Shapes
and Their
Interpretations

Scatter Diagram

scatter diagram
a graphical representation typically used to determine the relationship between two quantitative variables of interest, where the value of one variable is dependent on the value of the other variable

A **scatter diagram** is a two-dimensional graphical representation typically used to determine the relationship between two quantitative variables of interest, where the value of one variable is dependent on the value of the other variable. The pictorial representation of the data points on the scatter plot provides a visual indication of a relationship between the two variables. If a relationship exists between the two variables, the value of the one variable may influence the value of the other variable. Typically, the type of data represented in a scatter plot can take on any value along either axis. For example, consider a person's annual salary (in dollars) and experience (in years) performing a specialized information management job (see exhibit 10.9).

If a person's annual salary is plotted against their work experience, that is, their number of years working on a specific job, a relationship can be seen by the shape of the data points on the scatter plot (see exhibit 10.10). The independent variable, experience (in years), is usually represented on the x axis; the dependent variable, the person's annual salary (in dollars), is plotted on the y axis.

Linearity and direction are the two important concepts when analyzing scatter plots (see an example in exhibit 10.11). If the data points follow a path

EXHIBIT 10.9
Annual Salary and Job Experience

Job Experience (in years)	1	2	3	4	5	6	7	8	9	10
Annual Salary (in thousand US dollars)	$70.00	$72.80	$75.86	$80.41	$83.63	$86.80	$90.45	$99.49	$102.48	$106.27

EXHIBIT 10.10
Scatter Plot: Relationship of Annual Salary to Job Experience

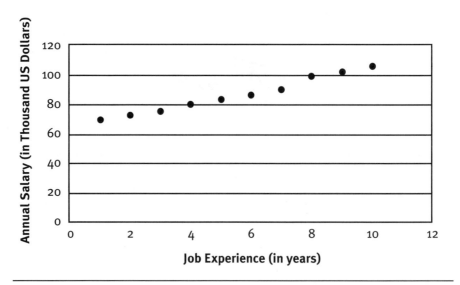

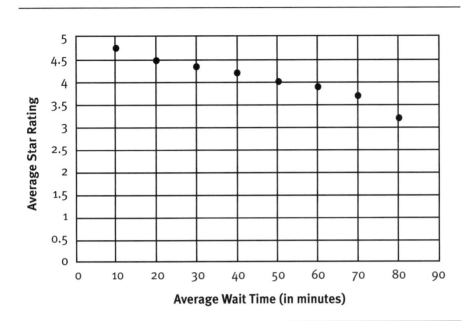

EXHIBIT 10.11
Scatter Plot:
A Hospital's
Star Rating
and Average
Monthly Wait
Time

approximating a straight line, the variables have a linear relationship. The direction determines whether the independent and dependent variables have a positive or negative relationship. The variables have a negative relationship if the value of the dependent variable, along the y axis, decreases as the value of the independent variable, along the x axis, increases. For example, consider a hospital's ED average monthly wait times (in minutes) and their impact on the hospital's performance rating (as indicated by the number of stars). One would expect to see a negative relationship between these two variables. The value of the dependent variable (hospital star rating) along the y axis tends to decrease as the value of the independent variable (ED wait time), along the x axis, increases.

Predictive Analytics

Predictive analytics is the branch of analytics used primarily to make future predictions about key performance measures. Using predictive analytics techniques such as logistic regression, neural networks, and support vector machines, healthcare leaders can predict strategically important associations, patterns, and trends in performance measures. Also, predictive analytics can help healthcare leaders in detecting utilization trends and anomalies that represent organizational improvement opportunities. For example, predictive analytics techniques can affect the health of the general public by helping leaders discover and predict potential public health threats.

predictive analytics
a branch of analytics used primarily to make future predictions about key performance measures

Another area for application of predictive analytics is competent workforce retention. Competent workforce retention is a big challenge for human resources managers. Managers can leverage predictive analytics techniques for their workforce, specifically in predicting flight risk for physicians and employees who may be on the verge of leaving their organization. The various predictive analytics techniques and applications are beyond the scope of this chapter (see Shmueli, Patel, and Bruce 2016 in the companion readings of this chapter for more details).

Numerical Summary Measures

Numerical measures are typically used to summarize a dataset. Numerical techniques are useful for providing an objective measure for comparing a performance measure at different points of time. For example, the manager in a nursing facility can measure the monthly rate of catheter-associated infections. When an improvement project is initiated to reduce these infections, numerical techniques such as monthly number of infections or monthly average can be compared preintervention and postintervention to objectively measure the impact of process change. The following section describes some of the commonly used numerical summary measures.

Measures of Central Tendency or Location

Central tendency or location is a single data point that refers to the central position in a given dataset. Given a list of data points, understanding the central value around which the values lie is helpful. For example, a manager could review raw data from patient satisfaction surveys, but knowing the central location of the responses for each survey question provides much more information about satisfaction levels. Some of the commonly used measures of central tendency are average (or mean), median, and mode.

The average or mean is a popular numerical technique used to describe the central location of the data. It is calculated by summing the value of the specific measurements of interest and dividing the sum by the total number of measurements in the dataset. For example, a dataset representing the time a primary care physician spends with each clinic patient during one day is shown in exhibit 10.12.

EXHIBIT 10.12
Time Physician Spent with Each Patient

Patient	1	2	3	4	5	6	7	8	9	10
Time spent (minutes)	20	30	25	18	12	16	23	18	19	15

To calculate the **average** time (measured by the number of minutes) the physician spent with each patient, simply sum the number of minutes spent with each patient (196) and divide the sum by the number of patients seen (10). The average time spent with patients on that day was 19.6 minutes.

The average is an easy calculation that only requires summing all the values and dividing the sum by the number of values. It requires no ordering of the values, no determining which one or two values occupy the middle location of all the values, no determining the frequency of each unique values occurrence, and no determining which unique value occurs most often. However, one of the shortcomings of the average is that it is seriously affected by extreme values called *outliers*. A small number of extreme values above or below the majority of the values can distort the mean and cause a misleading interpretation of the data's central tendency. For instance, what would happen if one patient suffering from multiple conditions was seen the day that clinic visit time data were gathered (see exhibit 10.12) and when the patient needed to spend 90 minutes with the physician? The mean patient visit times for the day would increase significantly to 26 minutes per patient.

Mean is a useful measure of central location when dealing with interval data. Because mean is extremely sensitive to outliers, managers must first understand the root cause of any outliers and then decide whether to include these outliers in the calculation of mean or discard them.

The **median** is another numerical summary measure used to describe a given dataset. It represents the central tendency of all values in a dataset. To calculate the median value in a dataset, first arrange all the measurements in order from lowest to highest. The measurement that lies in the middle is the median. If the dataset contains an odd number of measurements, the median is the value that occupies the middle position. If the dataset contains an even number of measurements, the median is the average of the two measurements that occupy the middle position.

Consider the dataset in exhibit 10.12. To calculate the median time a physician spends with each patient, arrange the values in order from lowest to highest (12, 15, 16, 18, 18, 19, 20, 23, 25, 30). Because the dataset contains 10 values—an even number—the median is the average (18.5 minutes) of the two values that occupy the middle position (18 and 19 minutes). Just like average or mean, median is a useful measure of central location when dealing with interval data.

The **mode** of a dataset is the value that occurs most frequently. The dataset in exhibit 10.12 has only one value, 18, that occurs most frequently. Some datasets are bimodal in nature, meaning that two distinct values in a dataset share the maximum frequency count. If more than two distinct values in a dataset share the maximum frequency count, the dataset is multimodal in nature.

average (or mean)
a popular numerical technique used to describe the central location of a dataset

median
the value that represents the central tendency of all values in a dataset

mode
the value that occurs most frequently in a dataset

Mode is a useful measure for all data types, though it is mainly used for nominal data. For nominal data values, counting the frequency of their occurrence is the most common numerical summary measure typically applied. For example, it may be useful to determine the most frequently occurring medical conditions (nominal data) of patients presenting to the ED over a specific span of time. For a very large dataset, one may wish to group the measurements from that dataset into distinct groups or classes based on a certain criteria. An example could be the age ranges of hospital patients. The modal class will be the age range that contains the largest number of patients.

Which measure—average or mean, median, or mode—should be used to measure central tendency or location in a set of data? In practice, the average or mean is often used as a default measure of choice; however, there are several circumstances in which the median is better. The median is a better representative of the central location when the data are skewed. Just one extreme high or low value may significantly alter the average or mean value of a set of measurements, whereas the median is not as sensitive to extreme values.

Mode is typically not considered the best measure of central location. Because the mode of a dataset is the value that occurs most frequently, it can occur at any point in the range of a set of values. A second problem with using mode as a measure of central location is that it can have more than one value, given that one or more values could share the highest frequency count in a dataset.

Measures of Variability

Measures of central tendency such as mean, median, and mode are useful measures to describe the data. However, these measures are not sufficient by themselves. For example, consider a hypothetical scenario in which a person's head is dipped in freezing liquid ($0°$ F) and his feet are dipped in ultrahot liquid ($196°$ F). Based on just these two data points, his average body temperature is $98°$ F, which is very close to normal human body temperature. However, in reality we know that because of extreme variation in the temperature at two different parts of the body, a human being will certainly be in great distress in this situation, despite the fact that average body temperature is close to normal. The key point is that we are describing the data just by the central location in this specific scenario. However, we are missing one important piece of information by not capturing the variability in the dataset.

Consider a dataset that contains the weights (in pounds) of people suffering from obesity or starvation. The mean weight for this disparate group of people may be similar to the mean weight of healthy individuals, but this does not imply these individuals are also healthy. To get a comprehensive picture of the people in the dataset, merely reporting the mean weight is not sufficient. One must also consider the variability associated with the weight measurements in the dataset. Some of the numerical measures that are commonly used to characterize variability in sets of data are range, standard deviation, and interquartile range. These measures of variability are used to determine how widespread the values of a dataset are.

Range is one of the simplest measures a manager can use to characterize variability in a dataset. It is simply computed by taking the difference between the largest and the smallest measurement in a given dataset. For example, the data representing the age (in months) of eight infants visiting a pediatrician is shown as {4, 10, 6, 2, 3, 3, 5, 1}. The range, computed as the difference between the largest (10) and the smallest (1) measurement, is 9 months.

range
the numerical difference between the largest and the smallest measurements in a given dataset

One of the main advantages of using range to capture variability is the ease with which it can be computed. However, the shortcoming of using range is its inability to capture information on the dispersion of the measurements between the two extreme end points. For example, consider two simple datasets of patient ages:

- Dataset 1: {4, 4, 4, 4, 50}
- Dataset 2: {4, 8, 15, 24, 39, 50}

The range is 46 for both datasets. However, the data points in the two datasets, except the smallest and largest values, have very different distributions in the middle, which is not typically captured by range. There are times when a manager needs to use a different measure of variability that incorporates all the data and not just two extreme measurements.

There are other measures of variability, such as **standard deviation**, that incorporate all the data points to capture overall variability in a dataset. In other words, standard deviation takes into account how far each data point in a dataset is away from the overall mean.

standard deviation
a measure of the variability in a given dataset

If the histogram or distribution of the dataset is approximately bell shaped (see exhibit 10.8), one can infer that approximately 68 percent of all measurements fall within one standard deviation of the mean; approximately 95 percent of all measurements fall within two standard deviations of the mean; and approximately 99.7 percent of all measurements fall within three standard deviations of the mean. Suppose the average age of patients admitted to a hospital is 40, with a standard deviation of 3. If the histogram representing the dataset is approximately bell shaped, then a manager can presume that approximately 68 percent of the patients fall between the ages of 37 and 43, approximately 95 percent of the patients fall between the ages of 34 and 46, and approximately 99.7 percent of the patients fall between the ages of 31 and 49.

It should be noted that the standard deviation is sensitive to outliers. To overcome this limitation, a robust measure of variability that is not sensitive to outliers is required. Interquartile range (IQR) is a measure that is not sensitive to outliers. To understand the IQR, understanding some of the basic statistics related to measures of relative standing—for example, percentile and quartile—is required. The next section covers a few basic statistics concepts related to measures of relative standing.

Measures of relative standing provide information about the position of particular values relative to the entire dataset. Specific measures of relative standing, such as percentiles and quartiles, are descriptive measures used to specify which value is greater than a specified percentage of all the other values. Some databases of aggregate measurement results use a measure of relative standing to report where a facility's performance ranks in relation to other facilities. For example, percentile rankings are calculated for the measurement results in home health performance data reported by the Centers for Medicare & Medicaid Services (CMS). The performance ranking stars awarded to each agency and reported on the CMS Home Health Compare website (www.medicare.gov/homehealthcompare) correspond to the agency's percentile ranking, with some adjustments for patient risk and other factors (CMS 2015; see exhibit 10.13).

Managers who rely on these comparative databases to evaluate performance of their department or organization should become familiar with the methodology used by the database sponsor to calculate the measures of relative standing.

percentile
a value (in percentage form) in the range of values in a dataset that is larger than the specified percentage of all the values in the dataset

A **percentile** is a value (in percentage) in the range of values in a dataset that is larger than the specified percentage of all the values in the dataset. Percentiles make it possible to determine how a single value from a dataset ranks in relation to all of the other values. For example, a monthly financial report for 100 medical clinics shows that net profits were evenly distributed between $100,000 and $200,000. Clinic A, one of the clinics included in the report, had a monthly profit of $135,000, which ranks it in the 35th percentile of profit. Another way to interpret "percentile" in this scenario is that 35 percent of the medical clinics had profits that were below the profit at Clinic A, while 65 percent of the medical clinics had profits that were above the profit at Clinic A.

EXHIBIT 10.13
Agency Star
Ratings on
CMS Home
Health Compare
Website

	Advanced Home Health NW of Portland	Adventist Home Health – Portland	Cascade Health Solutions	Oregon Average	National Average
Quality-of-care star ratings	★★★★⯪	★★★★★⯪	★★★★⯪ •	★★★⯪••	★★★⯪••

Source: Adapted from CMS (2016a).

Quartiles are values that divide a set of data into four equal parts. The first, second, and third quartiles, often expressed as Q1, Q2, and Q3, are the same as the 25th percentile, the 50th percentile, and the 75th percentile. The first quartile represents the value within the group that is greater than 25 percent of all the values. Likewise, it is less than 75 percent of all the values. The second quartile represents the value within the group that is greater than 50 percent of all the values. Likewise, it is less than 50 percent of all the values. The second quartile, the 50th percentile, and the median are the same value. The third quartile represents the value within the group that is greater than 75 percent of all the values. Likewise, it is less than 25 percent of all the values.

quartiles
values that divide a set of data into four equal parts

Many external stakeholders at the state and national levels are gathering and reporting performance data using percentile and quartile rankings. For example, the California Hospital Assessment and Reporting Taskforce publicly reports various nurse-sensitive patient outcome measures for California hospitals. The data are reported both in percentiles and quartiles to provide hospitals the opportunity to determine and compare their performance with specificity (Brown et al. 2010).

The quartiles can be used to create another measure of variability. The **interquartile range** (IQR) is the difference between the values found at first (Q1) and third (Q3) quartiles. The smaller the IQR, the less spread there is among all the values. The interquartile range measures the spread of the middle 50 percent of the observations. In other words, the smaller the range that contains the middle 50 percent of the values, the closer they are to the median, which means there is less dispersion. On the contrary, large values of this statistic mean that the 1st and 3rd quartiles are far apart, indicating a high level of variability. One of the advantages of using IQR is that it is not sensitive to outliers.

interquartile range (IQR)
the difference between the values found at first (Q1) and third (Q3) quartiles

Quantitative Measures of Linear Relationship

A scatter plot, one of the graphical methods covered earlier in this chapter, can be used to assess the linear relationship between the two variables of interest in a subjective manner. However, if the goal is to measure the direction and the strength of the relationship in a more objective manner, managers can use specific numerical summary measures to quantify the relationship. The strength of a relationship between two variables indicates how strongly one variable affects the other in a linear manner. The direction of the relationship indicates whether the effect is positive or negative. A statistical measure, the correlation coefficient, provides information about the strength and the direction of a linear relationship between two variables.

The **correlation coefficient** between two variables can be used to determine whether the two variables of interest are related to each other. The sign of the value of the correlation coefficient typically captures the direction

correlation coefficient
a statistical measure that provides information about the strength and the direction of a linear relationship between two variables

of the relationship between the two variables (positive or negative), and the strength of relationship is captured by its numerical value. The possible value of the correlation coefficient ranges from -1 to +1, where -1 indicates a strong negative relationship and +1 indicates a strong positive relationship. A correlation coefficient value of 0 indicates the variables are not related, meaning the two variables have little to no effect on one another.

It is important to keep in mind that correlation is not causation. A linear relationship between two variables, for example x and y, does not mean that one variable is causing change in another variable. It may be possible that a third variable is causing both x and y to change in the same manner. In other words, correlation does not imply causation. For example, if a patient is diagnosed with high blood pressure and osteoporosis, one may incorrectly assume that the osteoporosis is caused by the high blood pressure. However, the cause of both conditions is likely something else entirely.

Using Graphical and Numerical Methods to Analyze Process Performance

Measuring process performance involves several concepts and principles along with the analytics building blocks covered in the previous sections of the chapter. Analytics is vital to a manager's understanding of whether processes are meeting requirements.

process requirements
what is needed from a process; also known as *voice of the customer*

Process requirements, also referred to as the *voice of the customer*, define what is needed from the process. Process measurement quantifies process performance as it now exists. Performance improvement helps align process performance with process requirements.

Process requirements are the outputs the manager expects the process to deliver. In health services organizations, process requirements may be considered from the perspectives of patients, internal customers, other stakeholders, and the market in general. Clinical studies, guidelines, and practice standards are also sources of process requirements in health services. Customer, stakeholder, and market requirements are the foundation for and drive all work performed by the organization.

Process Capability and Process Measurement

process capability
what the process is able to deliver; also referred to as the *voice of the process*

Process capability, also referred to as the *voice of the process*, is what the process is able to deliver (Wheeler 2000). The run chart in exhibit 10.14 shows a change in process capability after improvement interventions. The hand-hygiene rates gradually yet steadily increased. Statistical analysis methods can be applied to the data to determine the rate of improvement and the variation before and after the interventions.

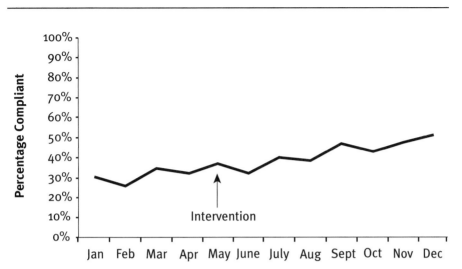

EXHIBIT 10.14
Run Chart:
Hand Hygiene
Compliance by
Percentage of
Staff Observed

Every process has a built-in capability to deliver outputs in a defined range. Process requirements guide the selection of metrics to quantify the process capability. Consider the example of a hospitalized patient experiencing pain. The voice of the customer (process requirement) in this case is a consistent, timely response when requesting assistance. The voice of the process (process capability) is how long it takes for the patient to receive assistance. The voice of the process may be measured in minutes from the time the patient asks for help to the time someone responds to the request. Collecting the response times for a defined period—say for a day—provides insight about the process capability. Exhibit 10.15 displays sample response-time data for two different hospitals with the minutes on the x axis and number of requests on the y axis.

Patients in Hospital 1 will receive help in 4 to 16 minutes and those in Hospital 2 in 2 to 6 minutes. The range of response times reflects the process capability at each hospital: the larger the range in minutes, the less dependable the process; the lower the range in minutes, the more dependable and predictable the process. In this example, Hospital 2 responds more quickly and more consistently than Hospital 1 to a patient's request for assistance. The voice of the Hospital 1 process shows a process designed in a manner that delivers inconsistent, rather than dependable, results. Adding training, working harder, or setting new goals will be ineffective strategies for improving the output of this process. The process delivers output in the range of its capability and will change only if the process itself is changed.

The frequency distribution may also be plotted as a line graph such as the one shown in exhibit 10.16. Displayed this way, the response times resemble normal distribution curves. Several calculations may be derived from the distribution, including a measure of central tendency (such as a mean or

EXHIBIT 10.15
Bar Graph:
Response Times
Frequency
Distribution

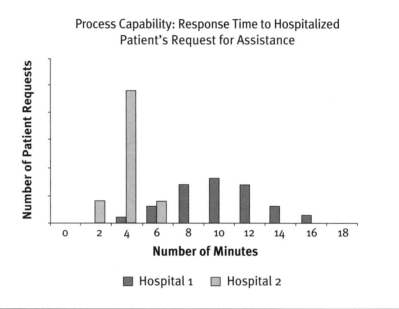

EXHIBIT 10.16
Line Graph:
Response Times
Frequency
Distribution

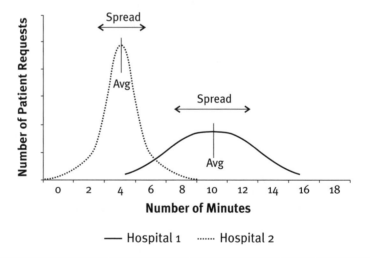

an average) and a measure of spread or distance from the average (such as a standard deviation). When the process is carried out, performance is expected to fall in the area under the curve.

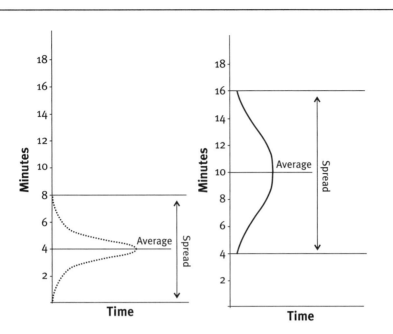

EXHIBIT 10.17
Converting
the Frequency
Distribution to a
Control Chart

Control Charts

Control charts, also known as **process behavior charts**, illustrate the difference between the voice of the customer and the voice of the process. While a frequency distribution shows process performance for a defined period, process performance may be plotted and tracked over time. Turning the frequency distribution on its side forms the basic process control chart, with the increments of time on the x axis and the units of performance on the y axis. This simple rotation to the frequency distributions in exhibit 10.16 is shown in exhibit 10.17. Three horizontal lines are added, representing the average and the upper and lower range of values also called *upper control limit* and *lower control limit*. In summary, a control chart is a line graph that contains a mean line and upper and lower limits of the normal range or control limits.

control chart (or process behavior chart) a line graph that contains a mean line and upper and lower limits of the normal range or control limits

Plotting the average response times (e.g., daily averages for a week, weekly averages for a month) provides additional insight about the process capability, its average level of performance, and the amount of variation in the process over time (exhibit 10.18).

A manager must be able to recognize the two types of variation illustrated by control charts. **Random variation**, also referred to as **noise** or **common cause variation**, is the natural variation present in all measures of healthcare processes (Neuhauser, Provost, and Bergman 2011). For example, in the Hospital 1 control chart in exhibit 10.18, the process did not suddenly deteriorate from Monday to Tuesday. The daily change simply represents the amount of random variation inherent in this process.

random variation (or noise, common cause variation) the natural variation present in all measures of processes (Neuhauser, Provost, and Bergman 2011)

EXHIBIT 10.18
Simple Control
Charts: Average
Daily Response
Times for
Hospitalized
Patients'
Requests for
Assistance

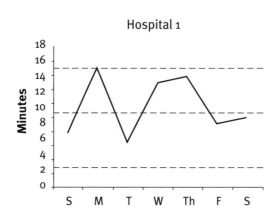

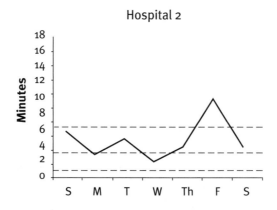

Assignable variation, also referred to as a **signal** or s**pecial cause variation**, appears as the result of causes outside of the core processes of the work (Neuhauser, Provost, and Bergman 2011). The presence of assignable variation in process measurement data indicates that something irregular (i.e., not inherent to the process) has occurred. The manager can distinguish random variation as those points that lie within the boundaries of the upper and lower control limits. Assignable or special cause variation is present when the manager sees any of the following situations (Wheeler 2000):

- A value that is above the upper control limit or below the lower control limit
- Three to four successive values that lie closer to the control limits than to the mean
- Eight or more consecutive points that lie on the same side of the mean

For example, in the Hospital 2 control chart in exhibit 10.18, the average response time on Friday is well above the upper limit. This instance is an example of a one-time irregularity, such as unexpected last-minute staff sick calls leaving the department short-handed for part of the day.

A manager must be able to distinguish between random and assignable variation because she will need to respond differently depending on the type of variation present. A manager cannot do anything to change the amount of random variation exhibited by the process, unless a systems approach is used to change, redesign, or improve the underlying process itself. On the other hand, assignable variation results from a distinct cause that warrants investigation by the manager. A one-time, assignable variation may be traced to its cause and explained. Assignable variation, represented by a series of points, is a clue that an intentional or unintentional change in the process has occurred. One expects to see a change in process capability after an improvement intervention. The desired impact is a more consistent and predictable process that results in a narrowing range of random variation and a shift in the average level of performance in a favorable direction.

When reading a control chart, remember the underlying curve and its measures of central tendency and spread. Control charts may be designed by establishing boundaries at plus or minus three standard deviations from the mean (capturing how the process performs about 99 percent of the time), or they may be designed by establishing boundaries at plus or minus two standard deviations from the mean (capturing how the process performs about 95 percent of the time). A detailed explanation of the statistical calculations of control charts is beyond the scope of this text. Readers are encouraged to consult a statistician or management engineer and refer to the references for more technical guidance on constructing control charts.

Bundling and Unbundling Data According to the User's Purpose

When different levels of the organization are telling different stories about the operating environment, unbundling or disaggregating the indicators can be useful. For example, administrators of a large tertiary care hospital tracked staff turnover rates as one of the hospital's performance measures. Turnover for the nursing department was 25 percent, which the administrators considered to be reasonable given the local employment and economic environments. However, the nurse managers and nurses consistently voiced their concerns about understaffing and turnover.

The aggregate turnover figures reflected the combined turnover of registered nurses, licensed practical nurses, certified nurse assistants, and unit secretaries. Unbundling the data revealed that although the departmental turnover was 25 percent, the registered nurse turnover was 15 percent, and the certified nurse assistant turnover was 43 percent. While studying the departmental turnover data, the human resources department realized that internal staff transfers were not included in the turnover calculations; only terminations were included. When staff movement in the organization was also taken into account, it became apparent that the original turnover data significantly underestimated the impact of staff changes on the nurse managers and the frontline nursing staff. Once these flaws in the performance measures were identified, the human resources department redesigned its measures and reporting mechanisms to account for changing activity at the unit level in addition to aggregate turnover at the departmental or organizational level.

The "distinction between data and information does not lie in the content of a given string of characters. It lies more in its relationship to required decisions. [Data are] measurements that enable us to judge the impact of a local decision on the company's goal" (Goldratt 1990, 4, 10). In the previous example, although the hospital administrators were receiving data, originally they were not receiving the information they needed to best understand the relationship between their decisions and the organization's goals.

The selection and presentation of metrics should match the level and purpose of its user. Consider the following four levels of decision making in a hospital: board, senior executive, nursing service line, and nursing unit. Now consider the following examples of Hospital Consumer Assessment of Healthcare Providers and Systems reports. The survey instrument contains the following questions (Agency for Healthcare Research and Quality 2016):

- During this hospital stay, how often did nurses treat you with courtesy and respect?
- During this hospital stay, how often did nurses listen carefully to you?
- During this hospital stay, how often did nurses explain things in a way you could understand?

The CMS Hospital Compare website combines these three questions into one value (CMS 2016b): patients who reported that their nurses "always" communicated well. The summary indicator is presented monthly to the board of a hospital and is shown in exhibit 10.19. A summary report, including the hospitalwide results for each question, is generated for the senior executives and shown in exhibit 10.20. Four inpatient units, reporting to one director, make up the medical-surgical inpatient nursing service line. A report containing the results for each question for all four units is generated for the nursing director. An example of one question is shown in exhibit 10.21. Finally, a unit-based

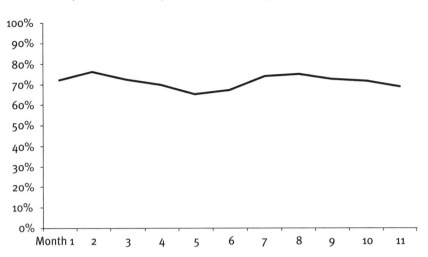

Inpatients Who Reported Nurses Always Communicated Well

EXHIBIT 10.19
Board-Level
Report: Nurse
Communication

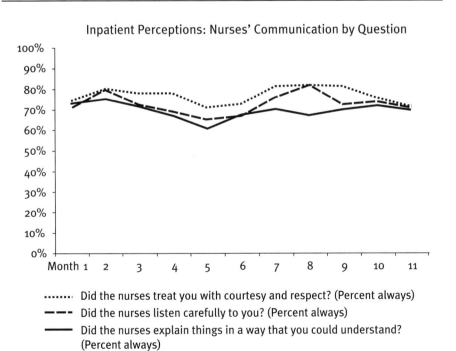

Inpatient Perceptions: Nurses' Communication by Question

EXHIBIT 10.20
Senior
Executive–Level
Report: Nurse
Communication
by Question

.... Did the nurses treat you with courtesy and respect? (Percent always)

━ ━ ━ Did the nurses listen carefully to you? (Percent always)

━━━ Did the nurses explain things in a way that you could understand?
(Percent always)

EXHIBIT 10.21
Service Line–
Level Report:
Individual
Question
Results by Unit
in the Service
Line

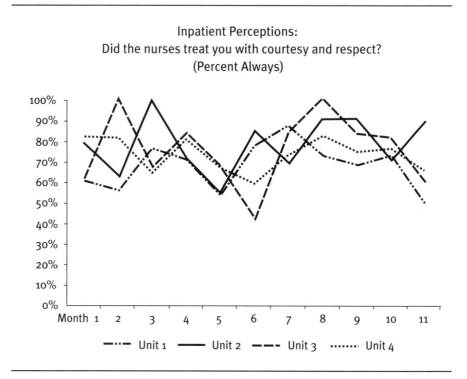

Inpatient Perceptions:
Did the nurses treat you with courtesy and respect?
(Percent Always)

report with results for each question is generated for each unit manager. An example of results for three questions for one unit is shown in exhibit 10.22.

The senior executive for quality and safety, responsible for designing and distributing the reports, understood the different data needs for the different decision makers. He also understood that as data are aggregated, some performance information may become buried in the data and that important opportunities for improvement may be missed. In this case, the unit manager–level report provided key information for system improvement. Presented in this way, the data revealed erratic performance in each of the four units. However, when one department is up, another is down, so when aggregated—as in the board-level and senior executive–level reports—the extremes canceled each other out. This key insight would be missed and leaders would be under the misimpression that patient perceptions were pretty consistent if the board-level or senior executive–level reports were the only ones reviewed in this organization. Overlaying multiple question results for Unit 4 on one graph demonstrates erratic performance on each question, indicating fundamental problems with how care is organized and delivered and a lack of consistency among caregivers.

Because the senior executive for quality and safety also understood the importance of communicating the story in the data, a brief explanation accompanied each report as data were aggregated. The director and unit

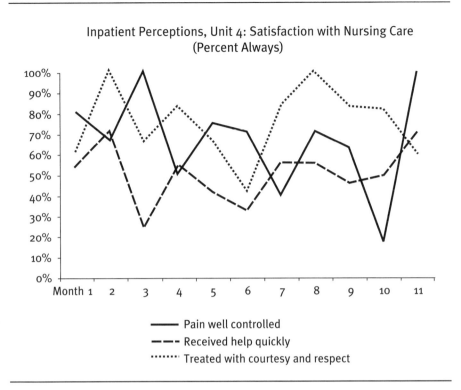

EXHIBIT 10.22
Unit Manager–
Level Report:
Individual
Question
Results for
Unit 4 Only

manager–level reports included all four levels of data so they could see how their performance fit in the performance of the organization overall. Segmenting data by healthcare service lines and workforce groups is often necessary to gain a deeper understanding of performance (BPEP 2015).

Many health services organizations have adopted a dashboard or scorecard approach to present a quick visual summary of the organization's current performance status to senior executives and the board. Many types of performance measurement data can be reported using this dashboard approach: "Examples of data that can be displayed in dashboard reports include financial indicators such as days cash on hand, patient satisfaction indicators such as average length of wait time, clinical indicators such as number of patients undergoing blood pressure exams, and provider performance indicators such as compliance with various clinical standards" (Health Resources and Services Administration 2011).

Analysis of the results is conveyed through red-yellow-green schematics or arrows pointing up, down, or horizontally. However, the desire for brevity sometimes leads to a loss of context. Exhibit 10.23 is an excerpt from a sample financial scorecard that maintains the balance between brevity and context. This example contains useful features such as a key and notes guiding readers to the context in which the ratings and trends should be interpreted.

EXHIBIT 10.23
Sample Hospital
Financial
Scorecard

	Hospital XYZ Year 1	Hospital XYZ Year 2	Bench mark facility	Regional Median	U.S. Median	Rating[1]	Rating Dashboard (see key)	Trend (see key)
Financial Overview								
Total Margin	0.40	(3.00)	2.00	2.07	3.70	Fair	★ ★	⇧
Market Factors								
Inpatient Revenue %	60.6	65.1	63.9	62.3	55.5	Fair	★ ★	Y
Investment Efficiency								
Days in A/R	54	55	80	56	56	Average	★ ★ ★	
Plant Obsolescence								
Average Age of Plant	17.0	N/A	8.2	N/A	9.6	Poor	★	
Capital Position								
Debt Financing %	104.0	104.8	48.7	57.7	47.8	Poor	★	
Labor Costs								
Staffing FTEs per Adjusted Patient Day	4.7	4.9	7.2	4.9	4.7	Average	★ ★ ★	⇩
Supply Costs								
Avg. Medical Supply Cost per Medicare Discharge (CMI = 1.0)	602	449	1,454	778	660	Average	★ ★ ★	↑
Non-Operating Income								
Days Cash on Hand	17	14	29	55	36	Fair	★ ★	⇧

Key:
Favorable trend, measure is increasing ⇧ Favorable trend, measure is decreasing ⇩
Unfavorable trend, measure is increasing ↑ Unfavorable trend, measure is decreasing ↓
The measure has increased by > 2%, but the change must be interpreted with respect to additional measures ⋏
The measure has decreased by > 2%, but the change must be interpreted with respect to additional measures Y
Rating Scale: poor, fair, average, good, and excellent, represented by 1–5 stars, respectively. Ratings are based on comparisons with national data.

Notes:
The far right column of the pages with the individual performance measures provides trend information, when available. This trend information should be interpreted cautiously. An arrow in this column is simply a mathematical indicator. It tells only whether this performance measure changed by more than two percent compared with the prior year. As such, there is no inherent judgment value contained in this information. *The purpose is simply to highlight measures that are changing so that, if appropriate, they can be studied further.* Even an unfavorable trend might not really be bad news. For example, suppose that some cost measure increased by 3%, which would be flagged as an unfavorable trend. If local, regional, and US hospitals experienced a 6% increase in this measure, this increase could be considered quite good relative to what was experienced elsewhere and probably reflects excellent managerial performance. *Furthermore, executives generally would want to avoid extreme values of any measure* (italics added).

Source: Reprinted with permission from Andrew Cameron, PhD, MBA. Principal, Mantium Consulting Services.

These examples illustrate two principles about data and complex systems (Wheeler 2000, 105):

1. As data are aggregated, they lose their context and usefulness.
2. Aggregated data may be used as a report card, but they will not pinpoint what needs to be fixed.

Summary

Analyzing data as a whole or in sufficiently large subsets can reveal useful information that otherwise may not be obvious. Multiple measures can be taken, and many ways to communicate the results both graphically and numerically exist. This information can help decision makers gain a better understanding of what is happening in the organization and determine what steps are needed to improve future performance.

In healthcare organizations, there are many variables in both business and clinical processes that can be examined using analytical methods. Applications of these methods could provide numerous opportunities to improve performance in health services organizations. This chapter covers the basic concepts of healthcare data analytics, with an overview of descriptive and inferential statistics. Commonly used types of performance data, such as categorical and continuous, are discussed, along with common graphical methods and numerical summary measures. The chapter also covers ways of reporting data to improve understanding of current performance.

Exercise 10.1

Background: This exercise further explores the principle about data and complex systems discussed in this chapter: "Graphs reveal interesting structures present in the data" (Wheeler 2000, 14, 79).

Objective: To evaluate graphic presentations of data and select the one that provides the most valuable feedback about the system's behavior.

Instructions: As the manager of an ED, you are faced with the challenge of improving flow and better matching your staffing plan to patient demand. Like the mammography center manager in this chapter, your monthly reports from the finance department present the ED's volume statistics in a spreadsheet according to this month, last month, year to date, and the same month in the previous year. You decide to graph the data. You experiment and come up with the following three graphs using the same information. Select the graph that provides you with the most insight and explain why you chose that graph.

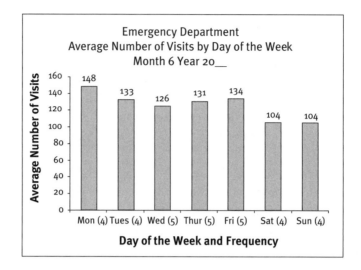

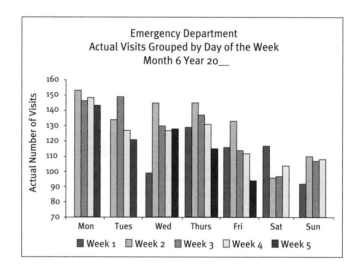

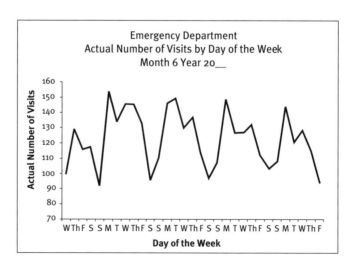

Exercise 10.2

Background: This exercise helps readers learn to identify specific types of data and choose the appropriate graphical techniques and numerical summary measures—critical components of making analytics-driven recommendations.

Objectives: The following dataset represents a small portion of a larger report about patients who visited an urgent care clinic on one day. Identify the type of data found in each column, and identify the numerical summary measures and graphical methods you would use to summarize the data in each column.

ID	Age (Years)	Gender (M/F)	Opinion	Visit Time (Min.)	Charges ($)	Payment Type	Prior Visits	Admission Blood Pressure	
								Systolic	Diastolic
1	33.5	M	5	64.2	158.00	Self-Pay	4	136	71
2	21.2	F	2	69.4	159.00	Medicaid	3	112	65
3	56.4	F	1	81.1	178.00	Medicaid	0	156	88
4	53.9	M	3	31.6	124.00	Blue Cross	1	125	80
5	51.2	F	5	48.5	146.00	Aetna	8	133	62

Instructions: You have been recently hired as the quality manager for an urgent care clinic and will spend the next two weeks reviewing all the patient records in this dataset. The information includes the identification number assigned to each patient, followed by patient age and gender. After this visit, the patients were mailed a survey to gather satisfaction scores. The results are represented in the opinion column. A score of 1 is very poor, 2 is poor, 3 is neutral, 4 is good, and 5 is very good. The clinic administrator has supplied the total time each patient spent in the clinic for this visit and the number of prior visits to the clinic for each patient. The billing department has provided the payment type and the charges billed for the visit in the charges column. The patient's admission blood pressure data come from his or her EHR.

The clinic administrator will ask you questions about these data, and your answers will be used to set performance goals and strategic objectives for the clinic. Considering the small portion of the dataset provided previously, answer the following questions:

1. What type of data is found in each column (e.g., categorical [nominal]; interval [continuous])?

2. Which numerical summary measures would you use to summarize the data in each column (e.g., mean, median, mode, range, standard deviation)?

3. What type of graphical methods would you use to represent the data in each column (e.g., bar chart, run chart)?

Companion Readings

Benneyan, J. C., R. C. Lloyd, and P. E. Plsek. 2003. "Statistical Process Control as a Tool for Research and Healthcare Improvement." *Quality and Safety in Health Care* 12 (6): 458–64.

Bronnert, J., J. S. Clark, L. Hyde, C. J. Solberg, S. White, and M. Wolin. 2011. *Health Data Analysis Toolkit.* American Health Information Management Association. Accessed November 16, 2016. http://library.ahima.org/PdfView?oid=103453.

Cline, J. S. 2014. "The Promise of Data-Driven Care." *North Carolina Medical Journal* 75 (3): 178–82.

Fernandes, L., M. O'Connor, and V. Weaver. 2012. "Big Data, Bigger Outcomes." *Journal of AHIMA.* Published October. www.ibmbigdatahub.com/whitepaper/big-data-bigger-outcomes-journal-ahima.

Health Resources and Services Administration. 2011. "Managing Data for Performance Improvement." Published April. www.hrsa.gov/quality/toolbox/508pdfs/managingdataperformanceimprovement.pdf.

Institute for Healthcare Improvement. 2016. "Building Skills in Data Collection and Understanding Variation." Training video. Accessed November 16. www.ihi.org/education/webtraining/ondemand/datacollection_variation/Pages/default.aspx.

———. 2016. "On Demand: Using Run and Control Charts to Understand Variation." Training video. Accessed November 16. www.ihi.org/education/webtraining/ondemand/run_controlcharts/Pages/default.aspx.

Lance, P., D. Guilkey, A. Hattori, and G. Angeles. 2014. *How Do We Know If a Program Made a Difference? A Guide to Statistical Methods for Program Impact Evaluation.* MEASURE Evaluation. Published May. www.cpc.unc.edu/measure/resources/publications/ms-14-87-en.

Liu, S. 2014. "Breaking Down Barriers: What Quality Professionals Need to Know to Survive and Thrive in the Age of Big Data." *Quality Progress* 47 (1): 17–22.

National Association for Healthcare Quality. 2015. *Essential Competencies: Health Data Analytics.* Retrieved July 10, 2016. www.nahq.org/uploads/NAHQ15_Health Data_Final.pdf.

Parikh, R. B., M. Kakad, and D. W. Bates. 2016. "Integrating Predictive Analytics into High-Value Care: The Dawn of Precision Delivery." *Journal of the American Medical Association* 315 (7): 651–52.

Perla, R., L. Provost, and S. Murray. 2013. "Sampling Considerations for Health Care Improvement." *Quality Management in Health Care* 22 (1): 36–47.

Raghupathi, W., and V. Raghupathi. 2014. "Big Data Analytics in Healthcare: Promise and Potential." *Health Information Science and Systems* 2 (3). https://hissjournal.biomedcentral.com/articles/10.1186/2047-2501-2-3.

Shmueli, G., N. R. Patel, and P. C. Bruce. 2016. *Data Mining for Business Analytics: Concepts, Techniques, and Applications in XLMiner.* New York: Wiley.

Ward, M. J., K. A. Marsolo, and C. M. Froehle. 2014. "Applications of Business Analytics in Healthcare." *Business Horizons* 57 (5): 571–82.

Wheeler, D. J. 2000. *Understanding Variation: The Key to Managing Chaos,* 2nd ed. Knoxville, TN: SPC Press.

Web Resource

Statistical Thinking for Managerial Decisions: http://home.ubalt.edu/ntsbarsh/Business-stat/opre504.htm

---

References

Adams, J., and J. Klein. 2011. *Business Intelligence and Analytics in Health Care: A Primer.* Washington, DC: Advisory Board Company.

Agency for Healthcare Research and Quality. 2016. "CAHPS Surveys and Guidance." Reviewed September. www.ahrq.gov/cahps/surveys-guidance/index.html.

Baldrige Performance Excellence Program (BPEP). 2015. *2015–2016 Baldrige Excellence Framework: A Systems Approach to Improving Your Organization's Performance (Health Care).* Gaithersburg, MD: US Department of Commerce, National Institute of Standards and Technology.

Brown, D. S., N. Donaldson, L. Burnes Bolton, and C. E. Aydin. 2010. "Nursing-Sensitive Benchmarks for Hospitals to Gauge High-Reliability Performance." *Journal of Healthcare Quality* 32 (6): 9–17.

Centers for Medicare & Medicaid Services (CMS). 2016a. "Find a Home Health Agency." Accessed November 16. www.medicare.gov/homehealthcompare/search.html.

———. 2016b. "Survey of Patients' Experiences (HCAHPS)." Accessed July 15. www.medicare.gov/hospitalcompare/Data/Overview.html.

———. 2015. "Home Health Star Ratings." Published July 14. www.cms.gov/Medicare/Quality-Initiatives-Patient-Assessment-Instruments/HomeHealthQualityInits/HHQIHomeHealthStarRatings.html.

Davenport, T. H., and J. G. Harris. 2007. *Competing on Analytics: The New Science of Winning.* Cambridge, MA: Harvard Business School Press.

Goldratt, E. M. 1990. *The Haystack Syndrome: Sifting Information Out of the Data Ocean.* New York: North River Press.

Health Resources and Services Administration. 2011. "Managing Data for Performance Improvement." Accessed July 10. www.hrsa.gov/quality/toolbox/methodology/performanceimprovement/part2.html.

National Association for Healthcare Quality (NAHQ). 2015. *Essential Competencies: Health Data Analytics.* Accessed July 10, 2016. www.nahq.org/uploads/NAHQ15_HealthData_Final.pdf.

Neuhauser, D., L. Provost, and B. Bergman. 2011. "The Meaning of Variation to Healthcare Managers, Clinical and Health-Services Researchers, and Individual Patients." *BMJ Quality and Safety* 20 (Suppl 1): i36–40.

Shmueli, G., N. R. Patel, and P. C. Bruce. 2016. *Data Mining for Business Analytics: Concepts, Techniques, and Applications in XLMiner.* New York: John Wiley.

Spath, P. L. 2013. *Introduction to Healthcare Quality Management,* 2nd ed. Chicago: Health Administration Press.

Wheeler, D. J. 2000. *Understanding Variation: The Key to Managing Chaos,* 2nd ed. Knoxville, TN: SPC Press.

Woodall, W. H. 2000. "Controversies and Contradictions in Statistical Process Control." *Journal of Quality Technology* 32 (4): 341–50.

DESIGNING AND IMPLEMENTING IMPROVEMENTS

Learning Objectives

After completing this chapter, you should be able to

- compare and contrast models used for systematic improvement;
- differentiate how, when, and why to use different improvement models;
- explain a framework for implementing improvements in complex systems; and
- identify strategies for sustaining improvement gains.

An employee is faced with choosing a new primary care physician when her employer changes health plans. This employee makes a list of the characteristics she wants in a physician (e.g., board certified) and in the physician's office (e.g., close to work). She asks fellow employees and friends if they know any of the physicians listed in the health plan handbook and what they think of their care experiences. She then selects a physician and makes an appointment for an annual physical. After her first experience with the new physician, she decides that the physician and the office staff meet her criteria and that she will continue to use the physician as her primary care physician.

She *planned* how to select a physician; *collected data* about her options; *compared* the various options against her criteria; *tested* her first choice; and, based on her impressions and experiences, *decided* to keep her first choice as her primary care physician. Although this employee may not have realized it, the continuous improvement approach used in her organization had "rubbed off" on her so that she automatically used the same systematic process for deciding what to do when faced with a personal problem or decision.

In the clinical setting, clinical providers use the scientific method and the evidence-based process (Guyatt et al. 2015) to systematically solve problems. For example, a patient presents with a complaint. The provider gathers subjective data (what the patient tells him) and objective data (e.g., vital signs, physical exam, diagnostic tests), diagnoses the problem on the basis of patient data, devises a patient plan according to the diagnosis, implements the plan, evaluates the patient's response (e.g., collects additional subjective and objective data and compares with previous data), and revises the plan as needed. When clinical professionals use the scientific method in decision making, it is often referred to as *professional judgment* (Coles 2002). Likewise, managerial professional judgment may be described by the concept of *critical thinking*.

This chapter presents systematic improvement approaches to aid managers in developing their improvement thinking and an implementation framework to enable managers to implement change in complex systems.

Systematic Critical Thinking in Designing Improvements

Critical thinking is essential in the management domain. "Everyone thinks; it is our nature to do so. But much of our thinking, left to itself, is biased, distorted, partial, uninformed or downright prejudiced. Yet the quality of our life and that of what we produce, make, or build depends precisely on the quality of our thought. Shoddy thinking is costly, both in money and in quality of life. Excellence in thought, however, must be systematically cultivated" (Scriven and Paul 2016).

critical thinking
"the art of analyzing and evaluating thinking with a view to improving it" (Scriven and Paul 2016)

The broader the scope of responsibility managers have in a health services organization, the greater the imperative to develop, cultivate, and refine their critical thinking skills. **Critical thinking** is essential if managers are to be effective stewards of limited human resources, financial resources, and the patients' lives and health that are entrusted to their organization or their community. In the context of quality management, managers have numerous approaches and tools to guide and maximize their critical thinking skills.

Applying critical thinking to a problem or performance gap is illustrated by the total quality principle of continuous improvement described in chapter 1: "a philosophy or an approach to management that can be characterized by its principles, practices, and techniques. Its three principles are customer focus, continuous improvement, and teamwork. . . . Each principle is implemented through a set of practices. . . . The practices are, in turn, supported by a wide array of techniques (i.e., specific step-by-step methods intended to make the practices effective)" (Dean and Bowen 2000, 4–5). Critical thinking is an important component of continuous improvement methodologies. The most common improvement models used in health services organizations are Plan, Do, Check, Act (PDCA); Six Sigma; and Lean strategies.

PDCA cycle (or Shewhart cycle)
an improvement cycle that consists of four continuous steps: plan, do, check or study, and act

Plan, Do, Check, Act

The employee in this chapter's opening example used an adaptation of what is referred to in the quality improvement literature as the **PDCA cycle or the Shewhart cycle** (exhibit 11.1).

Originating from industrial applications of quality improvement, the Shewhart cycle consists of four steps: planning, doing, checking or studying,

EXHIBIT 11.1
PDCA Cycle

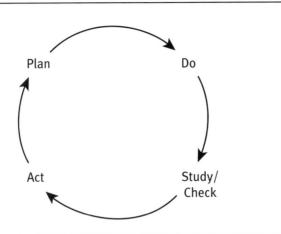

Source: Adapted from Deming (2000). © MIT Press.

and acting. The steps are linked to represent the cyclical nature of the approach. The steps in this systematic and continuous approach to improvement are as follows (American Society for Quality 2004):

- Plan: Identify an opportunity and plan for change.
- Do: Implement the change on a small scale.
- Check (or *study*): Use data to analyze the results of the change and determine whether it made a difference.
- Act: If the change was successful, implement it on a wider scale and continuously assess results. If the change did not work, begin the cycle again.

The PDCA cycle can be applied to most improvement projects as a means for honing in on a known problem, understanding its characteristics, and defining the system of solutions to bring about success. Good questions lead to good answers. Appendix 11.1 lists important process improvement questions to consider during each step of the PDCA cycle according to their relevance to the particular situation.

The improvement model recommended by the Institute for Healthcare Improvement (IHI) adds the following three questions before applying the PDCA cycle to a problem or performance gap (IHI 2016):

1. What are we trying to accomplish?
2. How will we know that a change is an improvement?
3. What change can we make that will result in an improvement?

rapid cycle improvement
"an accelerated method (usually less than six weeks per improvement cycle) of collecting and analyzing data and making changes on the basis of that analysis" (Spath 2013, 120)

Employees at all levels of an organization—from entry level to the executive suite—may use this simple continuous improvement thought process to promote critical problem solving in the work setting.

A PDCA improvement project involving five hospitals in a regional health system is summarized in exhibit 11.2.

A fast-track improvement model that uses the PDCA cycle to make small incremental changes is **rapid cycle improvement.** This "approach is an accelerated method (usually less than six weeks per improvement cycle) of collecting and analyzing data and making changes on the basis of that analysis" (Spath 2013, 120). Over a short period, small process changes are made and tested to evaluate their impact. For example, Varkey, Cunningham,

EXHIBIT 11.2
PDCA Improvement Project Aimed at Standardizing Computed Tomography Scan Protocols

Computed tomography (CT) scan protocols at the five hospitals in a regional health system had some scanning parameter differences primarily because of variations in the type of scanner at each site and radiologists' preferences. Different protocols at each site created the potential for quality problems such as

- the inability to accurately track radiation doses for patients who got scans at different sites,
- difficulty in comparing images of varying quality,
- the opportunity for confusion created by the use of different protocols at each site, and
- complications of the centralized scheduling process resulting from irregularity in appointment length and patient preparation.

To address these improvement opportunities, a team of representatives from each hospital—comprising radiologists, imaging administrators, and CT technologists—was formed to organize and standardize CT scan protocols at the five hospitals. The supervisor of imaging services at one of the hospitals served as the project leader. Activities that occurred at each step of the PDCA cycle are summarized in the following chart.

PLAN	All current CT scan protocols for various body areas were gathered. The technologists on the team identified the inconsistencies and, using current American College of Radiology scanner parameter recommendations, proposed standard protocols for each body area. The radiologists on the team reviewed the proposed standard protocols, made adjustments as needed, and gave final approvals for each protocol.
DO	Each hospital implemented the approved CT scan protocols. Technologists on the team communicated with and educated fellow technologists and oversaw loading of the new password-protected protocols into the computer systems. Radiologists on the team communicated with and educated fellow radiologists and created a survey to gather input from protocol users and referring physicians. The central scheduling manager trained clerical staff on the use of the protocols when scheduling exams.
CHECK	The project manager gathered data on the use of the protocols and sent surveys to referring physicians. The technologists and radiologists on the team gathered and reviewed feedback from their peers. The central scheduling manager gathered feedback from clerical staff.
ACT	The team reviewed feedback from referring physicians, technicians, radiologists, and clerical staff to determine whether any changes needed to be made. A PDCA cycle will be conducted again if more opportunities for improving the CT scanning protocols are identified.

and Bisping (2007) implemented a series of interventions in an ambulatory clinic that resulted in a reduction of prescribing errors and discrepancies by more than 50 percent. Each PDCA cycle of improvement lasted only 24 hours, with process changes based on what was learned in each previous cycle. At the end of one month, a new medication reconciliation process was standardized and implemented in the clinic.

Six Sigma Methodology

Another example of applying critical thinking in a systematic way to resolve a problem is Six Sigma. A **Six Sigma project** is a rigorous and disciplined approach using process improvement tools, methods, and statistical analysis. The idea is based on the philosophy that "views all work as processes that can be defined, measured, analyzed, improved and controlled" (Muralidharan 2015, 528).

Six Sigma project
a rigorous and disciplined approach to problem resolution using process improvement tools, methods, and statistical analysis

The most common steps in a Six Sigma project—define, measure, analyze, improve, and control—are illustrated in exhibit 11.3. The DMAIC (pronounced *dee-MAY-ick*) steps are intended to be an ongoing process similar to the PDCA cycle.

The DMAIC cycle adds more definition to the PDCA cycle, focuses improvement on root causes, and addresses ongoing evaluation and control. It encompasses the following five steps (Mukherjee 2008):

1. <u>D</u>efine the problem or improvement opportunity.
2. <u>M</u>easure key aspects of process performance.
3. <u>A</u>nalyze the data to determine the root causes of poor performance; determine whether the process can be improved or should be redesigned.
4. <u>I</u>mprove the process system.
5. <u>C</u>ontrol and sustain the improved process.

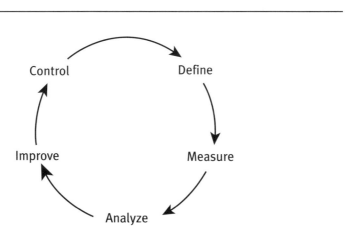

EXHIBIT 11.3
Six Sigma
DMAIC

The measurement and data analysis steps are often what differentiate a Six Sigma project from other improvement methodologies. Data are gathered to identify the extent of defects or errors in the process, which is reported as a sigma level. The higher the sigma level, the better the process is performing in terms of defect prevention (Lighter 2011). The "defect per million opportunities" (DPMO) rate is calculated and the current sigma level of the process identified.

six sigma level
the sigma level of a process that "has about 3.4 DPMO [defect per million opportunities] and is virtually error free (99.9996)" (Varkey, Reller, and Resar 2007, 737)

A process at the **six sigma level** "has about 3.4 DPMO and is virtually error free (99.9996%)" (Varkey, Reller, and Resar 2007, 737). The gap between desired sigma level and current level is used to establish an improvement goal.

In the measurement phase, the current process is studied to identify the extent of variation. In the analysis step, deviations from standards are identified and sources of process variation are hypothesized and evaluated using data analytic methods. A Six Sigma project in a hospital imaging department that followed the DMAIC cycle is summarized in exhibit 11.4.

Lean Strategies

In the mid-1980s, a research team at the Massachusetts Institute of Technology found that Toyota Motor Company in Japan made automobiles with fewer defects than did other manufacturers, and Toyota's production process required less inventory on hand, a smaller amount of capital investment, and fewer suppliers. The researchers coined the phrase *Lean manufacturing* to describe the unique attributes of the Toyota Production System, which was able to provide a customer-focused product while using fewer resources (Womack, Jones, and Roos 2007).

The Lean philosophy and tools that originated in manufacturing are being used in health services organizations to improve processes by removing non-value-added activities, also referred to as *waste*. Up to 40 percent of time spent in hospitals is estimated to be waste (Berczuk 2008). Seven different types of waste have been identified: "overproduction or underproduction, wasted inventory, rework or rejects (i.e., assembly mistakes), wasted motion (i.e., poor work area ergonomics), waste associated with waiting (i.e., patients waiting to be seen for appointments), waste associated with processing (i.e., outdated policies and procedures), and waste from transport or handlings (i.e., transporting patients unnecessarily)" (Varkey, Reller, and Resar 2007, 738).

kaizen event (or rapid process improvement project)
"a focused, short-term project aimed at improving a particular process" (McLaughlin and Olson 2012, 410)

A Lean project, which is often called a **kaizen event** or **rapid process improvement project** is "a focused, short-term project aimed at improving a particular process" (McLaughlin and Olson 2012, 410). The project follows steps similar to the PDCA cycle and is often completed in an accelerated fashion like a rapid cycle improvement project. Three core concepts are the basis of the Lean philosophy: standard work, user friendliness, and unobstructed throughput. These concepts are evident throughout a Lean project.

Define the problem	The telephone appointment process at the hospital's imaging center receives low customer satisfaction scores and racks up long hold times.	**EXHIBIT 11.4** Six Sigma Project Aimed at Improving an Imaging Center's Appointment Process
Measure key aspects of the process	Over the past six months, staff took an average of 2 minutes and 18 seconds to answer calls from customers wishing to schedule an imaging study. The center has received numerous customer complaints about long hold times and, as a result, lower satisfaction scores for the telephone appointment system.	
Analyze the data	• The imaging center appointment desk receives more than 2,000 calls per week. • Average customer satisfaction: 58 percent • Average hold time: 2 minutes, 18 seconds • Phone calls answered in less than 90 seconds: 55 percent • Overall call abandon rate: 26 percent; at peak time, 49 percent	
Improve the system	• Staffing changes were made to handle peak times. • Start and end times for shifts were revised to create a 45-minute overlap between day and evening shifts. • Registration forms for special imaging studies were modified to be easier for staff to complete. • The phone menu tree and call handling were improved. • Specifications for a future electronic scheduling system were defined.	
Control and sustain the improvement	• Overall average hold time decreased to 39 seconds. • Overall call abandon rate decreased to 11 percent. • Peak-time call abandon rate decreased to 27 percent. • Call volume decreased by 19 percent as a result of fewer callbacks. • Further improvements are expected after installation of the electronic scheduling system. The center will continue to monitor performance during and after transition to the new system.	

Source: Spath (2013). Used with permission.

standard work
"a process that has been broken down into a series of clearly defined tasks and is performed the same way every time by each individual involved in the process" (Lavallee 2011, 248)

"**Standard work** is a process that has been broken down into a series of clearly defined tasks and is performed the same way every time by each individual involved in the process" (Lavallee 2011, 248). Standardization improves efficiency because people can be more productive when the process steps remain stable. It also reduces errors by helping to ensure that steps do not get overlooked. Standardization of processes was ranked as the most effective action for reducing process errors by facility patient safety managers in the Veterans Health Administration (Bagian et al. 2011). An example of standard work could be a protocol for identifying hospital patients who are at high risk for falling. Standardized work is also the best starting point for process improvement. If the way things are being done is chaotic (people follow whatever steps they want), determining the cause of process output variation or what process changes will yield desired improvements is impossible.

Processes that are user friendly are easy for physicians and staff members to carry out. To achieve this goal, processes must be simple and direct, and supplies for completing tasks must be readily available. During a Lean project, the **5S methodology**—a philosophy and a way of organizing and managing the workspace by eliminating waste—is used to make the process more user friendly. The steps of the 5S methodology are as follows (Zidel 2007):

5S methodology
a philosophy and five-step way of organizing and managing the workspace by eliminating waste

1. *Sort*. Sort items in the work area and keep only those items that are frequently needed.
2. *Straighten*. Set work items in order of use after the workflow has been optimized.
3. *Scrub*. Clean the work area and inspect equipment for abnormal wear or defects.
4. *Standardize*. Systemize workflow processes.
5. *Sustain*. Maintain the gains made from the previous four steps.

unobstructed throughput
elimination of bottlenecks in a process

Unobstructed throughput, the third Lean core concept, relates to elimination of bottlenecks in the process. One tool that may be used in a Lean project is called a **value-stream map (VSM)**. "This tool graphically displays the process of services or product delivery with use of inputs, throughputs, and outputs" (Varkey, Reller, and Resar 2007, 738). A current VSM is created at the start of the project to identify process bottlenecks and other opportunities for improvement. Future-state VSMs are often designed during the project to illustrate proposed process changes.

value-stream map (VSM)
a diagram that "graphically displays the process of services or product delivery with use of inputs, throughputs, and outputs" (Varkey, Reller, and Resar 2007, 738)

Some organizations use a Lean problem-solving template, known as an **A3 report**, which has been adapted from the Toyota Production System model. The A3 report is a concise summary of the problem and solution with pictures and a few words (Dennis 2009). The report is named "A3" to denote the paper size used at Toyota for the report (the metric equivalent to 11-inch ×

A3 report
a concise summary of the problem and solution with pictures and a few words (Dennis 2009)

17-inch or B-sized paper). The report template standardizes project discussions using a structured storyboard format. Completing the report, question by question, helps engage people in collaborative, in-depth problem solving to address the root causes of performance problems. The A3 report format can be customized by an organization; thus, the structure and question wording may vary. Toyota actually uses several styles of A3 reports—for solving problems, for reporting project status, and for proposing policy changes—each with its own "storyline" (Sobek and Jimmerson 2006).

The problem-solving A3 report style is used most often in health services organizations. Generally, on the left side of the report answers to the following questions are recorded: Do we have a problem? What should be happening, and what is our gap? What is our history? What do we need to do? How will these actions help? On the right side of the report these questions are answered: What is our action plan? Are there any unresolved issues? Any additional resources required? Salem Health, a health system in Salem, Oregon, has conducted numerous Lean projects using an A3 report template and other Lean tools. A Lean project to decrease infections by improving hand hygiene in the system's 421-bed hospital is summarized in exhibit 11.5.

A number of health services organizations are combining tools from Six Sigma and Lean for process improvement projects aimed at reducing undesirable variation and controlling waste. Thus, the line between the two methodologies is becoming increasingly blurred.

		EXHIBIT 11.5
Problem Statement	Infection rates at Salem Health Hospital were rising and hand hygiene compliance, monitored through observation, was averaging 74%.	A Lean Journey to Decrease Hospital-Acquired Infections
Background/Evidence	Hand Hygiene is the single most important act to decrease hospital-acquired infections. Using Lean methodologies, such as Four Step Problem Solving (4SPS), Standard Work (SW), and bringing departmental accountability through Visual Management (VM), Salem Health Hospital implemented and sustained adoption of the World Health Organization's "Five Moments for Hand Hygiene."	
Aim/Objectives	The following hypothesis was tested: If this hospital utilizes Lean methodologies to improve hand hygiene compliance to 92%, then we will see a 50% reduction in hospital acquired infections.	

(continued)

EXHIBIT 11.5
A Lean Journey
to Decrease
Hospital-
Acquired
Infections
(continued)

Methods/Strategy	• An inter-professional team developed standard work for hand hygiene compliance (the best way we know how to do something right now) and created a standard audit process to reduce the risk of variation in measuring hand hygiene compliance. • Implementation of this standard work was championed by staff from every department. Champions conducted compliance observations and met monthly to share successes and problem-solve challenges. • To better understand the organizational barriers to hand hygiene compliance, the inter-professional team collaborated with unit champions using 4SPS, a Lean approach similar to PDCA (plan, do check, act), or the scientific method. • Compliance rates were made visible through a centralized database and frequent results reporting. • Process and outcome metrics were updated monthly, made visual in each department (VM), and addressed during staff huddles.
Outcomes and Takeaways	• By the end of the fiscal year, the organization achieved the goal of 92% hand hygiene compliance, with a 16% reduction in hospital-acquired infections. • While the hospital did not reach the 50% reduction in hospital-acquired infections, leaders learned to set stretch targets as opposed to easier-to-achieve goals.

Source: Reprinted from Nichols (2016). Used with permission.

Implementing Improvements

An understanding of systems provides implementation insights for managers. This section describes an implementation framework based on four system lessons: unintended consequences, small wins, begin with the end in mind, and creative tension.

Unintended Consequences

The principle of continuous improvement may be viewed as scalable; in other words, the size and scope of improvements may vary from very small to very large. While early efforts at improvement focused on continuously improving an individual process, an understanding of complex systems reveals that "we

EXHIBIT 11.6
Nested Systems

must almost always avoid focusing on just one element and pursuing only one goal; instead, we must pursue several goals at once" (Dörner 1996, 63–64). Managers must recognize that processes targeted for improvement interact with other processes in that system and are also "nested" in the larger system (exhibit 11.6). When implementing improvements, managers must also consider the effect of an improvement on the rest of the system.

In a large tertiary care hospital, one improvement effort was aimed at decreasing the amount of time patients spent on a ventilator after coronary bypass surgery. A patient's progress toward recovery could be greatly enhanced if she spent less time connected to a ventilator. The intensive care unit (ICU) improvement team thoughtfully took into account the upstream influences on the patient recovery process by inviting operating room staff and an anesthesiologist to be members of the improvement team. However, no acute care unit patient representative was included.

After bypass surgery, when a patient met the required clinical criteria, she was transferred from the ICU to the acute care unit. After the new ICU protocol was put into place, patients who had coronary bypass surgery began arriving in the acute care unit a day earlier and were sicker than patients who had been transferred under the old protocol. Although these patients were not on ventilators, the early transfer made a difference in other aspects of their care. The acute care unit found that although the same number of nurses was being scheduled, the higher patient acuity, which required more intense nursing care, led to inadequate staffing. After several weeks, the nurses in the acute care unit realized that a change had been made in the ICU's postoperative process. It took several months to hire additional acute care unit staff to meet the new patient acuity demands, during which time the existing nurses remained overworked, with the potential to compromise patient care quality.

Anticipating, identifying, measuring, and proactively managing unintended consequences should be considered in any improvement implementation

EXHIBIT 11.7
Anticipating
Unintended
Consequences

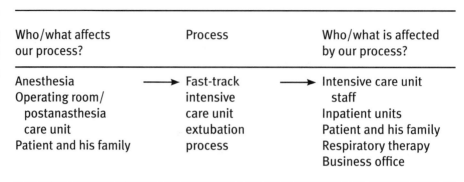

Who/what affects our process?	Process	Who/what is affected by our process?
Anesthesia Operating room/ postanasthesia care unit Patient and his family	→ Fast-track intensive care unit extubation process	→ Intensive care unit staff Inpatient units Patient and his family Respiratory therapy Business office

plan. Exhibit 11.7 illustrates how this ICU improvement team might have identified unintended consequences by asking not only "Who and what affects our process?" but also "Who and what is affected by our process?" Asking these questions early in the improvement effort would have allowed earlier coordination with those affected and reduced the negative impact of unintended consequences.

Another example of unintended consequences may be seen in how some institutions implement privacy policies required by the 1996 Health Insurance Portability and Accountability Act. An elderly patient with an infection was admitted to the hospital in a confused state. Her daughter was denied information about her condition, even though the daughter was her mother's designated medical proxy. Although the medical power of attorney documents were included in the patient's chart, the emergency department (ED) nurse refused to give out any information because the daughter was not on this patient's "approved visitor list" at the nurse's station. Because the well-intended privacy policies did not account for this particular circumstance, they actually interfered with communicating vital patient information to the ED care providers.

A lack of understanding and failure to anticipate unintended consequences may be considered a management planning error. Organizations may also consider inadequate monitoring of unintended consequences after implementing a change to be a management execution error (Reason 1995).

Small Wins

Using a small-wins strategy for implementing improvements in the larger system recognizes the dynamic complexity inherent in health services organizations. "Small wins provide information that facilitates learning and adaptation. Small wins are like miniature experiments that test implicit theories about resistance and opportunity and uncover both resources and barriers that were invisible before the situation was stirred up. . . . A series of small wins is also more structurally sound . . . because small wins are stable building blocks" (Weick 1984, 44).

Karl Weick (1984, 43), noted psychologist, defines a **small win** in the context of addressing social problems as "a concrete, complete, implemented outcome of moderate importance. By itself, one small win may seem unimportant. A series of wins at small but significant tasks, however, reveals a pattern that may attract allies, deter opponents, and lower resistance to subsequent proposals. Small wins are controllable opportunities that produce visible results."

small win
"a concrete, complete, implemented outcome of moderate importance" (Weick 1984, 43)

This approach promotes continuous improvement and also capitalizes on knowledge gained about system structure along the way. The benefits for managers are that small wins preserve gains and cannot unravel; they require less coordination to execute and are minimally affected by leadership, management, or administrative changes or turnover (Weick 1984). For employees, small wins are less stressful and are easier to comprehend and view as achievable. As a result, employees are more likely to comply with a small-wins intervention (Weick 1984).

Begin with the End in Mind

Consider two approaches to purchasing a new home. Every day for a week, Person A searches the real estate advertisements in the newspapers. His diligent search yields some properties that he is interested in, so he calls a Realtor for a tour of each. After seeing a certain property, he immediately knows it is his perfect house. The Realtor refers him to a mortgage company to work out the financing. Person A is confident that no problem will arise because, based on his own calculations, his salary will cover the monthly payments. But then he receives the bad news: He does not qualify for the financing. Payments on a new car bought six months earlier, outstanding credit card bills from a recent vacation, and insufficient savings all work against him. Person A only qualifies for a loan that is too small for his dream home.

Person A's coworker, Person B, has a hobby of scanning the real estate news. For years, Person B has been watching trends, so she has identified a particular area of the city in which she would like to purchase a house. Based on the average housing prices in that area, Person B calculates what she will need for a down payment and for monthly mortgage payments. She systematically accumulates the funds for the down payment, makes sure she pays her credit card balances down to zero every month, and prequalifies with a mortgage company. Although most of her friends and coworkers drive new cars, her car is five years old but completely paid for. When Person B's "perfect house" comes on the market, she is the first to see it and is able to complete the purchase without a problem. When Person A overhears Person B talking about her new address, Person A cannot believe it; he wonders, "How could she possibly afford that place when she makes the same salary as I do?"

The answer to Person A's question is that these coworkers used two entirely different approaches to planning and implementing their processes for buying houses. Person A used an approach called *forward planning*, which involves taking one step at a time and not knowing the next step until after the previous step is completed. Person B used an approach called **reverse planning** (Dörner 1996), which involves defining the desired result—in this case, her ideal house—and then working backward to determine a practical or logical starting point to the step-by-step process of getting to the result. In reverse planning, each step is a necessary precondition to the next step. By planning in this manner, Person B could make purposeful choices (e.g., not buying a new car, reducing her credit card debt) that would help her toward, rather than become barriers to, the goal of purchasing her ideal house.

Similar approaches have been described in the management literature. Habit 2 in *The Seven Habits of Highly Effective People* by Stephen Covey (1990) is to "begin with the end in mind." The "solution after next" principle, from Gerald Nadler and Shozo Hibino's *Breakthrough Thinking: The Seven Principles of Creative Problem Solving* (1994), indicates that more effective solutions may be generated "by working backward from an ideal target solution for the future."

reverse planning defining the desired result and then working backward to determine a practical or logical starting point to the step-by-step process of getting to the result

Creative Tension

Just as the medical specialty of surgery consists of such subspecialties as neurosurgery, orthopedic surgery, and plastic surgery, the field of systems thinking also consists of subfields. One of these subfields is called *structural dynamics*. Tension resolution is the fundamental building block in structural dynamics (Fritz 1996). When a difference exists between one thing and another, the resulting discrepancy creates the tendency toward movement. One type of tension found in organizations is called **creative tension**, which is formed by the discrepancy between an organization's current level of performance and its desired level of performance and vision for the future.

creative tension the state engendered by the discrepancy between an organization's current level of performance and its desired level and vision for the future

The rubber band metaphor has been used to illustrate the concept of creative tension (Senge 1990). Think of holding a rubber band, with one end in each hand and one hand above the other. Stretch the rubber band, and feel the tension of the pull. Think of the higher hand as vision—that is, the desired future state of the organization. Think of the lower hand as current reality—that is, the current level of the organization's performance. The tension may be released from the rubber band in only three ways.

The first way is to let go of the end clasped by the lower hand. As the tension is released, the rubber band snaps toward the top hand. The greater the tension, the faster and more forcefully the rubber band will return to the top hand. In organizations, this tension resolution may be seen as drawing the organization toward a vision. The second way to relieve tension is to let go of the end clasped by the higher hand. As the tension is released, the rubber band snaps toward the bottom hand. In organizations, this tension resolution may be seen as maintaining the status quo or stagnating. The third way to relieve tension is by stretching the rubber band beyond its natural limit and breaking it. In organizations, this type of tension resolution may be seen in situations where too much is expected, too fast, and without adequate resources; as a result, people and processes "break." Symptoms of this last type of tension resolution include employee turnover, morale problems, poor performance, and medical errors.

When organizational change and performance are viewed through a systems perspective, tension resolution is the key tool for changing behavior. The essential elements for creative tension to be present in an organization are current reality, vision, and an actual or perceived gap between the two. The manager's role is to consciously generate, make visible, and regulate creative tension in the organization to leverage the resulting tendency toward movement (Heifetz and Laurie 2001).

Performance measurement is one way managers describe current reality; organizational assessment is another. The Baldrige Performance Excellence Program (BPEP 2015) criteria for healthcare are a useful guide for organizational self-assessment. An organizational self-assessment conducted at regular intervals (e.g., annually, biannually) provides managers with the opportunity and impetus to systematically reexamine, document, and communicate current reality relative to desired organizational activities, strategies, and performance results.

People in an organization commonly define the organization's performance reality on the basis of their own mental models, knowledge, and previous experiences. As a result, some may hold an overly positive view of the organization's current reality and others may hold a disproportionately negative view. By using objective measurement and assessment techniques, a consistent and clearer picture of the performance reality can be developed. A shared understanding of current reality and performance gaps is necessary for creative tension. Creative tension creates tension resolution and, in turn, traction for change.

Framework for Implementation

Breakthrough technologies are most often associated with clinical breakthroughs in diagnosis (e.g., magnetic resonance imaging), intervention (e.g., minimally invasive surgery techniques), treatment (e.g., new drugs), or prevention (e.g., polio vaccination)—posing a challenge for healthcare managers. Unlike a breakthrough resulting from a technical invention, a managerial breakthrough may be defined through the vision or context of the department, service, or organization. The ideal vision may stretch as far as needed to illuminate the performance gap and thus establish creative tension. Management breakthroughs

EXHIBIT 11.8
Implementation
Framework:
Breakthrough
Vision,
Incremental
Implementation

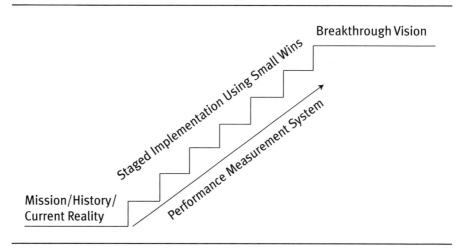

may be seen in (1) areas such as philosophies, approaches, and tools that enable managers to promote innovations in the operating environment, and (2) work processes that enable patients to fully realize the benefit of advancements in clinical technology.

Understanding the history of the organization, department, service, or technology helps managers identify and uncover issues, attitudes, or past events that may undermine implementation. An understanding of the past also promotes buy-in for change by grounding the change efforts in their continuity with past events.

A clear statement of vision describes the purpose and justifies the existence of an organization, department, service, or process. Implementing small wins in the direction of the vision represents continuous improvement in the system as it is defined. This conceptual framework for implementation, referred to as *breakthrough vision, incremental implementation*, is illustrated in exhibit 11.8.

The steps taken toward achieving the vision must not be so great that they distract the care providers' focus and attention and place patient safety and outcomes at risk (Reason 1990). However, the steps taken in implementation must be large enough so that slipping back to the previous way of doing things is not possible. A step may have one or several concurrent interventions. Some interventions may be completed quickly, and others may be broken down and achieved in several sequential steps. The diagonal line beneath the steps that points toward the ideal vision is labeled *Performance Measurement System*, indicating that progress toward the vision and measures of unintended consequences are continuously monitored and evaluated.

Summary

Just as providers use the scientific method to systematically solve problems in the clinical arena, managers also should use systematic critical thinking approaches when designing improvements. Approaches introduced in this chapter include the PDCA cycle, the Six Sigma DMAIC cycle, and Lean improvement strategies. Numerous improvement tools to document and understand processes, to organize and analyze contributing causes to process problems, to prioritize problems, and to monitor improvements are available to managers. The breakthrough vision, incremental implementation framework takes into account lessons from complex systems. The approaches, tools, and framework discussed in this chapter can strengthen managers' ability to design and implement successful improvements while decreasing the likelihood of managerial planning and execution errors.

Exercise 11.1

Objective: To plan a rapid cycle improvement project using the IHI improvement model.

Instructions: You will conduct a seven-day rapid cycle improvement project for the following problem: Food in your refrigerator is often not eaten by the "best before" date and has to be thrown out. You start the project by answering three improvement questions:

1. What am I trying to accomplish?
2. How will I know the change is an improvement?
3. What change can I make that will result in improvement?

You may choose to record your responses on the Improvement Questions Worksheet that follows or on one similar to it.

Improvement Questions Worksheet	
What Am I Trying to Accomplish? Write a short (one or two sentence), general statement describing what you want to accomplish.	
How Do I Know the Change Is an Improvement? Identify one numerical target for this improvement cycle, including expected time frame for achieving the target.	
What Change Can I Make That Will Result in Improvement? Describe one small process change you can implement and measure in seven days.	

Exercise 11.2

Objective: To practice anticipating unintended consequences.

Instructions: For questions *a* through *e*, you may choose to record your responses on the Unintended Consequences Worksheet that follows or on one similar to it.

a. Select any process that takes place in a health services organization. Write that process in the center column, column A.

b. In column B, identify who (person, group, department, stakeholder) influences the process. In other words, think about the activities and people upstream from your process.

c. Identify who is influenced by the process in column C. In other words, think about the activities and people downstream from your process.

d. Extend your response one more time. Identify who influences the items in column B. Write your response in column D.

e. Identify who is influenced by the items in column C. Write your response in column E.

f. Describe one or two unintended consequences created by a change in the process identified in column A.

Unintended Consequences Worksheet				
D	B	A	C	E
Who influences the entries in column B?	Who influences the process?	The process	Who is influenced by the process?	Who is influenced by the entries in column C?

Companion Readings

Bandyopadhyay, J. K., and K. Coppens. 2005. "Six Sigma Approach to Healthcare Quality and Productivity Management." *International Journal of Quality & Productivity Management.* Published December 2015. www.isqpm.org/2005%20 Journal/JRNLINDEX-05.htm.

Grosfeld, J. L. 2010. "Progress and Its Unintended Consequences." *American Journal of Surgery* 199 (3): 284–88.

MacInnes, R. L., and M. L. Dean. 2013. *The Lean Memory Jogger for Healthcare.* Milwaukee, WI: ASQ Quality Press.

Michigan Public Health Institute. 2012. *Embracing Quality in Public Health: A Practitioner's Quality Improvement Guidebook,* 2nd ed. Office of Accreditation and Quality Improvement. www.mphiaccredandqi.org/qi-guidebook.

Scoville, R., and K. Little. 2014. *Comparing Lean and Quality Improvement.* Institute for Healthcare Improvement. Accessed October 24. www.ihi.org/resources/ Pages/IHIWhitePapers.

Silver, S. A., Z. Harel, R. McQuillan, A. V. Weizman, A. Thomas, G. M. Chertow, G. Nesrallah, C. M. Bell, and C. T. Chan. 2016. "How to Begin a Quality Improvement Project." *Clinical Journal of the American Society of Nephrology* 11 (5): 893–900.

Sobek, D. K. II, and C. Jimmerson. 2016. "Innovating Health Care Delivery Using Toyota Production System Principles." Accessed October 24. www.montana .edu/dsobek/a3/ioc-grant/index.html.

Web Resources

American Society for Quality: http://asq.org/learn-about-quality
Institute for Healthcare Improvement: www.ihi.org

References

American Society for Quality. 2004. "Plan-Do-Check-Act (PDCA) Cycle." Accessed July 15, 2016. www.asq.org/learn-about-quality/project-planning-tools/ overview/pdca-cycle.html.

Bagian, J., B. King, P. Mills, and S. McKnight. 2011. "Improving RCA Performance: The Cornerstone Award and Power of Positive Reinforcement." *BMJ Quality and Safety* 20 (11): 974–82.

Baldrige Performance Excellence Program (BPEP). 2015. *2015–2016 Baldrige Excellence Framework: A Systems Approach to Improving Your Organization's Performance (Health Care)*. Gaithersburg, MD: US Department of Commerce, National Institute of Standards and Technology.

Berczuk, C. 2008. "The Lean Hospital." *Hospitalist*. Published June 1. www .the-hospitalist.org/article/the-lean-hospital.

Coles, C. 2002. "Developing Professional Judgment." *Journal of Continuing Education in the Health Professions* 22 (1): 3–10.

Covey, S. R. 1990. *The Seven Habits of Highly Effective People*. New York: Simon & Schuster.

Dean, J. W., and D. E. Bowen. 2000. "Management Theory and Total Quality: Improving Research and Practice Through Theory Development." In *The Quality Movement and Organization Theory*, edited by R. E. Cole and W. R. Scott, 3–22. Thousand Oaks, CA: SAGE Publications.

Deming, W. E. 2000. *Out of the Crisis*. Cambridge, MA: MIT Press.

Dennis, P. 2009. *Getting the Right Things Done*. Cambridge, MA: Lean Enterprise Institute.

Dörner, D. 1996. *The Logic of Failure: Recognizing and Avoiding Error in Complex Situations*. Reading, MA: Perseus Books.

Fritz, R. 1996. *Corporate Tides: The Inescapable Laws of Organizational Structure*. San Francisco: Berrett-Koehler Publishers.

Guyatt, G., D. Rennie, M. O. Meade, and D. J. Cook. 2015. *Users' Guides to the Medical Literature: A Manual for Evidence-Based Clinical Practice*, 3rd ed. New York: McGraw-Hill Education.

Heifetz, R. A., and D. L. Laurie. 2001. "The Work of Leadership." *Harvard Business Review* 79 (11): 131–40.

Institute for Healthcare Improvement (IHI). 2016. "How to Improve." Accessed July 15. www.ihi.org/IHI/Topics/Improvement/ImprovementMethods/ HowToImprove.

Lavallee, D. 2011. "Improve Patient Safety with Lean Techniques." In *Error Reduction in Health Care: A Systems Approach*, 2nd ed., edited by P. L. Spath, 245–65. San Francisco: Jossey-Bass.

Lighter, D. E. 2011. *Advanced Performance Improvement in Health Care: Principles and Methods*. Sudbury, MA: Jones & Bartlett.

McLaughlin, D. B., and J. R. Olson. 2012. *Healthcare Operations Management*, 2nd ed. Chicago: Health Administration Press.

Mukherjee, S. 2008. "A Dose of DMAIC: Hospital's Six Sigma and Lean Efforts Benefit Patients and Profitability." *Quality Progress* 41 (8): 44–51.

Muralidharan, K. 2015. *Six Sigma for Organizational Excellence: A Statistical Approach*. New York: Springer.

Nadler, G., and S. Hibino. 1994. *Breakthrough Thinking: The Seven Principles of Creative Problem Solving*. Rocklin, CA: Prima Publishing.

Nichols, J. 2016. Personal communication with author, August 16.

Reason, J. 1995. "Understanding Adverse Events: Human Factors." *Quality and Safety in Healthcare* 4 (2): 80–89.

———. 1990. *Human Error*. Cambridge, UK: Cambridge University Press.

Scriven, M., and R. Paul. 2016. "Defining Critical Thinking." Critical Thinking Community. Accessed July 15. www.criticalthinking.org/pages/defining-critical-thinking/410.

Senge, P. M. 1990. *The Fifth Discipline: The Art and Practice of the Learning Organization*. New York: Doubleday Currency.

Sobek, D. K., and C. Jimmerson. 2006. "A3 Reports: Tool for Organizational Transformation." Proceedings of the 2006 Industrial Engineering Research Conference, Orlando, FL. Accessed July 15, 2016. www.montana.edu/dsobek/a3/ioc-grant/documents/IERC_2006.pdf.

Spath, P. L. 2013. *Introduction to Healthcare Quality Management*, 2nd ed. Chicago: Health Administration Press.

Varkey, P., J. Cunningham, and S. Bisping. 2007. "Medication Reconciliation in the Outpatient Setting." *The Joint Commission Journal on Quality and Patient Safety* 33 (5): 286–92.

Varkey, P., M. K. Reller, and R. K. Resar. 2007. "Basics of Quality Improvement in Health Care." *Mayo Clinic Proceedings* 82 (6): 735–39.

Weick, K. E. 1984. "Small Wins: Redefining the Scale of Social Problems." *American Psychologist* 39 (1): 40–49.

Womack, J. P., D. Jones, and D. Roos. 2007. *The Machine That Changed the World*. New York: Free Press.

Zidel, T. 2007. *A Lean Guide to Transforming Healthcare*. Milwaukee, WI: ASQ Quality Press.

Appendix 11.1

Questions to Answer During PDCA Cycle Steps

Plan
Find an Opportunity

- What causes you the most trouble most often?
- What does the customer complain about most often?
- What would help make the job easier, the service faster, the process more efficient, the productivity greater, and the operation less costly?
- Can you measure success?

Organize the Team

- Who should be on the team to solve the problem?
- Do we have the right people involved?
- Are the necessary departments, or necessary shifts, represented?
- Will we need to bring in content experts to assist?
- Is the customer represented?

Clarify

- What is not happening?
- What is not known?
- How is the customer affected?
- Who should be included in this analysis?
- What are the known problems and the symptoms?
- What is the current condition?
- Does the process exhibit unnecessary performance variation? Can you distinguish between common cause and special cause variation?
- What influence does each component have on the others?
- Are there other areas, upstream or downstream, that are affected, and if so, how much?
- Can these areas be included in the problem definition and plan development?
- What methods are available to produce more information about the problem?

- Can the problem be broken into smaller, more predictable components?
- What new thinking or perspective might represent a breakthrough?
- What would be the ideal condition (one without any trace of barriers)?
- What are the elements of the ideal condition?
- What are the improvement priorities?

Derive a Solution

- Have you analyzed all the significant symptoms?
- Has the team formulated theories for the causes?
- How will you test the theories to confirm their causal relationship?
- Once tested, are the root causes either confirmed or rejected as not related?
- Have alternative solutions been identified?
- Have alternative solutions been prioritized?
- Who will implement the corrective actions?
- How will the corrective actions be implemented?
- How will you overcome change resistance?
- What can be done to anticipate and eliminate other potential roadblocks?
- Are the resource requirements known, and do they conflict with other efforts?
- What communications are required to minimize disruptions or surprises?
- Are the necessary incentives, facilities, and equipment in place to make the solution a success?

Do
Pilot the Change

- Is there a plan for implementing the corrective action(s)?
- How will you check the progress of the plan?
- Who are the most important people to ensure successful implementation?
- What factors will determine whether people will do what is needed?
- What is the adequacy (in terms of time, amount, effectiveness) of the feedback?
- What are the lessons learned that can be applied to the total rollout?

Check
Study the Results

- Can the results be verified?
- Who should collect the data and to whom should they be reported to maintain their effectiveness?
- Are there any other measurements that need to be in place?
- What will ensure that this new process is maintained and does not deteriorate over time?
- Who should collect the information to audit the process, and to whom should it be reported to maintain its effectiveness?
- Are there other improvements that can be made?
- When you check the results against the outcome measures early in the project, was the intended level of improvement attained?
- What would have made the implementation proceed more easily?
- How can what was learned be used in other improvement projects?

Act
Implement and Evaluate

- Was the pilot study successful? If yes, how will you implement the solution throughout the organization?
- If the pilot was unsuccessful, where was the breakdown? In the implementation phase? In the diagnosis of root causes?
- If there are other root causes, repeat the Plan phase.
- Once a successful solution is implemented throughout the organization, is there a need for additional improvement? If yes, begin the improvement cycle again.
- How will the process be kept current over time?
- Can you dismantle the old way to keep it from returning?

Source: Adapted from D. Rohe and P. L. Spath. 2005. *101 Tools for Improving Health Care Performance*. Forest Grove, OR: Brown-Spath & Associates. Used with permission.

USING IMPROVEMENT TEAMS AND TOOLS

Learning Objectives

After completing this chapter, you should be able to

- identify strategies for creating improvement project teams;
- describe the role of managers in team decision making;
- differentiate how, when, and why to use common improvement tools; and
- recognize what tools are best to use at each step of an improvement project.

The nursing shared leadership committee in a midsize hospital came up with a great idea for improving the work environment for bedside nurses, who spend time in face-to-face group meetings that take them away from patient care duties. The committee proposed using electronic message boards to reduce the need for these meetings. The nurses could use this medium to complete some group work during their downtime rather than depart from units to attend formal meetings. This change would potentially help nurses be more productive at the bedside and improve the way they get their work done. The electronic message boards could also be used to update everyone on the work of various committees and share evidence-based practice recommendations.

The information technology department set up electronic message boards for each unit, and nurses were instructed on how to use the medium and its purpose. However, what seemed like a great idea did not catch on with the bedside nurses. Simply making this new communication tool available was not enough to get people to start accessing the board to interact with one another. The value of using the message boards for communication was unclear to people at the grassroots level, and face-to-face meetings had been their usual way of interacting for years. The committee chairs, charge nurses, and clinical leaders were not made responsible for regularly posting content on the message boards. The staff nurses quickly stopped logging into the message boards when they found very little to read.

This change effort failed for several reasons. First, and most important, it was initiated with a top-down approach. The electronic message boards may have been a great idea; however, the frontline nurses were not engaged in the improvement project. The idea was pushed down from the upper levels of the nursing department, and the message boards were designed without any input from staff. Whether the frontline staff considered improved productivity and enhanced communication to be important goals was never fully explored before implementation.

Often, improvement projects result in people being asked to change the way they have always done things—thus, a bottom-up, team approach is more likely to be successful. This chapter describes how managers can reduce the likelihood of unsuccessful improvement projects. The first step is to charter the project, which involves clearly defining the project goals and scope. Next, the members of the improvement project team need to be carefully chosen. This chapter also discusses the various improvement tools that will be used by the team to understand the current process and select the best interventions for achieving the performance improvement goals.

Charter Improvement Projects

Before embarking on an improvement project, the manager or managers in the departments or units affected by an improvement project should establish clarity about the project scope (areas affected) and purpose (desired outcome). The more issues clarified up front, the less likely the team will be to experience false starts. A written project charter is essentially a contract between the organization's management and the improvement team.

The project leader and the sponsoring manager(s) may jointly create the chapter, or it may be created at the first team meeting. Issues that should be addressed in creating the project charter include these (Rohe and Spath 2005):

- Purpose: In one or two sentences, describe the purpose of the project. The brief explanations should define, in specific terms, what the project is expected to achieve.
- Objectives: List some of the measurable outcomes of the project. The objectives should answer the questions, "How will we achieve our purpose?" and "What are the signs of success?"
- Deliverables: What are the tangible milestones anticipated along the way? What are the progress points that can be expected? When defining deliverables, include dates—they add commitment and urgency to the project completion.

- Team and team resources: Identify the people and resources needed to analyze, create, and carry out the purpose.
- Success factors: These are the essential elements outside the team needed to make the project successful, such as buy-in from the staff or financial resources.

A typical charter consists of a one-page summary of critical details of the project, allowing all stakeholders to agree on the goals to be achieved, the scope, the time line, and the resources needed for the project to be successful. Exhibit 12.1 illustrates a project charter template.

EXHIBIT 12.1
Improvement Project Charter Template

Project Title	
Purpose What are we trying to achieve?	
Objectives What are we trying to achieve? How will we know we got there?	The new/redesigned process will (be specific): • • •
Deliverables What must be done to achieve the objectives?	The team is expected to complete the following: By __/__: By __/__: By __/__: By __/__:
Team and Resources	Core project team members: Leader: Other members: People who have knowledge or skills that will be helpful for completing the project:
Success Factors What leadership and resources are needed to make this improvement a success?	• • • •

Source: Adapted from Rohe and Spath (2005). Used with permission.

Once the initial project charter is drafted, its completeness can be evaluated using the following criteria:

- It specifies, in detail, the performance problem to be addressed.
- It contains measurable objectives that include target goals to be achieved.
- It sets realistic deadlines and expectations.
- It contains defined time lines for completion of the project.
- It is relevant to the organization's strategic quality goals.

If revisions are needed in the charter, the team should make them before the start of the project. Otherwise, the lack of clarity can eventually derail the improvement effort.

Performance Improvement Teams

Improvement methodologies such as Plan, Do, Check, Act and Six Sigma serve as critical thinking frameworks for managers studying any problems that may arise. Project teams also use these methodologies as they work to improve performance in a particular functional area. Regardless of the model used for an improvement project, assembling a team of people personally knowledgeable about the process to be improved is essential. Composition of the team (the number and identity of the members) and meeting frequency and duration are guided by the process purpose and scope. The questions that influence makeup of the team should include the following:

- What knowledge is required to understand the process and design the actual improvement intervention(s)?
- How should the team be designed to support the processes needed to accomplish implementation within the project constraints?

The number of team members needed to successfully achieve the project objective will vary. Managers need to take into account the number of staff members that can be taken away from their usual work without adversely affecting services. The optimal size of a team is between five and eight individuals. However, the size of the team is not as important as the diversity of its members. The team should include people who have different roles and perspectives on the process to be improved (Agency for Healthcare Research and Quality 2013). Individual contributions during a meeting tend to diminish as the size of the group grows beyond six members.

Just as managers use human resources practices that promote matching an employee's traits with the requirements of the job, managers may also match employees with the various roles and stages required in a change or improvement process. Problems in group processes tend to arise from a mismatch between a project stage and an individual rather than from problems inherent in the individuals themselves. Intentionally engaging individuals at the appropriate time, as well as offering support or requesting patience during other times, can enhance the effectiveness of both the team and the manager.

For instance, a team member favoring concrete thinking may get frustrated with creating a vision, though he will be essential in determining the logistics of implementing process changes. Someone with well-developed interpersonal or relational skills can be on the alert for any staff morale issues related to the changes. An employee who is good at seeing the big picture will be invaluable in identifying unintended consequences. A team member who is detail oriented can be an ideal choice for monitoring progress and ensuring follow-through; another member who is action oriented can make sure the project moves along on schedule.

Meeting Schedules and Frequency

Typically, team meetings are held weekly, biweekly, or monthly, and they generally last one to two hours. Some of the challenges associated with this approach in health services organizations include the time-consuming patient care duties required of clinical providers, the late arrival of team members because of other competing responsibilities, the need to devote portions of the meeting to updating team members, and dwindling interest as the project drags on.

Consider an alternative approach. If managers use a systematic method for approaching improvements, they will begin to get a sense for the total team time required for an improvement effort. For example, a team may take about 40 hours to complete the various phases of an improvement project. If the improvement effort is constrained by time or dollars, the team is faced with increasing its own productivity or reducing its own cycle time. With this limitation in mind, the 40 hours of time may be distributed in a variety of ways other than in one-to-two-hour segments. For example, ten four-hour meetings or five eight-hour meetings may better meet the needs of a particular project team. The meetings may occur once a week for ten weeks, twice a week for five weeks, or every day for one week. Based on the work environment, a strategy may be selected that balances project team productivity, daily operational capacity and requirements, the scope of the desired improvement, and project deadlines.

A concentrated team meeting schedule has several advantages:

- It demonstrates the organization's or management's commitment to change.
- It saves duplication and repeated work associated with bringing everyone up to speed at each meeting.
- It establishes traction by contributing to the elements of creative tension.
- It reduces the cycle time from concept to implementation.
- It forces managers and teams out of the "firefighting" mentality into one of purposely fixing not just the symptoms of problems but also the underlying problems themselves.

Decision Making

Consensus is a commonly employed approach to decision making in which the team seeks to find a proposal acceptable enough that all members can support it (Scholtes, Joiner, and Streibel 2003). Seeking consensus may, however, reduce decisions to the lowest common denominator (Lencioni 2002). In a team comprising primarily concrete, practical, linearly thinking members, how likely is it that an idea posed by the one creative, conceptual team member will gain enough acceptance to be considered a possible solution to a problem? Conversely, on a team of creative, conceptual innovators who are quickly moving forward on an idea without regard for the practical considerations of implementation, how likely will it be that they embrace the input from the one concrete, practical, linearly thinking team member? In either case, the result will be less than optimal. The best result (i.e., improvement intervention) in these two circumstances may come from listening to the "outlier"; perhaps that team member's perspective best matches the requirements of the decision at hand.

Using decision criteria is an alternative to consensus. For example, in one improvement effort, the criteria for pursuing an improvement idea include the following (Kelly 1998):

- Does it fit within the goal of the effort?
- Does it meet customer requirements?
- Does it meet regulatory or accreditation requirements?
- Does it remain consistent with the department's or organization's purpose?
- Does it support the vision?
- Does it demonstrate consistency with quality principles?

In this case, team members are expected to question and challenge each improvement idea. Those that meet the criteria are further evaluated by the team. All team members may not completely understand an idea the first time it is discussed, but the team can save time by quickly discarding ideas that do not meet criteria. Instead, they can then spend time on understanding and evaluating ideas that do meet criteria.

Managers can help support team decision making by staying informed about the progress of improvement projects. They can best keep up with events through periodic meetings with the team leaders. Unexpected "drop ins" by team managers in search of project updates can be disruptive to the team process. Some types of questions a project team leader would find helpful to discuss face-to-face with the manager or managers affected by the improvement project are listed in exhibit 12.2. These questions are especially useful during the action-planning stage of a project, when they can provide the team leader with a better understanding of leadership support, communication needs, and direction.

Improvement Tools and Techniques

In most improvement projects, regardless of the methodology followed, similar process improvement tools and techniques are used for understanding the performance problem and how to correct it. Appendix 12.1 provides descriptions of many frequently used tools and techniques. Some items in the list are described in greater detail in this chapter or covered in chapter 10.

EXHIBIT 12.2
Project Team Leader and Manager Discussion Questions

- Does the manager have any preset expectations about what needs to be done to improve performance? Is the manager open to accepting the team's recommendations, or does she have alternatives?
- Are the desired time frames for completing the improvement interventions realistic? Can the manager support these time frames?
- What resources (dollars, time, etc.) can be spent on the improvement interventions? What are the resource limitations?
- Is the manager willing to tolerate possible dips in productivity or service while the process changes are being implemented?
- Will the manager help prepare people to minimize disruptions during the implementation of improvement plans?
- What will make the manager anxious during the intervention design and implementation phase? How soon does he expect to see positive changes?
- If an individual or group resists making the needed changes, will the manager be willing to initiate appropriate pressure to correct the problem?
- Will the manager help dismantle the "old way" of doing things by holding fast to and reinforcing the redesigned way until it has had time to prove its effectiveness?

Source: Adapted from Rohe and Spath (2005). Used with permission.

Readers are encouraged to learn more about tools not explained in depth here by using the resources found at the end of this chapter.

Document the Process

Some of the most valuable improvement tools are those that help managers and teams better understand work processes. Often, a process is followed because "that's how we've always done it" or because a certain way of doing things has simply evolved over time. Before a process can be improved, it must be understood. The tools described in this section help managers and teams understand processes by documenting the steps involved.

process
"an organized group of related activities that work together to transform one or more kinds of input into outputs that are of value to the customer" (ASQ 2016a)

According to the American Society for Quality (ASQ), a **process** is "an organized group of related activities that work together to transform one or more kinds of input into outputs that are of value to the customer" (ASQ 2016a). This definition suggests the following key features of a process (ASQ 2016a; italics added):

- A process is a *group of activities*, not just one.
- The activities that make up a process are not random or ad hoc; they are *related and organized.*
- All the activities in a process must work together toward a *common goal.*
- Processes exist to create *results your customers care about.*

process flowchart
graphical representation of the steps in a process or project

A **process flowchart** is a graphical representation of the steps in a process or project. Types of activities in the process are represented by variously shaped symbols. An oval indicates the start and end of the process, a rectangle indicates a process action step, and a diamond indicates a decision that must be made in the process. Depending on the decision, the process follows different paths. A simple process flowchart is illustrated in exhibit 12.3. Clinical providers may already be familiar with this tool, as many clinical algorithms and guidelines are communicated using process flowcharts. Professionals from other specialties, such as laboratory, radiology, and information systems, may also be familiar with this tool, as more complex versions of a process flowchart are used to document technical standard operating procedures or data and information flow.

deployment flowchart
process flowchart diagram that indicates who is responsible for which steps of the process

At times, many individuals, departments, or organizations are involved in carrying out different steps of a single process. In such cases, a **deployment flowchart** (vertical flowchart) or "swim lanes" chart (horizontal flowchart) is used to indicate who is responsible for which steps of the process. Efforts to improve coordination of process steps may be enhanced by identifying, documenting, and understanding the essential handoffs that occur in a process.

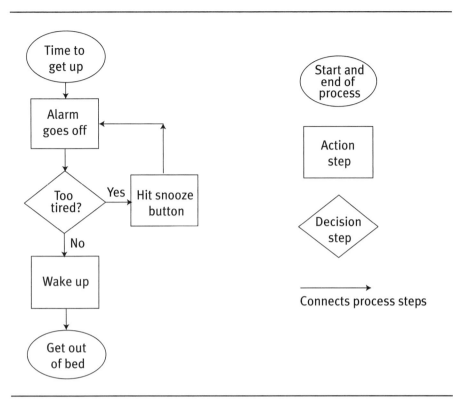

EXHIBIT 12.3
Simple Process
Flowchart

Exhibit 12.4 shows simple deployment flowcharts illustrating coordination between an orthodontist and an oral surgeon in providing care for a teenage patient.

Using a flowchart to document a process allows managers and teams to see a picture of the process. Often, just seeing a picture leads to obvious ideas for improvement. Additional benefits include the opportunity to distinguish the distinct steps involved; identify unnecessary steps; understand vulnerabilities where breakdowns, mistakes, or delays are likely to occur; detect rework loops that contribute to inefficiency and quality waste; and define who carries out which step and when. The process of discussing, reviewing, and documenting a process using a flowchart provides the opportunity for clarifying operating assumptions, identifying variation in practice, and establishing agreement on how work should be done.

Uncover Improvement Opportunities

A **cause-and-effect diagram** is a tool for organizing and documenting, in a structured format, the causes of a problem (Scholtes, Joiner, and Streibel 2003). The diagram may capture actual (observed) causes and possible (from brainstorming) causes. Kaoru Ishikawa, a Japanese quality management specialist, originally created this tool for use in product design and defect prevention.

cause-and-effect diagram (or fishbone or Ishikawa diagram) tool for organizing and documenting, in a structured format, the causes of a problem

EXHIBIT 12.4
Simple
Deployment
Flowcharts

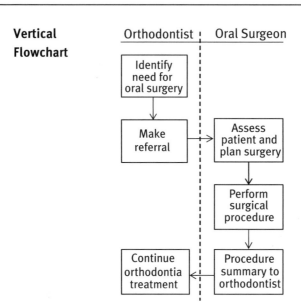

EXHIBIT 12.4
Simple
Deployment
Flowcharts

Vertical Flowchart

Horizontal Flowchart

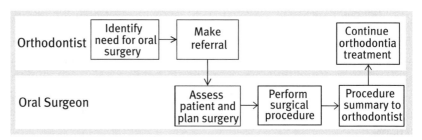

Because this diagram resembles a fish (the head represents the problem and the bones represent the causes), it is also referred to as a *fishbone diagram* (see exhibit 12.5). The problem is written on the far right of the diagram. Categories of causes are represented by the diagonal lines (bones) connected to the horizontal line (spine), which leads to the problem (head). The bones of the fish may be labeled in a variety of ways to represent categories of causes, including people, plant and equipment, policies, procedures, manpower, methods, and materials. Exhibit 12.6 is an example of a fishbone diagram.

EXHIBIT 12.5
How the
Fishbone
Diagram Got Its
Name

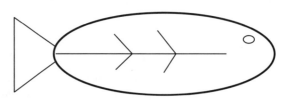

EXHIBIT 12.6
Fishbone
Diagram
Example

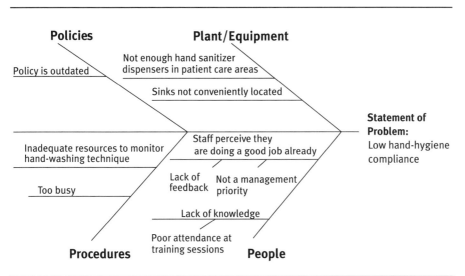

In exhibit 12.6, the problem is stated at the head of the fish (low hand-hygiene compliance) and the categories of causes are labeled as policies, procedure, people, and plant/equipment. Detailed causes are identified and represented by the small bones of the fish shown in the people category.

Stating the problem is the most important step in creating the fishbone diagram. Problem statements that are too narrow, vague, or poorly constructed can limit this tool's effectiveness in the improvement process. Users may be tempted to begin generating solutions (rather than documenting causes) in a fishbone diagram. However, users should take care to focus on cause, because identifying solutions too soon also limits the tool's usefulness and the opportunity to further investigate the problem.

A **causal loop diagram** is used to display the dynamic between cause and effect from a relational standpoint. While cause-and-effect diagrams elicit the categories of causes that affect a problem, causal loops show the interrelation between causes and their effects. When finished, a causal loop diagram provides an understanding of the positive and negative reinforcements that describe the system of behavior.

Exhibit 12.7 shows a simple causal loop diagram, including a problem statement: Maintaining qualified operating room (OR) staff during the nursing shortage is getting difficult. The causal loop diagram illustrates the behaviors that affect system outcomes. The cause-to-effect relationship is determined to be reinforcing (+) or negative (−). These designations do not indicate that the relationship is good or bad. They just mean that as the cause intensifies, effects do too, and as the cause diminishes, the effect does also.

An advantage of causal loops is that they depersonalize the process. People can point at the arrows in the loop that are reinforcing the problem

causal loop diagram
visual representation that displays the dynamic between cause and effect from a relational standpoint

EXHIBIT 12.7
Causal Loop
Diagram
Example

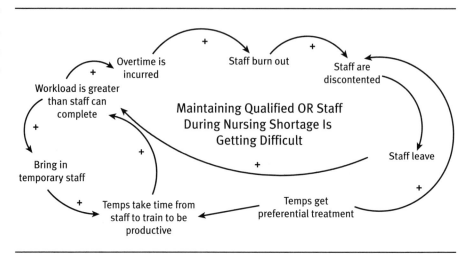

Maintaining Qualified OR Staff
During Nursing Shortage Is
Getting Difficult

Source: Adapted from Rohe and Spath (2005). Used with permission.

instead of pointing at people. The causal loop diagram illustrates the behaviors that affect system outcomes.

Not all identified causes influence the problem equally. Data about how important causes are or how often causes occur aid managers in prioritizing and selecting improvement interventions. A **Pareto chart** is a helpful tool in this process. In appearance, it is like a histogram, but with the data sorted in order of decreasing frequency of events; it also includes other annotations to highlight the *Pareto principle*. The Pareto chart is named after nineteenth-century economist Vilfredo Pareto and refers to the **Pareto principle**, which suggests "most effects come from relatively few causes; that is, 80 percent of the effects come from 20 percent of the possible causes" (ASQ 2016b).

Exhibit 12.8 is an example of a Pareto chart based on data collected about the causes in exhibit 12.6. Prior to collecting and displaying the data, a nursing manager plans an educational session (e.g., how to wash hands). However, after systematically analyzing the problem, the manager realizes that the cause is the availability of supplies. He installs more hand sanitizer dispensers and provides small bottles for staff to carry in their pockets.

Select Improvement Actions

Once the causes of a problem are understood and opportunities for improvement are clearly identified, actions intended to resolve the problems are selected. A team may have several ideas of what actions must be taken. However, a **decision matrix** that "evaluates and prioritizes a list of options" (ASQ 2016c) is an improvement tool that can help the team gain consensus.

To use a decision matrix, sometimes called a *prioritization matrix*, the team first comes up with criteria for judging the proposed actions (e.g., easy

Pareto chart
image similar to a histogram, but with the data sorted in order of decreasing frequency of events and with other annotations to highlight the Pareto principle

Pareto principle
theory that "most effects come from relatively few causes; that is, 80 percent of the effects come from 20 percent of the possible causes" (ASQ 2016b)

decision matrix
improvement tool that "evaluates and prioritizes a list of options" (ASQ 2016c)

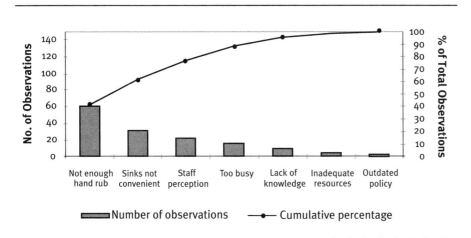

EXHIBIT 12.8
Pareto Chart
Example

or hard to implement, low or high cost, low or high impact). The members then judge actions against the goal of the project using these criteria and a numeric rating system. For instance, if the goal of a nursing care center's improvement project is to reduce resident falls by 20 percent, the criteria are applied individually by team members to each action being considered. An example of a simple decision matrix for the patient fall reduction project is illustrated in exhibit 12.9. Actions receiving higher scores are considered the best to implement. The team may ultimately implement all the actions being proposed, using the decision matrix to prioritize which actions to implement first.

If the criteria are not deemed by the team to be of equal importance, various statistical methods can be used to numerically weight each criterion (Minnesota Department of Health [MDH] 2016). For instance, "ease of implementation" may have a weight of 0.50, while "impact" might have a weight of 0.80.

An issue may come up during the action planning phase of an improvement project that relates to the expected success of the intervention. **Force field analysis** is "a technique for evaluating all the various forces for and against a proposed change" (McLaughlin and Olson 2012, 160). This technique can help the team determine whether a planned intervention can be successfully implemented. If the team has already chosen a particular intervention, a force field analysis can help in developing strategies for overcoming barriers to success.

Shown in exhibit 12.10 is a force field analysis developed by a hospital team involved in a project aimed at improving patient-centered care. The team had decided that moving the location of shift handoffs from the nurses' station to the patient's bedside would allow patients to be more involved in their care. The restraining forces were found to be significant; however, the team still chose to make this change. By using a force field analysis to identify

force field analysis
"a technique for evaluating all of the various forces for and against a proposed change" (McLaughlin and Olson 2012, 160)

EXHIBIT 12.9
Decision Matrix
Example

Project Goal: Reduce resident falls by 20 percent in one year.

Proposed Action	Ease of Implementation	Cost	Impact	Total
	Hard = 1 → Easy = 5	High = 1 → Low = 5	Low = 1 → High = 5	
"Ask for Help" signs in resident rooms	5	5	1	11
Bed alarms for high fall-risk residents	3	1	4	8
Change floor wax to a slip-resistant product	5	5	3	13
Add check that mobility devices are in the residents' reach to hourly resident rounds	5	5	3	13

EXHIBIT 12.10
Force Field
Analysis
Example

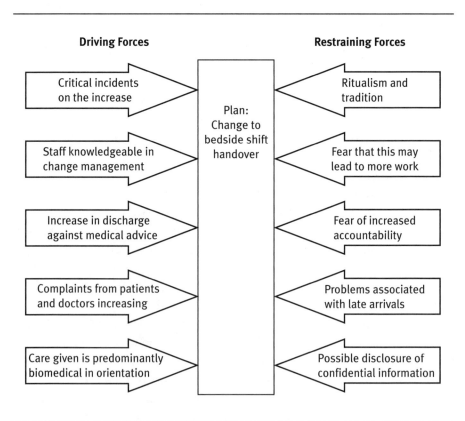

Source: Adapted from McLaughlin and Olson (2012). Used with permission.

the restraining forces prior to implementation, the team could then design the action plan in a way that would minimize these forces.

Monitor Progress and Hold the Gains

Following an improvement project, there must be a control system that allows management to measure progress toward goal attainment and identify unacceptable variances requiring action. One of the hallmarks of a good control system is that corrective action is taken as soon as it is found to be needed. Why wait until the end of the year to discover that an improvement project has not changed performance as expected? However, at the other end of the scale, should a manager check performance every week? That may make no sense, either. Monthly checking is probably about right unless the organization's leaders or healthcare regulators want more frequent checks.

A commonly used tool to monitor performance following an improvement project is a run chart, a graphic representation of data over time. This chart is described in chapter 10 and also discussed here because of its importance in monitoring the results of improvement projects. Run charts are useful for tracking progress after an improvement intervention and monitoring the performance of ongoing operations. On a run chart, the x axis represents the time interval (e.g., day, month, quarter, year) and the y axis represents the **variable** or **attribute** of interest. Displaying data on a run chart also enables a manager to more readily detect patterns or unusual occurrences in the data. Exhibit 12.11 shows a run chart tracking patient complaints about hospital noise at night. An intervention that involved some environmental changes—action that was taken as a result of an improvement project—is indicated with the arrow.

While managers should monitor performance following individual interventions, such as creating a quieter nighttime environment for hospitalized patients, changing system behavior often requires more than one intervention. Numerous factors contribute to consistent and successful practice, as illustrated in the simple cause-and-effect diagram in exhibit 12.6. Eliminating one of these causes can increase compliance a little; however, a problem with multiple causes requires a multifaceted improvement plan. For example, the World Health Organization (WHO) endorses a combination of interventions (exhibit 12.12) to improve the hand-hygiene compliance of health services workers.

Implementing the WHO guidelines involves improving multiple processes and engaging multiple stakeholders and departments throughout an organization on a continual basis.

Exhibit 12.13 provides an example of a control chart (sometimes called a *process behavior chart*). This graph provides a moving picture of the variation of key performance parameters. The control chart illustrates one organization's experience with continuous attention to and improvement of its

variable
number that "take[s] on different values on a continuous scale" (Carey and Lloyd 2001, 70)

attribute
tally of "events that can be aggregated into discrete categories" (Carey and Lloyd 2001, 70)

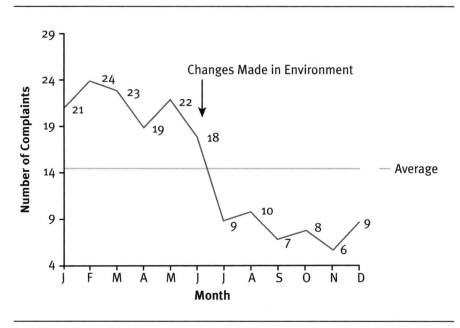

EXHIBIT 12.11
Run Chart of
Monthly Patient
Complaints
About Hospital
Noise at Night

EXHIBIT 12.12
WHO Hand-
Hygiene
Recommendations

System Change: ensuring that the necessary infrastructure is in place to allow healthcare workers to practice hand hygiene.

Training/Education: providing regular training on the importance of hand hygiene, based on the "My 5 Moments for Hand Hygiene" approach, and the correct procedures for hand rubbing and hand washing, to all healthcare workers.

Evaluation and Feedback: monitoring hand-hygiene practices and infrastructure, along with related perceptions and knowledge among healthcare workers, while providing performance and results feedback to staff.

Reminders in the Workplace: prompting and reminding healthcare workers about the importance of hand hygiene and about the appropriate indications and procedures for performing it.

Institutional Safety Climate: creating an environment and the perceptions that facilitate awareness-raising about patient safety issues while guaranteeing consideration of hand hygiene improvement as a high priority at all levels.

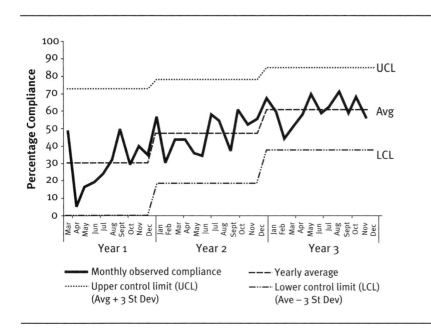

EXHIBIT 12.13
Three-Year
Hand-Hygiene
Compliance
Rates

multifaceted hand-hygiene initiative. System behavior, as measured by hand-hygiene compliance rates, has been tracked each month for a three-year period. As various interventions were implemented, the graph allowed managers to see how the interventions affected system performance. Over the three-year period, one sees an improvement of the average compliance rate per year and a narrowing of the range, indicating more predictable and dependable behavior in the direction of 100 percent compliance.

If an improvement project fails to achieve desired results and the performance issue continues to be of strategic importance to the organization, another project should be initiated with the same or different team members. The first step for this team should be to conduct a postmortem on the failed project to determine what went wrong so the repeat project will not fall into the same traps. A survey of 167 frontline leaders from four Midwest community hospitals found the top reasons improvement projects are not successful (Longenecker and Longenecker 2014, 150):

1. Poor implementation planning and overly aggressive time lines
2. Failure to create buy-in or ownership of the initiative
3. Ineffective leadership and lack of trust in upper management
4. Failure to create a realistic plan or improvement process
5. Ineffective, unilateral communications
6. A weak case for change, unclear focus, and unclear desired outcomes
7. Little or no teamwork or cooperation

8. Failure to provide ongoing measurement, feedback, and accountability
9. Unclear roles, goals, and performance expectations
10. Lack of time, resources, and support from upper management

Summary

Quality management is most successful when it is a bottom-up, team activity. The people personally involved in the process to be improved are best suited to identify the causes of performance problems and to propose and implement solutions. Involving frontline staff in improvement projects also reduces resistance to change. This chapter describes the role of managers throughout the life of an improvement project—from chartering the team to selecting the improvement strategies to monitoring the results.

Improvement tools and techniques are used during various steps of an improvement project. There are many different tools and techniques that can be used to document the process, uncover improvement opportunities, select improvement actions, monitor progress, and hold the gains. This chapter covers several of these tools and techniques, and students are encouraged to use the companion readings and web resources provided to learn more.

Exercise 12.1

Objective: To practice creating a project charter.

Instructions: Read the case study. Assume you are one of the two directors in the case study, and you are writing a team charter jointly with the other director to address the problems identified in the case study. Use the template in exhibit 12.1 or a similar format to document the project charter.

Case Study: The directors of imaging services and surgical services in a hospital are discussing an improvement opportunity involving care provided to patients with breast cancer. The hospital is encountering delays for procedures involving surgical removal of breast tissue (lumpectomy) in the area where an image-guided core needle biopsy has been performed. During the surgery, the removed tissue is imaged to ensure that the biopsy clip and microcalcifications are present in the specimen. The imaging must be done with a mammographic unit to provide visualization of the microcalcifications. Because the mammography machines are in the Breast Center, which is only open regular business hours, scheduling for the lumpectomy procedures is restricted to when a mammography technologist is available. This limitation causes delays as late as 8:00 pm, and technologists must be paid overtime for these evening procedures. In addition, even during Breast Center operating hours, the breast tissue has to be packaged and delivered by hand from the operating suite to the imaging department— and after the specimen is imaged, it must be returned to surgery, all while the surgeon waits with the patient still under general anesthesia. The hospital is not able to meet the needs of the surgeon for late cases, and even the requirements for cases during the day are not being fully met.

Exercise 12.2

Objective: To practice creating a process flowchart.

Instructions: Develop a flowchart for a healthcare process that you are familiar with. The flowchart should have a starting point and an end point. All key process steps should be included. Use the type of flowchart that will best display the steps in your chosen process. The flowchart can be hand drawn, or you can use software such as Microsoft Excel, Visio, or PowerPoint. Two examples of flowcharts are provided in this chapter, and the web resources included at the end of this chapter contain additional examples.

Companion Readings

Agency for Healthcare Research and Quality. 2013. *Practice Facilitation Handbook.* Published June. www.ahrq.gov/professionals/prevention-chronic-care/ improve/system/pfhandbook/index.html.

Harel, Z., S. A. Silver, R. F. McQuillan, A. V. Weizman, A. Thomas, G. M. Chertow, G. Nesrallah, C. T. Chan, and C. M. Bell. 2016. "How to Diagnose Solutions to a Quality of Care Problem." *Clinical Journal of the American Society of Nephrology* 11 (5): 901–7.

Health Resources and Services Administration. 2016. "Improvement Teams." Accessed November 16. www.hrsa.gov/quality/toolbox/methodology/ improvementteams/index.html.

Lenderman, H., H. Reffett, J. Moran, and M. Beaudry. 2014. "Selecting Quality Improvement Team Members." Public Health Foundation. Published May 19. www.phf.org/resourcestools/Documents/Team_Member_Selection_Tool.pdf.

McQuillan, R. F., S. A. Silver, Z. Harel, A. V. Weizman, A. Thomas, C. M. Bell, G. M. Chertow, C. T. Chan, and G. Nesrallah. 2016. "How to Measure and Interpret Quality Improvement Data." *Clinical Journal of the American Society of Nephrology* 11 (5): 908–14.

Minnesota Department of Health. 2016. "Public Health and Quality Improvement Resources and Tools." Accessed November 16. www.health.state.mn.us/divs/ opi/qi/toolbox.

Public Health Foundation. 2011. *Applications and Tools for Creating Healthy Teams.* Published April. www.phf.org/resourcestools/Documents/Applications_and_Tools_for_Creating_and_Sustaining_Healthy_Teams.pdf.

Silver, S. A., Z. Harel, R. McQuillan, A. V. Weizman, A. Thomas, G. M. Chertow, G. Nesrallah, C. M. Bell, and C. T. Chan. 2016. "How to Begin a Quality Improvement Project." *Clinical Journal of the American Society of Nephrology* 11 (5): 893–900.

Silver, S. A., R. McQuillan, Z. Harel, A. V. Weizman, A. Thomas, G. Nesrallah, C. M. Bell, C. T. Chan, and G. M. Chertow. 2016. "How to Sustain Change and Support Continuous Quality Improvement." *Clinical Journal of the American Society of Nephrology* 11 (5): 916–24.

Weston, M., and D. Roberts. 2013. "The Influence of Quality Improvement Efforts on Patient Outcomes and Nursing Work: A Perspective from Chief Nursing Officers at Three Large Health Systems." *OJIN: The Online Journal of Issues in Nursing* 18 (3). Published September. www.nursingworld.org/Quality-Improvement-on-Patient-Outcomes.html.

Web Resources

Agency for Healthcare Research and Quality flowcharts: https://healthit
.ahrq.gov/health-it-tools-and-resources/workflow-assessment-
health-it-toolkit/all-workflow-tools/flowchart
Institute for Healthcare Improvement: www.ihi.org

References

Agency for Healthcare Research and Quality. 2013. "Module 14: Creating Quality Improvement Teams and QI Plans." Reviewed May. www.ahrq.gov/professionals/prevention-chronic-care/improve/system/pfhandbook/mod14.html.

American Society for Quality (ASQ). 2016a. "Decision Matrix." Accessed July 15. http://asq.org/learn-about-quality/decision-making-tools/overview/decision-matrix.html.

———. 2016b. "Glossary—P." Accessed July 15. http://asq.org/glossary/p.html.

———. 2016c. "Process View of Work." Accessed July 15. http://asq.org/learn-about-quality/process-view-of-work/overview/overview.html.

Carey, R. G., and R. C. Lloyd. 2001. *Measuring Quality Improvement in Healthcare: A Guide to Statistical Process Control Applications.* Milwaukee, WI: Quality Press.

Kelly, D. 1998. "Reframing Beliefs About Work and Change Processes in Redesigning Laboratory Services." *The Joint Commission Journal on Quality Improvement* 24 (9): 154–67.

Lencioni, P. 2002. *The Five Dysfunctions of a Team: A Leadership Fable.* San Francisco: Jossey-Bass.

Longenecker, C. O., and P. D. Longenecker. 2014. "Why Hospital Improvement Efforts Fail: A View from the Front Line." *Journal of Healthcare Management* 59 (2): 147–57.

McLaughlin, D. B., and J. R. Olson. 2012. *Healthcare Operations Management,* 2nd ed. Chicago: Health Administration Press.

Minnesota Department of Health (MDH). 2016. "Public Health and QI Tool Box: Prioritization Matrix." Accessed July 15. www.health.state.mn.us/divs/opi/ qi/toolbox/prioritizationmatrix.html.

Rohe, D., and P. L. Spath. 2005. *101 Tools for Improving Health Care Performance.* Forest Grove, OR: Brown-Spath & Associates.

Scholtes, P. R., B. L. Joiner, and B. J. Streibel. 2003. *The Team Handbook,* 3rd ed. Madison, WI: Oriel.

Shiba, S., and D. Walden. 2002. "Quality Process Improvement Tools and Techniques." Massachusetts Institute of Technology and Center for Quality of Management. Published July 30. www.walden-family.com/public/iaq-paper.pdf.

UK Department of Trade and Industry. 2016. "Tools and Techniques for Process Improvement." Accessed July 15. www.businessballs.com/dtiresources/TQM_ process_improvement_tools.pdf.

World Health Organization (WHO). 2009. *A Guide to the Implementation of the WHO Multimodal Hand Hygiene Improvement Strategy.* Accessed July 15, 2016. www.who.int/gpsc/5may/Guide_to_Implementation.pdf.

Appendix 12.1

Frequently Used Improvement Tools

Tool Name	Description
Affinity diagram	Visualization that organizes ideas and issues to help in understanding the essence of a situation and possible actions
Arrow diagram	Graphical representation showing the network of tasks and milestones required to implement a project
Bar chart (or bar graph)	Display of data in which the height of the bars is used to show the relative size of the quantity measured
Benchmarking	Comparison of a process with a "best practice" or "best in class" to learn how to improve that process
Brainstorming	Process that allows a team to creatively generate ideas about a topic in a "judgment-free zone"
Capability measures	Various measures of the natural variation of process outputs (e.g., a limit of three standard deviations on a control chart) and specification limits (e.g., six sigma)
Causal loop diagram	Advanced type of relations diagram
Cause-and-effect diagram (or fishbone diagram or Ishikawa diagram)	Visualization that organizes and documents causes of a problem in a structured format
Check sheet (or tally sheet)	Form used to record and compile data from archives or observations to detect trends or patterns
Control chart	Display of data quantifying variation to monitor whether a process is continuing to operate reliably; also used to detect the effect of a process change
Decision matrix	Diagram used to evaluate and prioritize a list of options

(continued)

Tool Name	Description
Design of experiments	Systematic method that determines the relationship between factors affecting a process and the output of that process
Dot plot (or tally chart)	Visualization showing how often a particular value has occurred (frequency), with the shape of the plot giving a picture of the variation and highlighting unusual values
5S methodology	Philosophy and a five-step way of organizing and managing the workspace by eliminating waste
Five Whys	Process in which, when a problem occurs, its nature and source are discovered by asking "Why?" several times
Force field analysis	Examination that identifies forces that help or hinder change or improvement
Graphs and graphical methods	Many different techniques for showing data visually and analyzing the data
Histogram	Display showing the centering, dispersion, and shape of the distribution of a collection of data
Matrix diagram	Visualization showing multidimensional relationships
Pareto chart (or analysis diagram)	Visual representation similar to a histogram but with the data sorted in order of decreasing frequency of events and with other annotations to highlight the Pareto effect (i.e., the 20 percent of situations that account for 80 percent of results)
Poka-yoke (or mistake-proofing)	Methods for preventing mistakes
Process flowchart	Graphical representation of the steps in a process or project
Queuing theory	Analysis of delays and wait times
Regression analysis	Analysis of the relationship between response (dependent) variables and influencing factors (independent variables)
Relations diagram	Visualization showing a network of cause-and-effect relationships
Run chart (or line graph)	Graphical representation of data over time

(continued)

Tool Name	Description
Sampling	Statistical tool that selects a few instances from a set of events, from which characteristics of the entire set are inferred
Scatter diagram (or plot)	Graphical method of showing correlation between two variables
Stratification of data	Classification of data from multiple categories, such as what, where, when, and who
Tree diagram	Visualization that organizes a list of events or tasks into a hierarchy
Value-stream mapping	Graphical representation of the process of services or product delivery with use of inputs, throughputs, and outputs

Sources: Adapted from MDH (2016); Shiba and Walden (2002); UK Department of Trade and Industry (2016).

MAKING HEALTHCARE SAFER FOR PATIENTS

Learning Objectives

After completing this chapter, you should be able to

- explain types of human errors and error causes,
- differentiate characteristics of high-reliability organizations,
- describe reactive and proactive patient safety improvement models, and
- explain how managers can assist in improving patient safety.

A resident in a nursing care center sustained serious injuries when being transferred from her wheelchair to her bed. Two certified nursing assistants (CNAs) were using a portable mechanical lifting device (Hoyer lift) to move the 400-pound resident. The transfer was being supervised by a physical therapist because the lift being used was rated for use only for people weighing no more than 250 pounds. Rather than rent a larger and stronger lift for this one obese resident, the facility director determined that transferring the resident with improper equipment outweighed the risks associated with her confinement to a bed. To reduce the possibility of resident harm, the nursing supervisor requested a physical therapist supervise the transfers. On this occasion, the resident was placed in the lift and elevated into the air above her wheelchair. As the CNAs turned the lift toward the bed it began to sink because the lift arm could not handle the resident's weight. In an attempt to complete the transfer before the resident was below the level of the bed, the CNAs swung the lift quickly toward the bed. The lift tilted dangerously to the side and the legs started to move together, narrowing the base of support. The resident was dropped to the floor and the lift fell on top of her.

This unfortunate event illustrates how healthcare quality and patient safety are intertwined. The Institute of Medicine (IOM) defines quality as "the degree to which health services for individuals and populations increase the likelihood of desired health outcomes and are consistent with current professional knowledge" (Lohr 1990, 21). The facility in the scenario did not provide an environment that increased the likelihood of desired outcomes for the resident, nor was the care provided based on current professional knowledge. These quality problems affected patient safety, which is defined as "freedom from accidental or preventable injuries produced by medical care" (Agency for Healthcare Research and Quality [AHRQ] 2016a). The IOM (2001) identified safe care (avoidance of unintended patient injuries) as one of the key components of healthcare quality, the other components being effective, patient-centered, timely, efficient, and equitable care.

The importance of safe care received unprecedented public attention after the IOM released its groundbreaking report, *To Err Is Human: Building a Safer Health System* (IOM 2000). This report estimated 44,000 to 98,000 Americans die each year from medical mistakes. The report recommended a range of activities to improve patient safety and set some ambitious safety improvement goals for all parties in the healthcare system. Public pressures following the report resulted in development of patient safety improvement initiatives in all sectors of the healthcare field. Consumers, as well as regulatory and accreditation groups, now expect healthcare organizations to design safer patient care processes and investigate the cause of errors.

To achieve safe healthcare, health services organizations are working to protect healthcare recipients more effectively from being harmed. These initiatives are a component of an organization's overall quality management program. It can sometimes be difficult to differentiate between what is being done to improve patient safety and quality improvements that are being made for other purposes. In truth, there are no clear-cut distinctions. Improvements in most any healthcare process—clinical and nonclinical—are likely to affect some aspect of patient safety.

Like quality management, patient safety improvement requires a supportive culture—one that encourages highly reliable, safe practices. Patient safety improvement also involves activities that are used for quality management purposes: measuring and evaluating performance and designing and implementing improvements. This chapter describes the causes of errors that can harm patients, together with some concepts, tools, and techniques often associated with making healthcare safer for patients.

errors
"all those occasions in which a planned sequence of mental or physical activities fails to achieve its intended outcome" (Reason 1990, 9)

adverse event
"an injury caused by medical management rather than the underlying condition of the patient" (IOM 2000, 4)

Systems Model of Organizational Accidents

The systems model of organizational accidents developed by James Reason can help to explain how medical errors may occur in health services organizations. To understand Reason's model, one must first understand the definitions and assumptions on which it is based. **Errors** are "all those occasions in which a planned sequence of mental or physical activities fails to achieve its intended outcome" (Reason 1990, 9). An **adverse event** is defined as "an injury caused by medical management rather than the underlying condition of the patient"

(IOM 2000, 4). **Violations** are "deviations from safe operating practices, procedures, standards, or rules" (Reason 1997, 72).

Errors may be further categorized as **judgment errors** (improper selection of an objective or a plan of action), **execution errors** (proper plan carried out improperly), **errors of omission** (when something that should be done is not done), and **errors of commission** (when something that should not be done is done) (IOM 2000; Reason 1990). **Active errors** are those committed by frontline workers; the results of active errors are usually seen immediately (Reason 1990, 1997). For example, the CNAs in the nursing care home event described at the start of this chapter experienced an active error when the lift collapsed during a resident transfer. **Latent errors**, on the other hand, occur in the upper levels of the organization. The error may lie dormant for days or years until a particular combination of circumstances allows the latent error to become an adverse event (Reason 1990, 1997).

Violations may also be further categorized as routine, optimizing, and situation. **Routine violations** may be thought of as activities that cut corners. **Optimizing violations** are "actions taken to further personal rather than task related goals" (Reason 1995, 82). **Situation violations** occur when a person believes that the action "offers the only path available to getting the job done and where the rules or procedures are seen as inappropriate for the present situation" (Reason 1995, 82).

The distinction between errors and violations is important to managers because they have different contributing causes and, in turn, require different solutions, as summarized in exhibit 13.1.

Finally, **Reason's swiss cheese model** assumes a collection of defenses that act as buffers or safeguards to prevent a hazardous situation from becoming an adverse event, just as a thick oven mitt would prevent the restaurant worker from dropping a hot dish. The collection of defenses in an organization may be thought of as several slices of swiss cheese lined up next to each other. The holes in the slices of cheese represent the latent and active errors present in the organization. Even if an error may be present (i.e., a hole in one slice), it often does not result in an adverse event or accident because there are organizational defenses to stop it from continuing (i.e., the next slice). An example of an organizational defense is the standard practice of having a pharmacist review the appropriateness of all physician orders for medications to be dispensed. A physician may inadvertently write an incorrect dosage; however, when the pharmacist picks up the mistake and clarifies the order with the physician (organizational defense), a medical error (and potential adverse event) is prevented.

Exhibit 13.2 illustrates the slices of swiss cheese (or collection of defenses). The exhibit shows that under certain circumstances, the interplay between latent errors, local conditions, and active errors causes the holes in

violations
"deviations from safe operating practices, procedures, standards, or rules" (Reason 1997, 72)

judgment errors
errors resulting from improper selection of an objective or a plan of action

execution errors
problems that arise when a proper plan is carried out improperly

errors of omission
required tasks that are not done

errors of commission
tasks not required by the process that are done anyhow

active errors
errors committed by frontline workers; the results are seen immediately (Reason 1990, 1997)

latent errors
errors occurring in the upper levels of the organization; an error may lie dormant for days or years until a particular combination of circumstances allows the latent error to become an adverse event (Reason 1990, 1997)

EXHIBIT 13.1
Errors Versus
Violations

	Errors	Violations
Where	Cognitive domain (the mind)	Social domain (organizational context)
Why	Informational problem	Motivational problem
Prevention	Improve knowledge and information	Address motivational and organizational factors

Sources: Data from Reason (1995); Kelly (2009).

routine violations
steps in a process that are intentionally skipped; activities that cut corners

optimizing violations
"action taken to further personal rather than task related goals" (Reason 1995, 82)

situation violations
action undertaken when a person believes that the action "offers the only path available to getting the job done and where the rules or procedures are seen as inappropriate for the present situation" (Reason 1995, 82)

Reason's swiss cheese model
a model of how errors occur that "illustrates how analyses of major accidents and catastrophic systems failures tend to reveal multiple, smaller failures leading up to the actual hazard" (AHRQ 2016a)

the cheese to align so that a sequence of events may pass through all the holes and result in an adverse event.

Administrative and management professionals play key roles in medical errors, as they are the source of latent errors in organizations (Reason 1997, 10).

Latent conditions are to technical organizations what resident pathogens are to the human body. Like pathogens, latent conditions—such as poor design, gaps in supervision, undetected manufacturing or maintenance failures, unworkable procedures, clumsy automation, shortfalls in training, less than adequate tools and equipment—may be present for years before they combine with local circumstances and active failures to penetrate the system's many layers of defenses. They arise from strategic and other top-level decisions made by governments, regulators, manufacturers, designers and organizational managers. The impact of these decisions spreads throughout the organization, shaping a distinctive corporate culture and creating error-producing factors within the individual workplaces. . . . Latent conditions are an inevitable part of organizational life. Nor are they necessarily the products of bad decisions, although they may well be. Resources, for example, are rarely distributed equally between an organization's various departments. The original decision on how to allocate them may have been based on sound . . . arguments, but all such inequities create quality, reliability, or safety problems for someone, somewhere in the system at some later point.

Frontline employees or those in direct contact with patients, clients, and customers serve as the last layer of defense against an adverse event. While the results of a sequence of events leading to the adverse event may occur at the point of patient contact, the causes may be found throughout all levels of the organization. Reason (1990, 73) comments that the frontline staff, "rather than being the main instigators of an accident . . . tend to be the inheritors of system defects created by poor design, incorrect installation, faulty maintenance, and bad management decisions. Their part is usually that of adding the final garnish to a lethal brew whose ingredients have already been long in the cooking."

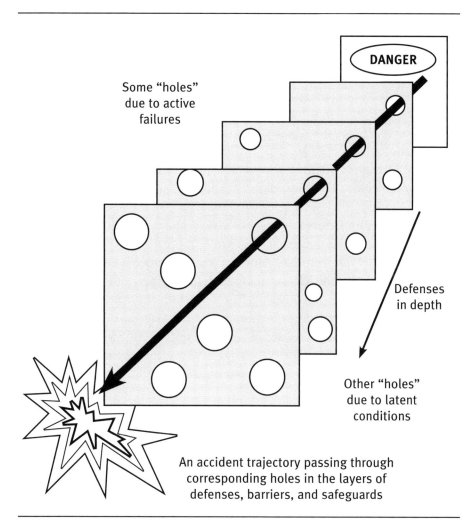

EXHIBIT 13.2
Systems Model of Organizational Accidents: Swiss Cheese Defenses

Some "holes" due to active failures

DANGER

Defenses in depth

Other "holes" due to latent conditions

An accident trajectory passing through corresponding holes in the layers of defenses, barriers, and safeguards

Source: © *Managing the Risks of Organizational Accidents*. Reason, J. 1997. Ashgate Publishing Limited. Reprinted with permission.

Latent errors may occur at the level of senior leaders who design organizational goals and priorities and determine how human, financial, and capital resources are allocated. Latent errors may occur at the level of frontline managers who translate and implement senior-level goals and priorities in their scope of responsibilities. Frontline management includes those responsible for departments that provide direct patient or client services, maintain and support the environment in which services are provided and the tools used by providers, and support the business functions of the organization. Decisions at the senior and frontline management levels of the organization, in turn, support preconditions for safe care in the form of appropriate, functioning, and reliable equipment; a knowledgeable, skilled, and trained workforce; appropriately designed work processes, communication mechanisms, and staffing plans; and effective supervision. Alternately, decisions at these two levels of the organization may promote the preconditions of error-prone work environments and processes.

While Reason's model represents a general organizational model, scholar Paul B. Hofmann examines specific sources, causes, types, and examples of latent management errors in health services organizations. For example, "inadequate preparation of/by decision maker(s), political pressure, flawed decision-maker process, and ignorance of legitimate alternatives" are causes of errors in the managerial domain of health services organizations (Hofmann 2005, 10). Errors of omission include "failure to delegate and hold subordinates accountable; failure to consider all options; failure to balance power interests; and failure to anticipate significant factors affecting decisions" (Hofmann 2005, 11). Errors of commission include "permitting decisions to be made without adequate analysis; choosing political, not business solutions; withholding negative information from individuals with the right to know; and making economic decisions that harm clinical care and outcomes" (Hofmann 2005, 11). An understanding of Reason's model emphasizes the imperative for managers' evidence-based knowledge, skill, and abilities. By complementing the safer practices of their clinical and technical counterparts, managers help safeguard the multiple levels of the organization in which errors may occur.

Creating High Reliability

It has been estimated that 210,000 patients are harmed each year by medication errors that occur in US hospitals (James 2013). A study of adverse events in skilled nursing facilities (SNFs) found that 33 percent of Medicare beneficiaries discharged from hospitals to SNFs experienced an adverse event during their SNF stays, and 59 percent of these events were preventable (Levinson 2014). Even amusement parks, with their potentially dangerous fun rides, do a better job of protecting the safety of consumers than do healthcare organizations (Clark 2012). The high rates of error in healthcare services could be a result of the system's complexity, yet fields outside of healthcare with complex processes have been able to achieve and maintain extraordinarily low levels of failure. The chance a person will die in a catastrophic accident involving civilian aviation, nuclear power, and railroad transportation is less than one in a million (Amalberti et al. 2005). Studies of these very safe industries have yielded an understanding of what is needed to produce safe and reliable performance in the delivery of healthcare services.

reliability
"measurable ability of a health-related process, procedure, or service to perform its intended functions in the required time under commonly occurring conditions" (Weick, Sutcliffe, and Obstfeld 1999, 82)

Reliability of healthcare services is defined as the "measurable ability of a health-related process, procedure, or service to perform its intended functions in the required time under commonly occurring conditions" (Weick, Sutcliffe, and

Obstfeld 1999, 82). When a process, procedure, or service does not perform as intended, it is considered unreliable, and this situation threatens patient safety. The nursing care home adverse event described at the start of this chapter illustrates at least two unreliable health-related activities. At the bedside, the procedure used to transfer the resident from her wheelchair to her bed did not perform its intended function. Contributing to the unreliable procedure at the bedside was the organization's unreliable process for securing the right equipment needed to care for its resident population.

An emerging context for health services organizations is **high-reliability organizations** (HROs), defined as "organizations with systems in place that are exceptionally consistent in accomplishing their goals and avoiding potentially catastrophic errors" (Hines et al. 2008, 5). In an HRO context, all individuals are encouraged to actively look for interdependencies in the system and to aggressively seek to know what they do not know (Roberts and Bea 2001). An HRO context influences managerial functions, as managers in HROs "design reward and incentive systems to recognize costs of failures as well as benefits of reliability . . . [and] consistently communicate the big picture of what the organization seeks to do and try to get everyone to communicate with others about how they fit in the big picture" (Roberts and Bea 2001, 71).

In the 1990s, researchers studying HROs in various industries outside of healthcare found several characteristics essential to avoiding or minimizing catastrophes in complex situations in which accidents might be expected to occur frequently. Health service managers seeking to improve patient safety by becoming an HRO should incorporate these characteristics—building a *learning environment* and practicing *collective mindfulness*—into daily practices.

high-reliability organizations (HROs)
"organizations with systems in place that are exceptionally consistent in accomplishing their goals and avoiding potentially catastrophic errors" (Hines et al. 2008, 5)

Learning Environment

Leaders in HROs place a high priority on maximizing learning opportunities in the organization and from other related organizations (Weick and Sutcliffe 2007). This learning aids in identifying and fixing underlying systemic faults before they can cause an accident. Health services managers can advance a learning culture by collecting, analyzing, and reporting safety-related information to staff and by providing opportunities for staff to discuss ways to prevent errors (Sammer and James 2011). In addition, lessons learned in one unit should be shared with managerial colleagues throughout the facility.

To support this learning environment, the organization's frontline staff members must share safety concerns with others and be commended by managers when they do so (Hines et al. 2008). This openness requires employees to be comfortable reporting mistakes so everyone can learn from them. The level of comfort in reporting mistakes is low when staff members are fearful of being punished for making a mistake, even when the mistake was triggered by a system problem. "A punitive approach shuts off the information that is needed to identify faulty systems and create safer ones. In a punitive system, no one learns from their mistakes" (Leape 2000).

An environment that encourages nonpunitive reporting of errors for learning purposes is described as a **Just Culture**, an aspect of organizational behavior that creates an atmosphere of trust, encouraging and rewarding people for providing essential safety-related information (Reason 1997). This organizational behavior is sometimes referred to as a *patient safety culture*. To support learning-driven improvement, management can encourage reporting of errors, and people who make honest mistakes or misjudgments do not incur blame. People are encouraged to come forward to help solve a problem rather than become defensive to avoid punishment (Sammer et al. 2010).

A Just Culture leads to improvements in reporting of errors, which in turn leads to revisions of unsafe systems and care processes. Leaders at all levels in an organization play an important role in supporting a Just Culture. This statement by the American Organization of Nurse Executives (AONE) is applicable to all managers, not just nurses: "The role of the nurse executive in patient safety is to help lead best practices and establish the right culture across multiple disciplines within the organization" (AONE 2007, 1).

To assist managers in evaluating their successful establishment of a Just Culture, the AHRQ has sponsored development of patient safety culture assessment tools for hospitals, nursing homes, ambulatory outpatient medical offices, community pharmacies, and ambulatory surgery centers (AHRQ 2016c). Exhibit 13.3 contains questions found in the "organizational learning/ response to mistakes" section of the AHRQ Ambulatory Surgery Center Patient Safety Culture.

Organizations that have administered AHRQ patient safety surveys can submit the results to AHRQ for inclusion in the agency's comparative databases. These central repositories can be used by managers to compare their patient safety survey results with those of other sites. An action plan to help survey users improve the patient safety culture and resources to help organizations administer the surveys and improve employee response rates are also available from AHRQ. A link to these materials is in the web resources section at the end of this chapter.

Collective Mindfulness

Weick and Sutcliffe (2007) found that HROs demonstrate the characteristic of **collective mindfulness**—all individuals in the organization are aware of the dire consequences of even a small error and are constantly alert to the potential for problems. To create collective mindfulness, the work culture in an HRO stresses open communication among individuals at all levels. Work teams have a more comprehensive picture of what is happening, which in turn allows for

Just Culture
an aspect of organizational behavior that creates an atmosphere of trust, encouraging and rewarding people for providing essential safety-related information (Reason 1997)

collective mindfulness
an organizational attribute in which all individuals are aware of the dire consequences of even a small error and are constantly alert to the potential for problems (Weick and Sutcliffe 2007)

How much do you agree or disagree with the following statements?	Strongly disagree	Disagree	Neither agree nor disagree	Agree	Strongly agree	Does not apply or Don't know
This facility actively looks for ways to improve patient safety	❑	❑	❑	❑	❑	❑
Staff are treated fairly when they make mistakes	❑	❑	❑	❑	❑	❑
We make improvements when someone points out patient safety problems	❑	❑	❑	❑	❑	❑
Learning, rather than blame, is emphasized when mistakes are made	❑	❑	❑	❑	❑	❑
Staff are told about patient safety problems that happen in this facility	❑	❑	❑	❑	❑	❑
We are good at changing processes to make sure the same patient safety problems don't happen again	❑	❑	❑	❑	❑	❑

EXHIBIT 13.3
Questions on the AHRQ Ambulatory Surgery Center Survey on Patient Safety Culture

Source: Reprinted from Smith et al. (2015).

identification and response to signs of rapidly escalating failure conditions before the onset of a full-scale disaster. Maintaining mindfulness is essential for high-quality, failure-free functioning. While accidents can happen in any organization, effective HROs are "known by their capability to contain and recover from the errors they do make and by their capability to have foresight into errors they might make" (Weick, Sutcliffe, and Obstfeld 1999, 51).

Five organizational characteristics contribute to collective mindfulness: preoccupation with failure, reluctance to simplify, sensitivity to operations, commitment to resilience, and deference to expertise (Hines et al. 2008). These characteristics, described in exhibit 13.4, guide the thinking of people in the organization and help create the condition of collective mindfulness.

EXHIBIT 13.4
Organizational
Characteristics
That Contribute
to Collective
Mindfulness

Characteristic	How This Is Demonstrated
Preoccupation with failure	• People are vigilant in observing and tracking small failures and anomalies. • People are encouraged to speak up about mistakes and incidents without fear of retribution. • People view small failures as opportunities to better understand what went wrong so more significant events can be prevented.
Reluctance to simplify	• People investigate the potential causes of problems and consider all potential solutions, rather than explain away problems or make excuses. • People do not apply simplistic fixes to complex system flaws. • People embrace diverse opinions and experiences to arrive at the best solutions for avoiding or minimizing catastrophes.
Sensitivity to operations	• People—from senior leaders to staff members—understand the big picture of current operations, so anomalies and potential mistakes can be quickly identified and addressed. • People constantly seek to understand what is happening right now and what is likely to happen next. • People use effective communication skills to help team members maintain situational awareness.
Commitment to resilience	• People are taught how to quickly address and contain evitable mistakes. • People are not caught by surprise when mistakes occur, and they know how to respond. • People closely monitor the ability of the work team to respond to situations regardless of what may happen.
Deference to expertise	• People seek input from the most knowledgeable individuals, regardless of where they are in the organizational hierarchy. • People with the most expertise can be given decision-making authority. • People de-emphasize hierarchy to prevent and respond to problems most effectively.

Source: Adapted from Spath (2013b). Used with permission.

Measuring and Evaluating Safe Performance

Measures of patient safety allow organizations to identify unsafe processes and practices that need investigating. Some measures alert managers to the existence of an adverse event. These are reactive measures because they notify managers after the fact that an undesirable event has occurred.

Reactive Measures

- Number of adverse events occurring during anesthesia use
- Number of medication errors per 1,000 doses dispensed
- Number of patients discharged with foreign body accidentally left in during procedure
- Ratio of transfusion reactions to total units transfused
- Number of patient falls with injury per 1,000 inpatient days
- Percentage of hospital patients who develop a hospital-acquired complication
- Percentage of nursing home residents with a catheter-related urinary tract infection

Proactive Measures

- Percentage of patients not identified by two identifiers prior to medication administration
- Percentage of staff not compliant with hand-hygiene requirements
- Number of patients with identification band missing or in an inappropriate location
- Percentage of behavioral health patients not adequately searched after returning from a leave of absence
- Percentage of patients who report not feeling safe at some point during their hospitalization
- Percentage of patients on anticoagulation therapy managed using the approved protocols
- Percentage of patients on infection control precautions with a sign posted at the doorway of the room to alert staff and visitors

EXHIBIT 13.5
Reactive and Proactive Patient Safety Measures

Some patient safety measures are proactive because they alert managers to potentially risky patient care conditions or situations, which if not acted on could result in an adverse event. For example, monitoring the rate of **near-miss events** is a proactive measure. A near miss is "an event or a situation that did not produce patient harm because it did not reach the patient, either due to chance or to [being] capture[d] before reaching the patient; or if it did reach the patient [did not cause harm], due to robustness of the patient or to timely intervention (for example, an antidote was administered)" (Wu 2011). Such events are also referred to as **close calls**.

Listed in exhibit 13.5 are examples of reactive and proactive patient safety measures.

The Joint Commission influences patient safety measurement activities in accredited health services organizations. To evaluate compliance with The Joint Commission's (2016a) annual National Patient Safety Goals (NPSGs), organizations often add measures related to the goal requirements. For example, to evaluate compliance with NPSGs related to accurate patient identification, a hospital might periodically measure the following:

near-miss event (or close call)
"an event or a situation that did not produce patient harm because it did not reach the patient, either due to chance or to [being] capture[d] before reaching the patient; or if it did reach the patient, [did not cause harm] due to robustness of the patient or to timely intervention (for example, an antidote was administered)" (Wu 2011)

- Percentage of blood draws in which the patient name and date of birth was confirmed by the phlebotomist prior to the blood draw
- Percentage of blood transfusions in which a two-person verification process was used to match the blood or blood component to the order and to match the patient to the blood or blood component

Healthcare organizations also gather and review performance data related to patient safety measures, which are publicly reported by the Centers for Medicare & Medicaid Services (CMS) on the Medicare data website (https://data.medicare.gov). For hospitals, these data include surgical complication measures and healthcare-associated infection measures. For nursing homes, these data include resident fall rates and percentage of residents who develop a pressure ulcer.

Safety Data Sources

Patient safety measures are derived from different data sources. For example, a hospital using the AHRQ Patient Safety Indicators gathers the data by electronically screening the hospital's computerized patient discharge database looking for ICD-10 diagnosis codes that signify that a potential complication or adverse event has occurred. The types of patient safety occurrences identified through this process include death in low-mortality diagnosis-related groups, hospital-acquired pressure ulcers, death among surgical inpatients with treatable serious complications, and foreign body left in patient during a procedure (AHRQ 2016b).

An organization's primary source of information for patient safety measures are **incident reports**. These are "instruments (paper or electronic) used to document occurrences that could have led or did lead to undesirable results" (Spath 2013b, 187). An incident report form used by caregivers to document patient falls is shown in exhibit 13.6. The types of incidents that should be reported to management by frontline staff are specific to each organization. There are similarities in the reporting requirements of health services organizations; however, there are no nationally mandated definitions of reportable occurrences. New employees often receive an orientation to the organization's incident reporting requirements, and managers may provide existing employees with periodic review sessions.

Although voluntarily reported incidents are the primary data source for patient safety measures, healthcare researchers have established that only 10–20 percent of adverse events in hospitals are reported (Levinson 2012; Milch et al. 2006). While similar studies have not been done in other types of facilities, the experience in all provider sites is most likely comparable. The reasons people do not report adverse events are multifactorial. A survey of physicians and nurses on their use of incident reporting found both groups

incident reports
"instruments (paper or electronic) used to document occurrences that could have led or did lead to undesirable results" (Spath 2013b, 187)

EXHIBIT 13.6
Patient Fall
Incident Report

Patient Name: _____ Room #: _____ Age: _____ Gender: _____

Admission Date: _____ Date of Fall: _____ Time of Fall: _____

Ask the Patient	
Do you remember falling?	❑ Yes
	❑ No (if patient cannot respond, his or her family may be able to provide information)
Were you injured?	❑ Yes (How and where?)
	❑ No
What were you doing when you fell?	
Other Information	
Was the nurse call light on?	❑ Yes (include the number of minutes call light was on)
	❑ No
The activated call light belonged to:	❑ Patient
	❑ Roommate
Contributing factors (specify all):	❑ Medication:
	❑ Equipment:
	❑ Footwear:
	❑ Confusion:
	❑ Urgency of bladder/bowels:
	❑ Environmental issues:
	❑ Other:
Did nursing follow the risk-for-falls protocol for this patient?	❑ Yes
	❑ No
Any other information from patient, family, or staff:	

(continued)

EXHIBIT 13.6
Patient Fall
Incident Report
(continued)

Number of hours since last patient assessment:	
Has this patient fallen previously during this stay?	☐ Yes
	☐ No
Age:	
Injury:	☐ Yes
	☐ No
Did staff witness the fall?	☐ Yes
	☐ No
Was the patient identified as at risk for falls?	☐ Yes
	☐ No
What fall prevention measures were used?	
Was the patient physically restrained?	☐ Yes
	☐ No

Source: Reprinted from Spath (2013b). Used with permission.

were more likely to report immediately visible events, such as patient falls, and less likely to report events that develop gradually and are not as obvious, such as hospital-acquired deep-vein thrombosis or pressure ulcers (Evans et al. 2006). There are many additional barriers to reporting events, including uncertainty about what to report, a lack of confidence that reporting actually makes a difference, "embarrassment, lack of time, fear of reprisal, and fear of medico-legal repercussions" (Kilbridge and Classen 2008, 401).

To increase the number of voluntarily reported incidents, instead of relying on sporadic reminders, managers should engage staff in ongoing education on the merits of reporting. One way to keep incident reporting in the limelight is to include nonpunitive event discussions as a regular agenda item at unit meetings. Staff will see the value of reporting incidents when it becomes clear the information provides a worthwhile learning opportunity and will also help to make healthcare safer for patients (Benn at al. 2009).

To supplement voluntary incident reporting, some organizations use a focused patient record–review process to identify **triggers** that are "clinical data related to patient care indicating a reasonable probability that an adverse event

triggers
"clinical data related to patient care indicating a reasonable probability that an adverse event has occurred" (AAP 2011, 1206)

has occurred" (American Academy of Pediatrics [AAP] 2011, 1206). Because record reviews are time consuming, researchers at the Institute for Healthcare Improvement (IHI) suggest screening a percentage of records for triggers or clues that suggest a patient has been harmed. The definition for **patient harm** used in the IHI Global Trigger Tool (GTT) is "unintended physical injury resulting from or contributed to by medical care that requires additional monitoring, treatment or hospitalization, or that results in death" (Griffin and Resar 2009, 5). For example, using the screening process recommended in the GTT, hospital staff members (often nurses or pharmacists) would review a minimum of 20 charts from surgical inpatients each month looking for triggers such as the following:

patient harm
"unintended physical injury resulting from or contributed to by medical care that requires additional monitoring, treatment or hospitalization, or that results in death" (Griffin and Resar 2009, 5)

- Change of anesthetic during surgery
- Insertion of arterial or central venous line during surgery
- Intraoperative administration of epinephrine or norepinephrine
- Unplanned X-ray, intraoperatively or in postanesthesia recovery unit

Further investigation into whether an adverse event occurred and how severe the event was comes next. A physician ultimately has to examine and sign off on the conclusions (Classen et al. 2011).

The GTT has proven to be a useful adjunct to incident reporting. For example, a veterans hospital reviewed a sample of patient records for 17 weeks using the GTT and found that one in five hospitalizations (21 percent) were associated with an adverse event and 69 of the GTT-detected 109 adverse events (88 percent) were not identified through incident reporting or other means (Mull et al. 2015). The estimated cost of the screening process necessary for identifying the GTT-detected events was $140 per event. The majority of GTT-detected adverse events (60 percent) were minor harms, and there were no deaths attributable to medical care. Managers and the organization's senior leaders must decide whether the costs associated with screening patient records for triggers is worth the effort.

A growing number of health services organizations encourage patients and families to report adverse events. A combination of closed-ended questions and open-ended narratives is suggested as the most effective way to solicit these reports and obtain data for analysis (King et al. 2010). Scholars have found that patient and family reports are trustworthy and could help managers identify safety problems that currently go unreported. One study found that patient-reported incidents in hospitals are strongly correlated with patient harm rates calculated using the IHI GTT (Bjertnaes et al. 2015).

Designing and Implementing Safety Improvements

Improving patient safety requires managers to apply *critical thinking*, which is "the art of analyzing and evaluating thinking with a view to improving it" (Scriven and Paul 2016). In the context of quality management there is a wide array of step-by-step methods managers can use as a framework for critical thinking. The most common quality improvement methods—Plan, Do, Check, Act (PDCA); Six Sigma; and Lean—can also be used to identify the cause of safety problems and select the best actions for resolving these problems (Spath 2013b). For example, leaders at the nursing care home that experienced the adverse event could form a team to conduct an improvement project using the PDCA cycle (American Society for Quality 2016):

- Plan: To improve the safety of morbidly obese residents, develop a new protocol for overseeing activities of daily living, including transfers.
- Do: Train nurses, CNAs, and therapists on a unit in the new protocol, and implement it for a two-month trial.
- Check or Study: Gather data to determine whether the new protocol makes a difference.
- Act: If the protocol proves to be successful, implement it on a wider scale and continuously evaluate the results. If the protocol fails to reduce safety problems for morbidly obese residents, repeat the improvement cycle.

In addition to using quality improvement methods to make healthcare safer for patients, two other methods are commonly associated with patient safety projects: root cause analysis and failure mode and effects analysis. These methods are described in the next sections.

Root Cause Analysis

root cause analysis (RCA) method used to "identify hazards and systems vulnerabilities so that actions can be taken that improve patient safety by preventing future harm" (NPSF 2016, 2)

Singular adverse events and serious unsafe situations can be investigated using **root cause analysis (RCA)**, a method used to "identify hazards and systems vulnerabilities so that actions can be taken that improve patient safety by preventing future harm" (National Patient Safety Foundation [NPSF] 2016, 2). The Joint Commission (2016b) requires accredited organizations to conduct an RCA following a sentinel event—a patient safety event that reaches a patient and results in death, permanent harm, or severe temporary harm and intervention required to sustain life. This RCA must include implementation of risk-reduction strategies that target the root causes of the event and measurement of the effectiveness of the interventions (Joint Commission 2016b). The RCA should be conducted by a project team comprising people personally involved in the event or personally familiar with the systems and processes that need to be examined.

An RCA focuses primarily on systems and processes. Even though the mistakes of individuals often precipitated the adverse event, the goal of the RCA is to find the problematic system or processes that set up people to make these mistakes. Team members examine what happened and use various methods to uncover the underlying causes of the event. A simplistic root cause analysis method is **Five Whys**, "a questioning process designed to drill down into the details of a problem . . . and peel away the layers of symptoms" (Bialek, Duffy, and Moran 2016). Exhibit 13.7 is an illustration of how Five Whys might be

Five Whys
"a questioning process designed to drill down into the details of a problem . . . and peel away the layers of symptoms" (Bialek, Duffy, and Moran 2016)

EXHIBIT 13.7
Five Whys of Resident Injury in a Nursing Care Home

Problem to be investigated: Resident injured during transfer from wheelchair to bed

↓

Why?

↓

Mechanical lift collapsed

↓

Why?

↓

Only mechanical lift available was not intended for use with obese residents

↓

Why?

↓

Facility did not purchase mechanical lift that would accommodate obese residents

↓

Why?

↓

Care requirements of current residents are not known by board of directors during budget discussions for equipment purchases

↓

Why?

↓

Nursing director's input not actively solicited by board of directors during the equipment budgeting process

---

Source: Adapted from CMS (2016).

used to identify a root cause of the nursing care home resident injury described earlier (CMS 2016).

The team starts the Five Whys process by clarifying the problem and then proceeds to ask and answer "Why?" questions. It may take fewer or more than five times to reach the root cause (Bialek, Duffy, and Moran 2016). The Five Whys process is designed to uncover only one root cause for a problem, whereas "there are generally many contributing factors that must be considered in understanding why an event occurred" (NPSF 2016, 2). Managers may find the Five Whys process most useful for analyzing less complex problems.

A more in-depth RCA requires a systematic analysis of what happened. This examination often involves the development of a time line showing the process steps or happenings that led to the adverse event. Next, the team begins to explore why the event happened by identifying the active failures. These can be categorized into human factors, equipment factors, and environmental factors. Last, the team drills down to identify the underlying systemic structures (latent failures) that caused the event. The sequencing of this investigative process is illustrated in exhibit 13.8.

The RCA project does not end when the root causes of an event are identified. Like all performance improvement models, once the causes of problems are identified, the next steps are to design and implement actions to eliminate the causes and then measure the effects after implementing the actions. Common ways of preventing mistakes in the delivery of health services fall into

EXHIBIT 13.8
Root Cause
Analysis:
Systematic
Investigation

What happened? What are the details of the event?	Why did it happen? What were the most proximate factors?	Why did it happen? What systems and processes underlie those proximate factors?
• When • Where • What • Who	• The process or activity in which the event occurred • Human factors • Equipment factors • Controllable environmental factors	• Human resources issues • Information management issues • Environmental management issues • Leadership issues (corporate culture, encouragement of communication, clear communication of priorities) • Uncontrollable factors
Events	*Patterns*	*Systemic Structures*

Source: Adapted from The Joint Commission (2013).

three major categories: eliminate the chance for failures, make it easier for people to do the right thing, and make it easier to identify failures quickly and take appropriate action. Exhibit 13.8 shows examples of safety improvement actions in each action category. Efforts to catch human errors or other process failures before they occur or to prevent them from causing patient harm ultimately will be more fruitful than actions that seek to somehow create flawless caregivers (Spath 2013a).

To meet The Joint Commission's requirements, accredited organizations must conduct a comprehensive systematic analysis of adverse events that identifies the causal and contributory factors and designs and implements "corrective actions to eliminate or control system hazards or vulnerabilities directly related to causal and contributory factors" (Joint Commission 2016c, SE-6). The individuals responsible for implementing the actions and time lines for completion are to be identified, as well as "strategies for evaluating the effectiveness of the action and strategies for sustaining the change" (Joint Commission 2016c, SE-6).

Many accredited organizations voluntarily self-report their adverse events to The Joint Commission, the data from which contribute to the creation of its anonymized Sentinel Event Database (Joint Commission 2014). This database provides health services organizations and the public with information about the incidence of sentinel events in US facilities, event types, and root causes. "Event reporting also enables The Joint Commission to validate that the organization has completed a thorough and credible RCA and that the implementation and monitoring of action items will enhance patient safety by mitigating future risk" (Joint Commission 2014, 11). The companion readings at the end of this chapter include a link to The Joint Commission's "Framework for a Root Cause Analysis and Action Plan."

Failure Mode and Effects Analysis

Problems may also be anticipated and processes improved in advance of an adverse event occurring. This proactive, preventive approach is referred to as a **proactive risk assessment**, "an improvement model that involves identifying and analyzing potential failures in healthcare processes or services for the purpose of reducing or eliminating risks that are a threat to patient safety" (Spath 2013b, 192). **Failure mode and effects analysis (FMEA)** is a commonly used tool for this assessment.

Anyone who lost documents and wasted hours of work in the early days of personal computers can appreciate the periodic autosave, the pop-up warning of a low battery, and the rescued document feature that are commonplace for users of contemporary computers. These features illustrate computer designers' understanding of the consequences of hardware and software failures and the subsequent incorporation of product designs that prevent failures from

proactive risk assessment
"an improvement model that involves identifying and analyzing potential failures in healthcare processes or services for the purpose of reducing or eliminating risks that are a threat to patient safety" (Spath 2013b, 192)

failure mode and effects analysis (FMEA)
a systematic process used to conduct a proactive risk assessment

occurring (e.g., plug in the laptop before the battery runs out) or the user from incurring the consequences of the failure (e.g., document saved in the event of a sudden and unexpected power failure). Such is the premise of the FMEA.

This proactive risk assessment tool, FMEA, represents an organized way of thinking of patient safety and medical errors. "Systemic analysis . . . requires a simultaneous imagining of all possible stories. . . . FMEA [does not] refer to a specific methodology; instead . . . [it] defines terms of inquiry . . . 'what has failed, what could fail, and how?'. . . . Given the various possibilities for failure, what are the potential consequences of each?' . . . In general, a failure is said to occur if a component or a collection of components of a system behaves in a way that is not included in its specified performance criteria" (Senders and Senders 1999, 3.2–3.3).

This type of assessment has been used for many years by chemical, structural, mechanical, software, and aerospace engineers. Use of FMEA in healthcare is growing, particularly because The Joint Commission (2015) requires accredited organizations to conduct at least one proactive risk assessment project periodically. Common applications of the FMEA tool include high-risk processes involving medication and intravenous fluid administration, technology implementation, communications handoffs, and prevention of patient falls. An FMEA is most effective when used in the context of a multidisciplinary team. There are various FMEA models; however, the team process often follows these steps:

1. Organize information about the process by creating a simple flowchart of the process steps.
2. Identify what could go wrong (the **failure modes**) at each step of the process.
3. Identify the **critical failures** in the process.
4. Identify what needs to be done to prevent bad results when critical failures occur.
5. Implement preventive actions, and evaluate success at preventing failures.

failure modes
"different ways a process step or task could fail to provide the anticipated result" (Spath 2013b, 194)

critical failures
based on the assessment of the FMEA team, "the most important process failures to prevent" (Spath 2013b, 194)

Actions to improve the safety of healthcare processes following an adverse event are also used to proactively prevent critical failures that may cause an adverse event (exhibit 13.9).

Various forms, charts, and matrices to aid in conducting and documenting an FMEA may be found in the web resources box at the end of this chapter.

Action Category	Examples of Improvement Actions
Eliminate the chance for failures	• Restructure tasks so the error-prevalent step is no longer performed. • Automate the process to change the role of human involvement. • Purchase error-proof equipment.
Make it easier for people to do the right thing	• Create visible displays of acceptable actions (e.g., checklists, computer alerts, instructional posters). • Conduct preuse inspections, such as double-checks prior to administration of high-risk medications. • Reduce the number of process steps, thus reducing the chances of error. • Standardize the process steps to improve consistency of performance. • Make ergonomic changes (e.g., improve lighting, reduce workplace clutter). • Maintain equipment according to manufacturers' recommendations (e.g., regularly monitor compliance with routine maintenance schedules). • Limit the number of people who are permitted to do a critical task.
Identify failures quickly and take appropriate action	• Improve human intervention (e.g., train people to better recognize and deal with unusual situations). • Institute response teams (e.g., specialized teams that are prepared to deal with predefined consequences). • Create backups (e.g., provide equipment or human intervention to mitigate the consequences of the adverse event). • Introduce automation (e.g., visual/auditory feedback indicating "off-normal" situations).

EXHIBIT 13.9
Actions to Improve the Safety of Healthcare Processes

Source: Reprinted from Spath (2013b). Used with permission.

Summary

Patient safety is a component of the overall quality management activities in a health services organization. Keeping patients safe from harm requires an understanding of what causes errors and how to prevent them. By incorporating the characteristics of HROs into the delivery of health services, the rate of adverse events can be reduced. This decline requires the commitment and involvement of people at all levels of the organizational hierarchy—from senior leaders to managers to frontline staff. Root cause analysis and failure mode and effects analysis are two of the many improvement models that can be used to fix system and process problems that cause people to make mistakes.

Exercise 13.1

Objective: To practice identifying different types of errors described in Reason's swiss cheese model.

Instructions:

- Consider the following scenario: In Florida, Clara, an active 94-year-old great-grandmother who still worked as a hospital volunteer two days a week, was admitted to the hospital for a bowel obstruction. She and her family, along with nurses from the hospital, said that there were too few nurses to check on her during the night when her eldest son went home to sleep for a couple of hours. Clara called the nurses to help her use the bathroom but when no one came, she climbed over the bed railing. Still groggy from surgery 20 hours earlier, Clara fell to the floor and broke her left hip. She died two days later during surgery to repair the hip fracture. "It was just too much for her," said her grandson. "For want of one nurse, she died" (Gibson and Singh 2003, 101).

- Review the following list of latent errors, active errors, and preconditions that could have contributed to the event described in this scenario.

  - Absence of one nurse and one nurse aide because of illness that night
  - Clara's advanced age not taken into consideration by caregivers
  - Unavailability of staff to fill in for the two people calling in sick
  - Falls risk assessment not complete on patient's chart
  - Decision to upgrade computed tomography scanner over purchasing safer patient beds
  - Lack of training for nurses about specialized needs of elderly patients, especially related to their responses to medications
  - The departure of Clara's son
  - Consistent scheduling of the night shift with minimum staff needed on the unit
  - Bioengineering's skipping of last month's preventive maintenance check on the call light system (because the department was six weeks behind on its work)
  - Admission of three new patients to this unit from the emergency department between 7:00 pm and 10:00 pm
  - Falls precautions not implemented for this patient

  Write the errors and risk factors in column 2 beside the appropriate category.

Category/Type of Failure	Error
Latent errors at the level of senior decision makers	
Latent failures at the level of frontline management	
Circumstances or conditions present when the patient's accident occurred	
Active errors associated with this event	

Exercise 13.2

Objective: To practice addressing the questions in The Joint Commission's "Framework for Conducting a Root Cause Analysis and Action Plan."

Instructions:

- Download The Joint Commission framework from www.jointcommission. org/framework_for_conducting_a_root_cause_analysis_and_action_plan.
- Read the following case study.
- Follow the instructions at the end of the case study.

Case Study: The letter in this case study is adapted with permission from Trina Bingham, a student in the nursing master's degree program at Duke University School of Nursing in 2005.

You are the risk manager of a tertiary care hospital and have just received the following letter from a patient who was recently discharged from your facility.

Dear Risk Manager,

Last month, I had surgery at your hospital. I was supposed to have a short laparoscopic surgery with a discharge by lunch, but it turned into an open surgery with complications. This led to a four-day hospital stay and discharge with a Foley catheter. Overall, my hospital stay was OK, but I had a situation when the call bell was broken. It was during the night, and I was alone. I needed pain meds. I kept ringing the call bell and no one answered. I used my phone to call the switchboard and no one answered. I didn't want to yell. My IV began beeping (to be honest I kinked the tubing to make it beep), but no one came with that noise either. Eventually the certified nursing assistant came to routinely check my vitals and she got a nurse for me. They switched call bells, but apparently there was an electrical problem, and the call bell couldn't be fixed until the next day, when maintenance was working. The CNA told me to "holler if I needed anything" as she walked out, closing the door. I was so mad, but by this time, the IV pain med was working and I was dozing off. I reported the situation again on day shift and spoke to the director of nursing and the quality assurance manager. Upon discharge, I included this dangerous and unethical situation on my patient satisfaction survey. For me, it worked out OK. All I needed was pain medicine, but what if I had needed help for something more serious? But I have to wonder, when these data are combined with all the other data, if my experience will be minimized. Depending on the layout of satisfaction and quality of care survey results, this situation could look very minor. For all I know, my dissatisfaction was under the heading "dissatisfied with room."

I am writing to you because I have not heard from the director of nursing or the quality assurance manager about what they have done to fix the problems. I believe it is important that you hear my complaint so other patients will not have to go through the terrible experience that I did.

To fix the problems described in this patient's letter, you realize you must first understand the root causes of the problems. Brainstorm possible responses to the questions in "A Framework for Conducting a Root Cause Analysis and Action Plan" by The Joint Commission (2013).

Companion Readings

Centers for Medicare & Medicaid Services (CMS). 2016. *Guidance for Performing Failure Mode and Effects Analysis with Performance Improvement Projects.* Accessed November 8. www.cms.gov/Medicare/Provider-Enrollment-and-Certification/QAPI/downloads/GuidanceForFMEA.pdf.

———. 2016. *Guidance for Performing Root Cause Analysis (RCA) with Performance Improvement Projects (PIPs).* Accessed November 8. www.cms.gov/Medicare/Provider-Enrollment-and-Certification/QAPI/downloads/GuidanceforRCA.pdf.

Chassin, M. R., and J. M. Loeb. 2013. "High-Reliability Health Care: Getting There from Here." *Milbank Quarterly* 91 (3): 459–90.

Coles, G., B. Fuller, K. Nordquist, S. Weissenberger, L. Anderson, and B. DuBois. 2010. "Three Kinds of Proactive Risk Assessments for Health Care." *The Joint Commission Journal on Quality and Patient Safety* 36 (8): 365–75.

Grout, J. 2007. *Mistake-Proofing the Design of Health Care Processes.* Agency for Healthcare Research and Quality. Published May. http://archive.ahrq.gov/professionals/quality-patient-safety/patient-safety-resources/resources/mistakeproof/index.html.

Health Research and Educational Trust, the Institute for Safe Medication Practices, and the Medical Group Management Association. 2008. "Module 1: Working as a Team." Medical Group Management Association. Accessed November 15, 2016. www.mgma.com/practice-resources/tools/patient-safety-tools-for-physician-practices/pathways-for-patient-safety.

———. 2008. "Module 2: Assessing Where You Stand." Medical Group Management Association. Accessed November 15, 2016. www.mgma.com/practice-resources/tools/patient-safety-tools-for-physician-practices/pathways-for-patient-safety.

———. 2008. "Module 3: Working as a Team." Medical Group Management Association. Accessed November 15, 2016. www.mgma.com/practice-resources/tools/patient-safety-tools-for-physician-practices/pathways-for-patient-safety.

Hines, S., K. Luna, J. Lofthus, M. Marquardt, and D. Stelmokas. 2008. *Becoming a High Reliability Organization: Operational Advice for Hospital Leaders.* Agency for Healthcare Research and Quality. Published April. http://archive.ahrq.gov/professionals/quality-patient-safety/quality-resources/tools/hroadvice/hroadvice.pdf.

Hughes, R. G. (ed.). 2008. *Patient Safety and Quality: An Evidence-Based Handbook for Nurses.* Agency for Healthcare Research and Quality. Published April. www.ncbi.nlm.nih.gov/books/NBK2651.

Joint Commission. 2013. "Framework for Conducting a Root Cause Analysis and Action Plan." Revised March 21. www.jointcommission.org/framework_for_conducting_a_root_cause_analysis_and_action_plan.

Makary, M. A., and D. Michael. 2016. "Medical Error—the Third Leading Cause of Death in the US." *British Medical Journal* 353: i21–39.

National Patient Safety Foundation (NPSF). 2016. *RCA²: Improving Root Cause Analyses and Actions to Prevent Harm.* Published January. www.npsf.org/?page=RCA2.

Spath, P. L. 2003. "Using Failure Mode and Effects Analysis to Improve Patient Safety." *AORN Journal* 78 (1): 16–37.

Spath, P. L., and W. Minogue. 2008. "The Soil, Not the Seed: The Real Problem with Root Cause Analysis." Agency for Healthcare Research and Quality. Published July. https://psnet.ahrq.gov/perspectives/perspective/62/the-soil-not-the-seed-the-real-problem-with-root-cause-analysis.

Vincent, C., and R. Amalberti. 2016. *Safer Healthcare: Strategies for the Real World.* New York: Springer.

Weaver, R. R. 2015. "Seeking High Reliability in Primary Care: Leadership, Tools, and Organization." *Health Care Management Review* 40 (3): 183–92.

Web Resources

Improvement Tools

Minnesota State Department of Health Root Cause Analysis Toolkit: www.health.state.mn.us/patientsafety/toolkit

Patient Safety

Agency for Healthcare Research and Quality Patient Safety Network: https://psnet.ahrq.gov

American Hospital Association hospital engagement network: www.hret-hen.org

American Nurses Association 2010 position statement on Just Culture: http://nursingworld.org/psjustculture

Institute for Healthcare Improvement: www.ihi.org/Topics/Patient Safety/Pages/default.aspx

Institute for Safe Medication Practices: www.ismp.org

The Joint Commission on patient safety: www.jointcommission.org/topics/patient_safety.aspx

National Patient Safety Foundation: www.npsf.org

Veterans Administration National Center for Patient Safety: www.patient safety.va.gov

---

References

Agency for Healthcare Research and Quality (AHRQ). 2016a. "Patient Safety Network Glossary." Accessed June 25. www.psnet.ahrq.gov/glossary.aspx.

———. 2016b. "Patient Safety Indicators: Overview." Accessed July 20. www.quality indicators.ahrq.gov/Modules/psi_resources.aspx.

———. 2016c. "Surveys on Patient Safety Culture." Accessed July 20. www.ahrq.gov/professionals/quality-patient-safety/patientsafetyculture/index.html.

Amalberti, R., Y. Auroy, D. Berwick, and P. Barach. 2005. "Five System Barriers to Achieving Ultrasafe Health Care." *Annals of Internal Medicine* 142 (9): 756–64.

American Academy of Pediatrics (AAP). 2011. "Principles of Pediatric Safety: Reducing Harm Due to Medical Care." *Pediatrics* 127 (6): 1199–210.

American Organization of Nurse Executives (AONE). 2007. "AONE Guiding Principles: The Role of the Nurse Executive in Patient Safety." Accessed July 30, 2016. www.aone.org/resources/role-nurse-executive-patient-safety.pdf.

American Society for Quality. 2016. "Plan-Do-Check-Act (PDCA) Cycle." Accessed July 15. www.asq.org/learn-about-quality/project-planning-tools/overview/pdca-cycle.html.

Benn, J., M. Koutantji, L. Wallace, P. Spurgeon, M. Rejman, A. Healey, and C. Vincent. 2009. "Feedback from Incident Reporting: Information and Action to Improve Patient Safety." *Quality and Safety in Health Care* 18 (1): 11–21.

Bialek, R., G. L. Duffy, and J. W. Moran. 2016. "Five Whys and Five Hows." American Society for Quality. Accessed August 1. http://asq.org/healthcare-use/why-quality/five-whys.html.

Bjertnaes, O., E. T. Deilkås, K. E. Skudal, H. H. Iversen, and A. M. Bjerkan. 2015. "The Association Between Patient-Reported Incidents in Hospitals and Estimated Rates of Patient Harm." *International Journal of Quality Health Care* 27 (1): 26–30.

Centers for Medicare & Medicaid Services (CMS). 2016. "Guidance for Performing Root Cause Analysis (RCA) with Performance Improvement Projects (PIPs)." Accessed November 8. www.cms.gov/Medicare/Provider-Enrollment-and-Certification/QAPI/downloads/GuidanceforRCA.pdf.

Clark, C. 2012. "Hospital Care '3,000 Times Less Safe Than Air Travel,' Says TJC Chief." *HealthLeaders Media*. Published December 20. www.healthleaders media.com/quality/hospital-care-3000-times-less-safe-air-travel-says-tjc-chief.

Classen, D. C., R. Resar, F. Griffin, F. Federico, T. Frank, N. Kimmel, J. C. Whittington, A. Frankel, A. Seger, and B. C. James. 2011. "'Global Trigger Tool' Shows That Adverse Events in Hospitals May Be Ten Times Greater Than Previously Measured." *Health Affairs* 30 (40): 581–89.

Evans, S. M., J. G. Berry, B. J. Smith, A. Esterman, P. Selim, J. O'Shaughnessy, and M. DeWit. 2006. "Attitudes and Barriers to Incident Reporting: A Collaborative Hospital Study." *Quality & Safety in Health Care* 15 (1): 39–43.

Gibson, R., and J. P. Singh. 2003. *Wall of Silence: The Untold Story of the Medical Mistakes That Kill and Injure Millions of Americans*. Washington, DC: LifeLine Press.

Griffin, F. A., and R. K. Resar. 2009. *IHI Global Trigger Tool for Measuring Adverse Events*, 2nd ed. IHI Innovation Series white paper. Institute for Healthcare

Improvement. Accessed November 8, 2016. www.ihi.org/resources/Pages/Tools/IHIGlobalTriggerToolforMeasuringAEs.aspx.

Hines, S., K. Luna, J. Lofthus, and M. Marquardt. 2008. *Becoming a High Reliability Organization: Operational Advice for Hospital Leaders.* Agency for Healthcare Research and Quality. Published April. http://archive.ahrq.gov/professionals/quality-patient-safety/quality-resources/tools/hroadvice/hroadvice.pdf.

Hofmann, P. B. 2005. "Acknowledging and Examining Management Mistakes." In *Management Mistakes in Healthcare: Identification, Correction and Prevention,* edited by P. B. Hofmann and F. Perry, 3–27. New York: Cambridge University Press.

Institute of Medicine (IOM). 2001. *Crossing the Quality Chasm: A New Health System for the 21st Century.* Washington, DC: National Academies Press.

———. 2000. *To Err Is Human: Building a Safer Health System.* Washington, DC: National Academies Press.

James, J. T. 2013. "A New, Evidence-Based Estimate of Patient Harms Associated with Hospital Care." *Journal of Patient Safety* 9 (3): 122–28.

Joint Commission. 2016a. "2016 National Patient Safety Goals." Accessed July 30. www.jointcommission.org/standards_information/npsgs.aspx.

———. 2016b. "Sentinel Event Policy and Procedures." Accessed June 26. www.jointcommission.org/sentinel_event_policy_and_procedures.

———. 2016c. "Sentinel Events (SE)." Published January. www.jointcommission.org/assets/1/6/CAMH_24_SE_all_CURRENT.pdf.

———. 2015. "Patient Safety Systems (PS) Chapter for the Hospital Program." In the 2015 Update 2 to the *Comprehensive Accreditation Manual for Hospitals.* Published January 5. www.jointcommission.org/patient_safety_systems_chapter_for_the_hospital_program.

———. 2014. "Why Organizations Self Report Sentinel Events to The Joint Commission." *The Joint Commission Perspectives* 34 (9): 11–12.

———. 2013. "Framework for Conducting a Root Cause Analysis and Action Plan." Published March 22. www.jointcommission.org/framework_for_conducting_a_root_cause_analysis_and_action_plan.

Kelly, D. 2009. "Creating and Leading Error-Free Management Systems." Seminar presented by the American College of Healthcare Executives, Atlanta, GA, September 16–17.

Kilbridge, P. M., and D. C. Classen. 2008. "The Informatics Opportunities at the Intersection of Patient Safety and Clinical Informatics." *Journal of the American Medical Informatics Association* 15 (4): 397–407.

King, A., J. Daniels, J. Lim, D. D. Cochrane, A. Taylor, and J. M. Ansermino. 2010. "Time to Listen: A Review of Methods to Solicit Patient Reports of Adverse Events." *Quality and Safety in Health Care* 19 (2): 148–57.

Leape, L. 2000. *Joint Hearings Before the Subcommittee on Labor, Health and Human Services, and Education, and Related Agencies: Committee on Appropriations;*

the Committee on Health, Education, Labor, and Pensions; and the Committee on Veterans' Affairs. 106th Cong, 1st and 2nd Sess. Testimony.

Levinson, D. R. 2014. *Adverse Events in Skilled Nursing Facilities: National Incidence Among Medicare Beneficiaries.* US Department of Health and Human Services. Published February. https://oig.hhs.gov/oei/reports/oei-06-11-00370.pdf.

———. 2012. *Hospital Incident Reporting Systems Do Not Capture Most Patient Harm.* Department of Health and Human Services. Published January. http://oig.hhs.gov/oei/reports/oei-06-09-00091.asp.

Lohr, K. N. (ed.). 1990. *Medicare: A Strategy for Quality Assurance.* Washington, DC: National Academies Press.

Milch, C. E., D. N. Salem, S. G. Pauker, T. G. Lundquist, S. Kumar, and J. Chen. 2006. "Voluntary Electronic Reporting of Medical Errors and Adverse Events." *Journal of General Internal Medicine* 21 (2): 165–70.

Mull, H., C. W. Brennan, T. Folkes, J. Hermos, J. Chan, A. K. Rosen, and S. R. Simon. 2015. "Identifying Previously Undetected Harm: Piloting the Institute for Healthcare Improvement's Global Trigger Tool in the Veterans Health Administration." *Quality Management in Health Care* 24 (3): 140–46.

National Patient Safety Foundation (NPSF). 2016. *RCA²: Improving Root Cause Analyses and Actions to Prevent Harm.* Published January. www.npsf.org/?page=RCA2.

Reason, J. 1997. *Managing the Risks of Organizational Accidents.* Hampshire, UK: Ashgate Publishing Company.

———. 1995. "Understanding Adverse Events: Human Factors." *Quality and Safety in Healthcare* 4 (2): 80–89.

———. 1990. *Human Error.* New York: Cambridge University Press.

Roberts, K., and R. Bea. 2001. "Must Accidents Happen? Lessons from High Reliability Organizations." *Academy of Management Executives* 15 (3): 70–78.

Sammer, C. E., and B. James. 2011. "Patient Safety Culture: The Nursing Unit Leader's Role." *OJIN: The Online Journal of Issues in Nursing* 16 (3).

Sammer, C. E., K. Lykens, K. P. Singh, D. A. Mains, and N. A. Lackan. 2010. "What Is Patient Safety Culture? A Review of the Literature." *Journal of Nursing Scholarship* 42 (2): 156–65.

Scriven, M., and R. Paul. 2016. "Defining Critical Thinking." Critical Thinking Community. Accessed July 15. www.criticalthinking.org/pages/defining-critical-thinking/410.

Senders, J. W., and S. J. Senders. 1999. "Failure Mode and Effects Analysis in Medicine." In *Medication Errors*, edited by M. R. Cohen, 3.1–3.8. Washington, DC: American Pharmaceutical Association.

Smith, S., J. Sorra, M. Franklin, and J. Behm. 2015. *Ambulatory Surgery Center Survey on Patient Safety Culture: User's Guide.* Agency for Healthcare Research and Quality. Published April. www.ahrq.gov/professionals/quality-patient-safety/patientsafetyculture/asc/index.html.

Spath, P. L. 2013a. "FMEA: A Proactive Resident Safety Technique." *MMDA Topics in Geriatric Medicine and Medical Direction* 35 (2): 1–4.

———. 2013b. *Introduction to Healthcare Quality Management.* Chicago: Health Administration Press.

Weick, K. E., and K. M. Sutcliffe. 2007. *Managing the Unexpected: Assuring High Performance in an Age of Complexity*, 2nd ed. San Francisco: Jossey-Bass.

Weick, K. E., K. M. Sutcliffe, and D. Obstfeld. 1999. "Organizing for High Reliability: Processes of Collective Mindfulness." *Research in Organizational Behavior* 21: 81–123.

Wu, A. 2011. "Near Miss with Bedside Medications." *WebM&M Cases and Commentaries.* Published November. https://psnet.ahrq.gov/webmm/case/254/near-miss-with-bedside-medications#references.

PRACTICE LAB

When asked the way to Carnegie Hall, a famous musician replied, "Practice, practice, practice!"

The end-of-chapter exercises throughout the book are designed to aid students with remembering, understanding, and applying various system concepts and improvement techniques. Section 4 includes additional exercises and case studies designed to help students further apply, evaluate, and synthesize the content and to individualize the application of concepts to their own practice setting.

PRACTICE EXERCISE 1: REFLECTIVE JOURNAL

Although reflection plays an important role in personal learning, it is not practiced often in today's demanding work environments. To individualize learning and enhance the relevance of the content, this journal assignment is offered as a teaching tool to tailor the content to the reader's practice environment, professional experience, and learning needs. This journal exercise section provides a structured opportunity for reflecting on how the concepts discussed and the readings recommended in this book can be applied to circumstances and challenges in the work setting.

Readers may use the journal to reflect on an individual chapter or article or to synthesize content from a group of assigned readings that make up a lesson or module.

Name: Date:

Citation(s):

1. Key points to remember from this reading and my reason(s) for selecting these points:

2. This information has prompted the following questions:

3. How can I use the information in my professional practice, in my work setting, or for my own personal effectiveness?

Part 1: Key Points to Remember

Depending on a reader's experience and current circumstances, one topic may be particularly relevant to one reader, but the same concept may be repetitive or routine to another reader. This part of the template asks readers what lessons are important to them rather than instructing them to consider someone else's perspective.

Part 2: New Questions

Asking readers to list the questions that arise as a result of the readings emphasizes the importance of posing questions and helps develop critical thinking. Although readers, particularly students, may be accustomed to striving for the correct answers, this part of the journal is intended to encourage the practice of formulating good questions.

Part 3: Application

Part 3 encourages readers to think about how the content may be applied to their own work environment or professional practice. Sometimes, the content is relevant personally; a personal application is appropriate to include. The key is to be specific and concrete to solidify the understanding of the material and its practical uses.

PRACTICE EXERCISE 2: THE MANAGER'S ROLE

Objective

To explore how managers influence the quality of products, services, and the customer experience.

Instructions

1. Think of an instance in which you had or observed an experience of excellent quality. You may have had this experience as a customer, a patient, a provider, or an employee. Describe the factors that made this experience excellent and how you felt as a result. Include a description of management's influence on your experience. Do the same for a situation in which you experienced poor quality. Record your responses in the following table or one similar to it.

	Quality of Experience: Excellent	Quality of Experience: Poor
Briefly describe the experience.		
Describe what made this experience excellent or poor.		
How did you feel as a result?		
What was management's role or influence?		

2. On the basis of the observations you recorded in the table, describe why understanding quality is important for health services managers.

PRACTICE EXERCISE 3: DYNAMIC COMPLEXITY

Objective

To practice identifying dynamic complexity in a patient care experience.

Instructions

1. Read the case study.
2. Review the system characteristics that contribute to dynamic complexity:
   - Change
   - Trade-offs
   - History dependency
   - Tight coupling
   - Nonlinearity

For further explanation on these system characteristics, please refer to J.D. Sterman, 2006, "Learning from Evidence in a Complex World," *American Journal of Public Health* 96 (3): 505–14.

3. Explain how these system characteristics are expressed in the case study.

Case Study

This case is adapted from D. L. Kelly and S. L. Pestotnik's 1998 unpublished manuscript "Using Causal Loop Diagrams to Facilitate Double Loop Learning in the Healthcare Delivery Setting."

Mrs. B was a 66-year-old widow living on a fixed income. She had been diagnosed with high blood pressure and osteoporosis. Her private doctor knew her well. When he selected the medication with which to treat her high blood pressure, he took into account her age, the fact that she had osteoporosis, and other issues. He chose a drug that had proven beneficial for patients such as

Mrs. B and had minimum side effects. Mrs. B did well on the medication for ten years. Her insurance covered the cost of her medication, except for a small out-of-pocket copayment.

The last time Mrs. B went to her local pharmacy to refill her prescription, the pharmacist informed her that her insurance company had contracted with a pharmacy benefits management (PBM) company. (The role of a PBM company is to perform a variety of cost-cutting services for health insurance plans. One of these services is to decide which drugs an insurance company will pay for; the PBM company's preferred-product list is known as a *formulary*.) If Mrs. B wanted to continue to take the same medication, it would cost her five times her usual copayment. She was quite disturbed because she could not afford this price increase and did not fully understand her insurance company's new policy. The pharmacist offered to call Mrs. B's doctor, explain the situation, and ask him whether he would change her prescription to the PBM-preferred brand. When the physician was contacted, he was not aware of the PBM company's action and was not completely familiar with the preferred product. The pharmacist discussed Mrs. B's predicament with the physician and described the financial consequences of continuing to receive her original prescription. After this discussion with the pharmacist, the physician concluded that his only option was to approve the switch, which he did.

Mrs. B began taking the new brand of high blood pressure medicine. One week after starting on the new drug, she developed a persistent cough that aggravated her osteoporosis and caused her rib pain. When the cough and pain continued for another week, Mrs. B began to take over-the-counter medicines for the pain. She unknowingly opened herself to a reaction between her blood pressure medication and the pain medication: orthostatic hypotension (lightheadedness when rising from a lying to an upright position). One morning on her way to the bathroom, she fainted, fell, and broke her hip. She was admitted to the hospital for surgery, where she developed a urinary tract infection. The infection spread to her repaired hip, which resulted in a bloodstream infection that eventually led to her death.

PRACTICE EXERCISE 4: SYSTEM RELATIONSHIPS

Objective

To practice identifying relationships within systems.

Instructions

1. This exercise builds on Exercise 2: The Manager's Role. To begin, review your responses to that exercise.
2. Review these three systems models presented in chapter 5:
   - Three core process model
   - The Baldrige Performance Excellence Program framework
   - Socioecological framework
3. Choose the model you can best relate to at this time.
4. Look at both your excellent experience and your poor experience, paying particular attention to how you described the manager's role or influence. Transfer what you wrote about the manager's role or influence to the following Systems Model Worksheet.
5. Now, think about those experiences from the perspective of the systems model you chose in question 3. Describe any additional insights gained about this experience by viewing it in the context of the systems perspective represented by the model. Write your responses in the following Systems Model Worksheet.

Systems Model Worksheet

	Quality of Experience: Excellent	Quality of Experience: Poor
Manager's role/influence		
Additional understanding by viewing through systems perspective		

PRACTICE EXERCISE 5: MEETING CUSTOMER EXPECTATIONS

Objective

To encourage practice managers or care providers to identify customer expectations and measure whether these expectations are being met.

Instructions

1. Write a brief description of your organizational setting in the following Customers Worksheet. This setting may be a practice, department, or program.
2. Identify your customers (recipients or beneficiaries of your services, such as patients or clients, other caregivers, providers, and stakeholders), and write them in the first column of the Customers Worksheet.
3. Complete the remaining columns of the worksheet for each customer listed in the first column.

Customers Worksheet

Organizational Setting:

Customer	Expectation	What I Do to Meet That Expectation	How I Can Measure Whether I Met That Expectation

PRACTICE EXERCISE 6: ORGANIZATIONAL SELF-ASSESSMENT

Objectives

- To practice using an organizational assessment as a means of documenting current reality and identifying performance gaps.
- To practice using the Baldrige Performance Excellence Program Health Care Criteria for Performance Excellence as a guide for completing an organizational assessment.
- To conduct a miniassessment of an organization using questions from the Baldrige Excellence Builder self-assessment tool.

  Note: Working managers may complete this exercise by basing it on the practices of their own organizations. Students may complete this exercise by basing it on the practices of a current or previous employer.

Instructions

1. Select and describe the boundaries of the system of interest; the term "organization" will be used to refer to this system. You may select a team, a department, a small organization (e.g., an office practice), or an entire organization.
2. To familiarize yourself with the criteria, review the section called "Health Care Criteria Category and Item Commentary" in the Baldrige Health Care Criteria for Performance Excellence, available at www.nist .gov/baldrige/enter/health_care.cfm.
3. The Baldrige Excellence Builder self-assessment provides a general description of the criteria category followed by questions from the self-assessment (pp. 5–13) from the 2017–2018 Health Care Criteria for Performance Excellence.
4. Based on the system selected in question 1, write brief replies to the Baldrige questions.

Organizational Assessment Worksheet

Organizational Profile

This category of the self-assessment is a snapshot of your organization, including the key influences on how it operates, and of your competitive environment.

- Briefly describe your organization, including its services; size; geographic community; key patient or customer groups; and current facilities, equipment, and technology, as well as the number of patients or clients it serves.

- Briefly describe your organization's key challenges and current performance improvement system.

Leadership

This category examines how the personal actions of your organization's senior leaders guide and sustain your organization. It also examines your organization's governance system and how your organization fulfills its legal, ethical, and societal responsibilities and supports its key communities.

- How do senior leaders deploy your organization's vision and values through your leadership system, to the workforce, to key suppliers and partners, and to patients and stakeholders, as appropriate?

- How do senior leaders encourage frank, two-way communication throughout the organization?

Strategy

This category examines how your organization develops strategic objectives and action plans. It also examines how your chosen strategic objectives and action plans are deployed and changed, if circumstances require, and how progress is measured.

- How does your organization conduct strategic planning?

- Summarize your organization's action plans, how they are deployed, and key action plan performance measures or indicators.

Customers

This category examines how your organization engages its customers—the users of your healthcare services (e.g., patients, families, insurers, other third-party payers)—for long-term marketplace success. This engagement strategy includes how your organization listens to the voice of its customers, builds customer relationships, and uses customer information to improve and identify opportunities for innovation.

- How do you identify customers and market requirements for service offerings?

- How do you build and manage relationships with customers to meet their requirements and exceed their expectations at each stage of their relationship with you?

Measurement, Analysis, and Knowledge Management

This category examines how your organization selects, gathers, analyzes, manages, and improves its data, information, and knowledge assets and how it manages its information technology. It also examines how your organization uses review findings to improve its performance.

- What are your key organizational performance measures?

- How do you use this information to support organizational decision making and innovation?

Workforce Focus

This category examines your ability to assess workforce capability and capacity needs and to build a workforce environment conducive to high performance. This category examines how your organization engages, manages, and develops your workforce to use its full potential in alignment with your organization's overall mission, strategy, and action plans.

- How do you assess your workforce capability and capacity needs, including skills, competencies, and staffing levels?

- How do you address workplace environmental factors to ensure and improve workplace health, safety, and security?

Operations

This category examines how your organization designs, manages, and improves its work systems and work processes to deliver patient and stakeholder value and achieve organizational success and sustainability. It also examines your readiness for emergency.

- How do you design and innovate your work processes to meet all the key requirements?

- How do you improve your work processes to improve healthcare outcomes, to achieve better performance, to reduce variability, and to improve healthcare services?

Results

This category examines your organization's performance and improvement in all key areas: healthcare and process outcomes, customer-focused outcomes, workforce-focused outcomes, leadership and governance outcomes, and financial and market outcomes. Performance levels are examined relative to those of competitors and other organizations with similar healthcare services offerings.

- Provide data for one key measure or indicator of performance and process effectiveness.

- Provide data for one key measure or indicator of patient or stakeholder satisfaction.

- Provide data for one key measure or indicator of workforce capability.

- Provide data for one key measure or indicator of achievement of organizational strategy and action.

- Provide data for one key measure or indicator of financial performance.

- Provide data for one key measure or indicator related to operational performance.

- Provide data for one key measure related to achieving legal, regulatory, and accreditation requirements.

Prioritizing Improvement Opportunities

1. Review the responses to the organizational assessment questions.
2. Note any questions for which you could not provide a response (i.e., the organization does not have a defined process or approach to address the topic of the question).
3. Review the results data and select one or more measures that demonstrate less-than-desirable results.

PRACTICE EXERCISE 7: IMPROVING A PERFORMANCE GAP IN YOUR ORGANIZATION

Objectives

- To provide an opportunity for managers to be involved in a performance improvement effort using the actual identified needs in their own organizations.
- To practice improvement approaches in a safe and controlled setting.

   Note: Implementing the results of this exercise in your own organization is not required. However, the exercise requires you to think through and document all of the steps in the exercise as if you were actually conducting this effort in your organization.

Instructions

1. Describe one of the performance gaps you identified in Exercise 6: Organizational Self-Assessment or a performance gap that you are aware of in the scope of your defined work unit or responsibilities.

2. Briefly describe the process(es) or function(s) that makes up this performance area.

3. List whom you would invite to participate in your improvement effort and why you selected them.

4. a. State and critique several possible goal statements for this improvement effort. Use the following Goals Worksheet to organize your thinking.

   b. Based on your critique, select the goal you will use for the improvement effort.

Goals Worksheet

Goal Statement	Type of Goal	Pros	Cons

5. Practice the purpose principle (chapter 6) by asking yourself the following questions:
   - What am I trying to accomplish?

   - What is the purpose of the process(es) identified in question 2?

- Have I further expanded the purpose? What is the purpose of my previous response?
- Have I further expanded the purpose? What is the purpose of my previous response? (Continue expanding the purpose, if needed.)

- What larger purpose may eliminate the need to achieve this smaller purpose altogether?

- What is the right purpose for me to be working on? (Describe how this purpose differs or does not differ from the original purpose.)

6. Review your selected goal from question 4. After completing the purpose questions in question 5, does this goal still seem appropriate? If not, redefine the goal of your improvement effort.

7. Is the process (or processes) from question 2 still the appropriate process to improve? If not, describe the process(es) you will improve.

8. Describe the customers of the process and their expectations or requirements.

9. Describe a performance measure for this process, how the data are collected, and a graph that could be used to display the measurement results. This performance indicator may be the original from which you determined this performance gap.

10. Document the process steps as they are currently carried out using a high-level flowchart.

11. Practice identifying mental models (chapter 8):
    - Identify at least two mental models that may be interfering with achieving a higher level of performance from your process. What actions are associated with these mental models?

    - Describe an alternative mental model for each that could enhance the improvement of your process. What actions are associated with the alternative mental model?

12. Identify and apply any additional quality improvement tools (see chapter 12) that may help you better understand how to improve your process. Show your work.

13. If your process is to be the best practice for the community, describe your ideal vision for this process. To help create your vision, ask yourself the following questions:
    - What would your process contribute to the overall organizational performance or effectiveness?

– What would patients and families who are receiving care as a result of your process, or who are influenced by your process, say about their experience with your organization?

– What would employees involved in your process say about the process?

– What would colleagues around the country who came to learn from your best practice say about your process?

14. Improve your process.
   – Determine if you are solving a problem associated with an existing process or creating a new process.

   – Review your original and revised improvement goal(s).

   – Review the purpose of your process.

   – Review your customers' expectations.

- Review the mental models you selected.

- Review what you learned from question 12.

- Redefine the starting and ending points of your process as needed to support the purpose.

- Based on the previous information, document the ideal process that will achieve the purpose you described, using a high-level flowchart.

- Check your process against the goal you set for your improvement effort.

15. Review the measure from question 9. Is this measure still appropriate for your ideal process? If not, what should you measure?

16. Review your goal and your purpose. Will these measure(s) help you determine if you are working toward your goal and carrying out your purpose?

17. Describe any unintended consequences to any other area, department, process, or entity inside or outside of your organization if you change your process. What measure(s) would help you to be on the alert for them?

18. Describe how the measures from questions 15 and 17 fit into a balanced set of performance measures for the organization.

19. For your defined performance measures, describe
    - How you would collect the data

    - What type of graph you would use to report the data

    - How often you would report the data

    - With whom and how you would share the data for review on a regular basis

20. You have defined the purpose and described the ideal process. Determine the ideal structure to carry out this process—that is, by whom and how the process should be carried out to best achieve the purpose.

21. Describe an implementation plan that takes into consideration the concepts described in chapter 12.

PRACTICE EXERCISE 8: TEAMWORK AND PATIENT SAFETY

Objective

To better understand how inadequate teamwork practices can cause a sentinel event and what needs to be done to prevent similar events from occurring.

Instructions

1. Common teamwork barriers that can lead to a sentinel event include these problems:
   - Inconsistency in team leaders
   - Lack of time to meet and interact as a team
   - Hierarchy
   - Defensiveness
   - Not speaking up
   - Conventional thinking
   - Varying communication styles
   - Unresolved conflict
   - Distractions
   - Fatigue
   - Heavy workload
   - Misinterpreting cues
   - Lack of role clarity

Source: M. Leonard, A. Frankel, T. Simmonds, and K. Vega. 2005. *Achieving Safe and Reliable Healthcare: Strategies and Solutions*. Chicago: Health Administration Press.

2. Read the sentinel event in the case study.

3. Considering the list of teamwork barriers in question 1, describe which barriers existed in this case and how the barriers contributed to the eventual adverse event.

4. Suggest ways the process can be changed to improve teamwork and thus reduce the likelihood another event of this type will occur.

Case Study

An orthopedic clinic phones the hospital to schedule a left-knee arthroscopy procedure for a 66-year-old man. On receipt of the procedure reservation, the hospital sends an electronic copy of the surgery booking back to the clinic for verification. According to procedure, the clinic is to confirm the accuracy of the information, but this confirmation is not done. It is later discovered the surgeon's medical assistant had incorrectly scheduled the procedure for the left knee when the patient's right knee was to be operated on.

One week later the patient arrives at the hospital's outpatient surgery unit. The operating room (OR) schedule and the patient's registration information indicate he is scheduled for a left-knee arthroscopy. The patient's history and physical (H&P) from his primary care physician indicates his right knee is to be operated on. The patient's H&P from the orthopedic surgeon indicates the procedure will be done on the left knee. Throughout the entire stay, no one notices the inconsistencies in laterality present in the two H&Ps.

The patient is taken to the preoperative area, where a nurse obtains routine information from the patient and asks the patient to state the surgery he is having. The patient says he has been having pain in both knees but thinks it is his left knee that will be operated on today. This statement is confirmed by the nurse by comparing what the patient said to the procedure listed on the OR schedule.

The anesthesiologist scheduled to participate in the case is running behind schedule with another procedure, so a covering anesthesiologist conducts the patient's preoperative anesthesia assessment. During the assessment, the anesthesiologist notices the patient seems to be confused about which knee is to be operated on, but this observation is not documented in the assessment notes nor is it communicated to the surgeon. The covering anesthesiologist only notes "knee arthroscopy" in the patient's record and does not indicate which knee.

In the preoperative area, the surgeon talks with the patient and discusses the right-knee arthroscopy he will be doing. The patient agrees and signs the consent form for a right-knee procedure, and the surgeon marks the patient's right knee as the correct surgery site. The circulating nurse witnesses the patient's signature on the consent form. The OR room is set up for the procedure. The anesthesiologist scheduled to participate in the case reads the preoperative anesthesia assessment done by the covering anesthesiologist to determine what is needed for the procedure.

The patient is brought in to the OR. The patient's identity is validated and documented on the time-out form. Although the patient's right knee has markings indicating it is the site for surgery, the surgeon places the patient's left knee in a stirrup for prepping. The circulating nurse preps the patient's left knee and the surgeon drapes the left knee. The circulating nurse verbally initiates the time-out and receives verbal confirmation of the planned surgery and surgery site from the technical staff. Although no verbal responses are received from the surgeon or anesthesiologist, the nurse documents completion of all time-out steps.

The surgeon proceeds with the arthroscopy, which is performed on the patient's left knee. When the patient awakens from the procedure he asks why his left knee is painful as he expected to have surgery on his right knee. The surgeon immediately discusses the mistake with the patient and family.

PRACTICE EXERCISE 9: IMPROVEMENT CASE STUDY

Objective

To practice quality improvement tools by applying them to an improvement effort in an ambulatory care setting.

Instructions

1. Read the following case study.
2. After you have read the case study, follow the instructions continued at the end of the case.

Case Study

Background

You have just been brought in to manage a portfolio of several specialty clinics in a large multiphysician group practice in an academic medical center. The clinics reside in a multiclinic facility that houses primary care and specialty practices, as well as a satellite laboratory and radiology and pharmacy services. The practice provides the following centralized services for each of its clinics: registration, payer interface (e.g., authorization), and billing. The CEO of the practice has asked you to initially devote your attention to Clinic X to improve its efficiency and patient satisfaction.

Access Process

A primary care physician (or member of the office staff), patient, or family member calls the receptionist at Clinic X to request an appointment. If the receptionist is in the middle of helping a patient in person, the caller is asked to hold. The receptionist then asks the caller, "How may I help you?" If the caller is requesting an appointment within the next month, the appointment date and time are made and given verbally to the caller. If the caller asks additional questions, the receptionist provides answers. The caller is then given the toll-free preregistration phone number and asked to preregister before the date of the scheduled appointment. If the requested appointment is beyond a 30-day period, the caller's name and address are put in a "future file" because physician availability is given only one month in advance. Every month, the receptionist reviews the future file and schedules an appointment for each person on the list, and a confirmation is automatically mailed to the caller.

When a patient preregisters, the financial office is automatically notified and performs the necessary insurance checks and authorizations for the appropriate insurance plan. If the patient does not preregister, when the patient arrives at the clinic on the day of the appointment and checks in with the specialty clinic receptionist, she is asked to first go to the central registration area to register. Any obvious problems with authorization are corrected before the patient returns to the specialty clinic waiting room.

Receptionist's Point of View

The receptionist has determined that the best way not to inconvenience the caller is to keep her on the phone for the shortest period possible. The receptionist expresses frustration with the fact that there are too many tasks in the office to do at once.

Physician's Point of View

The physician thinks too much of his time is spent on paperwork and chasing down authorizations. The physician senses that appointments are always running behind and that patients are frustrated, no matter how nice he is to them.

Patient's Point of View

Patients are frustrated when asked to wait in a long line to register, which makes them late for their appointments, and when future appointments are scheduled without their input. As a result of this latter factor, and work or childcare conflicts, patients often do not show up for these scheduled appointments.

Office Nurse's Point of View

The office nurse feels that he is playing catch up all day long and explaining delays. The office nurse also wishes there was more time for teaching.

Billing Office's Point of View

The billing office thinks that physicians are giving some care that is not reimbursed because of inaccurate or incomplete insurance or demographic information, and observes that some care is denied authorization after the fact.

Patient Satisfaction Measures

All clinics in the multiphysician group contract with a customer satisfaction measurement firm that administers customer surveys. This survey is sent to a random sample of patients at each clinic to determine their satisfaction ratings for eight dimensions of outpatient and inpatient care for adults and children:

- Respect for patients' values, preferences, and expressed needs
- Coordination and integration of care
- Information and education
- Physical comfort
- Emotional support and alleviation of fear and anxiety
- Involvement of family and friends
- Transition and continuity
- Access to care

Performance Data

The last quarter's worth of performance data for Clinic X are found in the following table.

Overall satisfaction with visit rated as very good or excellent	82%
Staff courtesy and helpfulness rated as very good or excellent	90%
Waiting room time for patients is less than 15 minutes	64%
Examination room waiting time is less than 15 minutes	63%
Patient no-show rate	20%
Patient appointment cancellation rate	11%
Provider appointment cancellation rate	10%
Rate of initial insurance claim rejections because of inaccurate or incomplete patient record documentation	4%
Patient preregistration rate	16%
Average number of patient visits per day	16
Range of patient visits per day	10–23

Instructions (continued)

3. Before continuing, completely read all of the remaining instructions.

4. Decide which problem you want to focus on as your first priority for Clinic X. Describe the problem and why you chose this problem.

5. State the goal for the improvement effort.

6. Identify the fundamental knowledge required by the improvement project team to solve this problem. Identify the people (professional group or service area) that should be represented on the team and the fundamental knowledge they bring to the team.

7. Document the current process (as it is described in the case narrative) using a process flowchart.

8. Identify the customers of the process to be improved and their expectations.

9. Explore and prioritize root causes of the problem by doing the following:
   a. Brainstorm root causes and document the causes on a fishbone diagram.

b. Describe how you would collect data about how frequently the root causes contribute to the problem.

10. Review the following process improvement techniques. Select and explain the ones that apply to improving your process. Be sure to take into account what you have learned in steps 6 through 8.

a. Eliminate waste (e.g., things that are not used, intermediaries, unnecessary duplication)

b. Improve workflow (e.g., minimize handoffs, move steps in the process closer together, find and remove bottlenecks, do tasks in parallel, adjust to high and low volumes)

c. Manage time (e.g., reduce setup time and waiting time)

d. Manage variation (create standard processes where appropriate)

e. Design systems to avoid mistakes (use reminders)

11. Incorporating what you learned in steps 6 through 9, describe the changed process using a process flowchart or workflow diagram.

12. Decide what you will measure to monitor process performance to be sure your changes were effective and briefly describe how you would collect the data.

13. You have completed the "Plan" phase of the Shewhart cycle. Describe briefly how you would complete the rest of the Plan, Do, Check, Act cycle.

14. Save your answers to each part of this exercise. This material will become the documentation of your improvement effort.

PRACTICE EXERCISE 10: SYSTEMS ERROR CASE STUDY AND ANALYSIS

Objectives

- To better understand Reason's Model of Organizational Accidents and actions to make healthcare safer by identifying different types of errors and interventions.
- To prevent actual sentinel events.

Instructions

1. Read Katherine Eban's 2008 article "Your Hospital's Deadly Secret," available at http://katherineeban.com/2008/03/01/your-hospitals-deadly-secret-conde-nast-portfolio.

2. Based on the information provided in the article, identify specific actions or decisions that proved to be errors at the different levels of the system. Write your responses in the first column of the following Organizational Errors Worksheet. Complete this column before moving on to question 3.

3. Identify specific interventions that would have helped the organization monitor or prevent the failures identified in the first column from occurring. Write your response in the second column of the worksheet. Be very specific and concrete in your responses.

4. Refer to chapter 13 and the chapter 13 companion readings for assistance in completing this exercise.

Organizational Errors Worksheet

Latent failures in the healthcare system level external to the hospital and its parent company:	Intervention(s) to prevent failure from occurring:
Latent failures at the level of the organization's leadership:	Intervention(s) to prevent failure from occurring:
Latent failures at the level of frontline management:	Intervention(s) to prevent failure from occurring:
Workplace preconditions surrounding this event:	Intervention(s) to prevent failure from occurring:
Active errors associated with this event:	Intervention(s) to prevent failure from occurring:

PRACTICE EXERCISE 11: FAILURE MODE AND EFFECTS ANALYSIS

Objective

To practice completing a failure mode and effects analysis (FMEA). FMEA is a proactive risk assessment technique that includes identification of failure modes (things that could go wrong) for the steps of a process, selection of failure modes that most need to be prevented, and identification of how the process can be changed to reduce the likelihood of these failures occurring. This exercise involves completion of a simplified FMEA that follows steps similar to those outlined in the following Centers for Medicare & Medicaid Services article "Guidance for Performing Failure Mode and Effects Analysis with Performance Improvement Projects," available at www.cms.gov/Medicare/Provider-Enrollment-and-Certification/QAPI/downloads/GuidanceForFMEA.pdf.

Instructions

1. Evaluate the process of administering pneumococcal vaccinations for eligible hospitalized patients. The four steps of this process are as follows:
   a. On admission, a nurse assesses whether the patient has received a pneumococcal polysaccharide vaccine or pneumococcal conjugate vaccine, and how recently.

   b. The nurse records the patient's vaccination status in the electronic health record.

   c. The nurse identifies patients eligible for vaccination and adds vaccine administration to the patient's plan of care.

d. The vaccine is administered to eligible patients by the nurse (per standing orders) prior to the patient's discharge.

2. Identify two failure modes (things that could go wrong) in each step of the process. Record the failure modes on part 1 of the following FMEA worksheet.

3. Review all the failure modes you have identified and pick two that are very important to prevent. This decision will be your "best guess" using the following criteria:

    a. How often the failure probably happens

    b. Whether the failure is likely to be corrected before causing harm

    c. How severe the results could be, should the failure occur and not be corrected

4. Record the two failure modes you select (as written in part 1) in the first column in part 2 of the FMEA worksheet under the heading Critical Failure Modes.

5. Determine what would cause each critical failure mode to occur. Base this answer on your personal experiences, knowledge of why such failures have occurred in the past, or input you get from people currently involved in similar processes. Record the causes for each critical failure mode in the space provided.

6. Identify actions to eliminate or reduce the chance each critical failure will happen. For this step, consider recommendations in exhibit 13.9 in chapter 13. Record the actions in the space provided.

FMEA Worksheet, Part 1

Process Step	Failure Mode (What Could Go Wrong)
On admission, a nurse assesses the patient's status re: pneumococcal polysaccharide vaccine or pneumococcal conjugate vaccine	
Nurse records the patient's vaccination status in the electronic health record	
Nurse identifies patients eligible for vaccination and adds vaccine administration to the patient's plan of care	
Vaccine is administered to eligible patients by nurse (per standing orders) prior to the patient's discharge	

FMEA Worksheet, Part 2

Critical Failure Modes	Cause(s)	Actions to Eliminate/ Reduce Failures

GLOSSARY

accountable care organization (ACO): a network of providers (primarily doctors and hospitals) that share financial and medical responsibilities for providing coordinated care to patients in hopes of limiting unnecessary spending (Gold 2015)

accreditation: "a public recognition by a healthcare accreditation body of the achievement of accreditation standards by a healthcare organization, demonstrated through an independent external peer assessment of that organization's level of performance in relation to the standards" (Smits, Supachutikul, and Mate 2014, 2)

active errors: errors committed by frontline workers; the results are seen immediately (Reason 1990, 1997)

adverse event: "an injury caused by medical management rather than the underlying condition of the patient" (IOM 2000, 4)

analysis: "extracting larger meaning from data and information to support evaluation, decision making, improvement, and innovation" (BPEP 2015, 43)

assignable variation (or signal, special cause variation): variation that appears as the result of causes outside of the core processes of the work (Neuhauser, Provost, and Bergman 2011)

A3 report: a concise summary of the problem and solution with pictures and a few words (Dennis 2009)

attribute: tally of "events that can be aggregated into discrete categories" (Carey and Lloyd 2001, 70)

average (or mean): a popular numerical technique used to describe the central location of a dataset

balanced scorecard (BSC): an organization-defined set of measures that provides leaders with a concise but comprehensive view of business performance

bar chart (or bar graph): a graphical representation that is primarily used to describe a single set of categorical data

causal loop diagram: visual representation that displays the dynamic between cause and effect from a relational standpoint

cause-and-effect diagram (or fishbone or Ishikawa diagram): tool for organizing and documenting, in a structured format, the causes of a problem

certification: a form of external quality review for health services professionals and organizations; when applied to individuals, it represents advanced education and competence; when applied to organizations, it represents meeting predetermined standards for a specialized service provided by the organization (Rooney and Ostenburg 1999)

change management: a "systematic approach that prepares an organization to accept, implement, and sustain the improved processes" (Chassin and Loeb 2013, 481)

clinical microsystem: a "small group of people who work together on a regular basis to provide care to discrete subpopulations of patients" (Godfrey, Nelson, and Batalden 2004, 5)

clinical value compass: a balanced scorecard for evaluating outcomes of a clinical process that includes four categories: functional status and well-being of the patient (north), direct and indirect healthcare costs (south), patient and family satisfaction and perceived benefit (east), and clinical results (west)

cognitive psychology: the branch of psychology "concerned with mental processes (as perception, thinking, learning, and memory) especially with respect to the internal events occurring between sensory stimulation and the overt expression of behavior" (Merriam-Webster 2016)

collaborative team: "health care professionals assuming complementary roles and cooperatively working together, sharing responsibility for problem-solving and making decisions to formulate and carry out plans for patient care" (O'Daniel and Rosenstein 2008, 2-272)

collective mindfulness: an organizational attribute in which all individuals are aware of the dire consequences of even a small error and are constantly alert to the potential for problems (Weick and Sutcliffe 2007)

complex: having a large number of variables that interact with each other in innumerable, and often unpredictable, ways

context: "the unquestioning assumptions through which all experience is filtered" (Davis 1982, 26)

continuous data: numeric (real number) data that can be broken down into smaller and smaller subunits of measurement

continuous improvement: steady, incremental improvement in the organization's overall performance

control chart (or process behavior chart): a line graph that contains a mean line and upper and lower limits of the normal range or control limits

correlation coefficient: a statistical measure that provides information about the strength and the direction of a linear relationship between two variables

creative tension: the state engendered by the discrepancy between an organization's current level of performance and its desired level and vision for the future

critical failures: based on the assessment of the FMEA team, "the most important process failures to prevent" (Spath 2013b, 194)

critical thinking: "the art of analyzing and evaluating thinking with a view to improving it" (Scriven and Paul 2016)

customer: the user or potential user of services or programs

customer-focused quality: a type of quality in which key patient and other customer requirements and expectations are identified and drive improvement efforts

data analytics: "the extensive use of data, statistical and quantitative analysis, explanatory and predictive models, and fact-based management to drive decisions and actions" (Davenport and Harris 2007, 7)

decision matrix: improvement tool that "evaluates and prioritizes a list of options" (ASQ 2016c)

deployment flowchart: process flowchart diagram that indicates who is responsible for which steps of the process

descriptive statistics: a catch-all term used to summarize and describe data using techniques such as mean, standard deviation, bar graph, and histogram

discrete data: numeric (real number) data that can take on values that cannot be broken into smaller subunits of measurements

double-loop learning: a type of learning in which, if one is not satisfied with the results or consequences, before taking further action, underlying assumptions are examined, clarified, communicated, or reframed based on what the assumptions reveal. Only then is subsequent action, based on lessons revealed, taken (Argyris 1991; Tagg 2007)

dynamic complexity: complexity in which "cause and effect are subtle, and where the effects over time of interventions are not obvious" (Senge 2006, 71)

errors: "all those occasions in which a planned sequence of mental or physical activities fails to achieve its intended outcome" (Reason 1990, 9)

errors of commission: tasks not required by the process that are done anyhow

errors of omission: required tasks that are not done

execution errors: problems that arise when a proper plan is carried out improperly

external customer: a user outside the organization

failure mode and effects analysis (FMEA): a systematic process used to conduct a proactive risk assessment

failure modes: "different ways a process step or task could fail to provide the anticipated result" (Spath 2013b, 194)

5S methodology: a philosophy and five-step way of organizing and managing the workspace by eliminating waste

Five Whys: "a questioning process designed to drill down into the details of a problem . . . and peel away the layers of symptoms" (Bialek, Duffy, and Moran 2016)

force field analysis: "a technique for evaluating all of the various forces for and against a proposed change" (McLaughlin and Olson 2012, 160)

health policies: policies that "pertain to health or influence the pursuit of health" (Longest 2010, 6)

high-reliability organizations (HROs): "organizations with systems in place that are exceptionally consistent in accomplishing their goals and avoiding potentially catastrophic errors" (Hines et al. 2008, 5)

histogram: a graphical representation that is primarily used to describe a single set of continuous data

hospital-acquired conditions (or never events): medical conditions that "could reasonably have been prevented through the application of evidence-based guidelines" (CMS 2015b)

incident reports: "instruments (paper or electronic) used to document occurrences that could have led or did lead to undesirable results" (Spath 2013b, 187)

inferential statistics: numeric information used to make an estimate, prediction, or decision about a population on the basis of a sample using techniques such as confidence intervals and hypothesis tests

internal customer: a user inside the organization

interquartile range (IQR): the difference between the values found at first (Q1) and third (Q3) quartiles

judgment errors: errors resulting from improper selection of an objective or a plan of action

Just Culture: an aspect of organizational behavior that creates an atmosphere of trust, encouraging and rewarding people for providing essential safety-related information (Reason 1997)

kaizen event (or rapid process improvement project): "a focused, short-term project aimed at improving a particular process" (McLaughlin and Olson 2012, 410)

key components of quality care: quality care is safe, effective, patient centered, timely, efficient, and equitable (IOM 2001)

latent errors: errors occurring in the upper levels of the organization; an error may lie dormant for days or years until a particular combination of circumstances allows the latent error to become an adverse event (Reason 1990, 1997)

Lean (or Lean thinking): an improvement philosophy and set of tools that "is about finding and eliminating waste in all processes" (Black 2016, 6)

licensure: status granted by a governmental body and confirming minimum standards

macrosystems: organizations providing health services, such as hospitals, nursing homes, community health clinics, and emergency medical services

median: the value that represents the central tendency of all values in a dataset

megasystem: a complex variety of interdependent organizations

mental model: a deeply ingrained way of thinking that influences how a person sees and understands the world as well as how that person acts

microsystems: "people, machines, and data at the level of direct patient care (the treatment team within the hospital or the physician office practice, for example)" (Schyve 2005, 2)

mission: statement that defines the system's identity

mode: the value that occurs most frequently in a dataset

near-miss event (or close call): "an event or a situation that did not produce patient harm because it did not reach the patient, either due to chance or to [being] capture[d] before reaching the patient; or if it did reach the patient, [did not cause harm] due to robustness of the patient or to timely intervention (for example, an antidote was administered)" (Wu 2011)

nominal data: text or numeric values used to categorize or classify qualitative attributes with no implied rank or order given to the individual values

nonlinear: relating to a system in which the "effect is rarely proportional to the cause" (Sterman 2000, 22)

optimizing violations: "actions taken to further personal rather than task related goals" (Reason 1995, 82)

ordinal data: text or numeric values used to categorize or classify qualitative attributes in a fixed set of possible values with an implied rank or order given to the individual values

organization: a structured system designed to accomplish a goal or set of goals

organizational culture: a consistent, observable pattern of behavior in an organization; the way things get done

organizational effectiveness: the ability to accomplish goals

organizational structure: the manner in which responsibility and authority are distributed throughout an organization (Shortell and Kaluzny 2006)

outcome: "a change in a patient's current and future health status that can be attributed to antecedent healthcare" (Donabedian 1980, 83)

Pareto chart: image similar to a histogram, but with the data sorted in order of decreasing frequency of events and with other annotations to highlight the Pareto principle

Pareto principle: theory that "most effects come from relatively few causes; that is, 80 percent of the effects come from 20 percent of the possible causes" (ASQ 2016b)

patient care microsystem: "the level of healthcare delivery that includes providers, technology, and treatment processes" (McLaughlin and Olson 2012, 9)

patient experience: a patient's "report of observations of and participation in health care, or assessment of any resulting change in their health" (AHRQ 2016a)

patient harm: "unintended physical injury resulting from or contributed to by medical care that requires additional monitoring, treatment or hospitalization, or that results in death" (Griffin and Resar 2009, 5)

patient safety: "freedom from accidental or preventable injuries produced by medical care" (AHRQ 2016b)

PDCA cycle (or Shewhart cycle): an improvement cycle that consists of four continuous steps: plan, do, check or study, and act

percentile: a value (in percentage form) in the range of values in a dataset that is larger than the specified percentage of all the values in the dataset

performance management: "an umbrella term that describes the methodologies, metrics, processes and systems used to monitor and manage the business performance of an enterprise" (Buytendijk and Rayner 2002)

performance management cycle: ongoing cycle in which performance standards, performance measurement, performance improvement, and reporting progress are linked

pharmacogenomics: "a biotechnological science that combines the techniques of medicine, pharmacology, and genomics and is concerned with developing drug therapies to compensate for genetic differences in patients which cause varied responses to a single therapeutic regimen" (Medline Plus and Merriam-Webster 2016)

pharmacotherapeutics: "the study of the therapeutic uses and effects of drugs" (Medline Plus and Merriam-Webster 2016)

pillars of performance excellence: general categories of performance that function as "the foundation for goal setting and results reporting, leadership evaluation, meeting agendas, and departmental communications" (Spaulding, Gamm, and Griffith 2010, 4)

predictive analytics: a branch of analytics used primarily to make future predictions about key performance measures

primary prevention: the effort to prevent a disease or disorder before it happens (Merrill and Timmreck 2006, 16)

proactive risk assessment: "an improvement model that involves identifying and analyzing potential failures in healthcare processes or services for the purpose of reducing or eliminating risks that are a threat to patient safety" (Spath 2013b, 192)

process: "an organized group of related activities that work together to transform one or more kinds of input into outputs that are of value to the customer" (ASQ 2016a)

process capability: what the process is able to deliver; also referred to as the *voice of the process*

process flowchart: graphical representation of the steps in a process or project

process of care: "a set of activities that go on within and between practitioners and patients" (Donabedian 1980, 79)

process requirements: what is needed from a process; also known as *voice of the customer*

public policy: "authoritative decisions made in the legislative, executive, or judicial branches of government that are intended to direct or influence the actions, behaviors, or decisions of others" (Longest 2010, 5)

purpose: an identity or reason for being

purpose principle: a tool to aid managers in identifying the right purpose to address

qualitative data: any data that cannot be easily expressed as a number or quantified

quality: "the degree to which health services for individuals and populations increase the likelihood of desired health outcomes and are consistent with current professional knowledge" (Lohr 1990, 21)

quality assurance (QA): actions performed to eliminate defective outputs

quality control (QC): "the operational techniques and activities used to fulfill requirements for quality" (ASQ 2016)

quality improvement (QI): "ongoing improvement of products, services or processes through incremental and breakthrough improvements" (ASQ 2016)

quality indicators: statistical measures that give an indication of process or output quality

quality management: the manager's role and contribution to organizational effectiveness; how managers working in various types of health services organizations and settings understand, explain, and continuously improve their organizations to allow them to deliver quality and safe patient care, promote quality patient and organizational outcomes, and improve health in their communities

quality measure (or metric): "any type of measurement used to gauge a quantifiable component of performance" (Spath 2013, 34)

quantitative data: data that can be expressed as a number or quantified

quartiles: values that divide a set of data into four equal parts

random variation (or noise, common cause variation): the natural variation present in all measures of processes (Neuhauser, Provost, and Bergman 2011)

range: the numerical difference between the largest and the smallest measurements in a given dataset

rapid cycle improvement: "an accelerated method (usually less than six weeks per improvement cycle) of collecting and analyzing data and making changes on the basis of that analysis" (Spath 2013, 120)

Reason's swiss cheese model: a model of how errors occur that "illustrates how analyses of major accidents and catastrophic systems failures tend to reveal multiple, smaller failures leading up to the actual hazard" (AHRQ 2016a)

reliability: "measurable ability of a health-related process, procedure, or service to perform its intended functions in the required time under commonly occurring conditions" (Weick, Sutcliffe, and Obstfeld 1999, 82)

repair service behavior: a type of problem solving where organizations or individuals solve a problem they know how to solve, regardless of whether it is the problem they need to solve (Dörner 1996)

reverse planning: defining the desired result and then working backward to determine a practical or logical starting point to the step-by-step process of getting to the result

root cause analysis (RCA): method used to "identify hazards and systems vulnerabilities so that actions can be taken that improve patient safety by preventing future harm" (NPSF 2016, 2)

routine violations: steps in a process that are intentionally skipped; activities that cut corners

run chart (or line graph): a graphical representation that is primarily used to describe a single set of data over a period of time

scatter diagram: a graphical representation typically used to determine the relationship between two quantitative variables of interest, where the value of one variable is dependent on the value of the other variable

schema: a "mental codification of experience that includes a particular organized way of perceiving cognitively and responding to a complex situation or set of stimuli" (Merriam-Webster 2016)

secondary prevention: activities "aimed at health screening and detection activities [to] block the progression of disease" (Merrill and Timmreck 2006, 17)

sentinel event: a patient safety event that affects a patient and results in death, permanent harm, or severe temporary harm and intervention required to sustain life (Joint Commission 2016)

situation violations: action undertaken when a person believes that the action "offers the only path available to getting the job done and where the rules or procedures are seen as inappropriate for the present situation" (Reason 1995, 82)

Six Sigma: a rigorous and disciplined process improvement approach using defined tools, methods, and statistical analysis with the goal of improving the outcome of a process by reducing the frequency of defects or failures

six sigma level: the sigma level of a process that "has about 3.4 DPMO [defect per million opportunities] and is virtually error free (99.9996)" (Varkey, Reller, and Resar 2007, 737)

Six Sigma project: a rigorous and disciplined approach to problem resolution using process improvement tools, methods, and statistical analysis

small win: "a concrete, complete, implemented outcome of moderate importance" (Weick 1984, 43)

stakeholder: "all groups that are or might be affected by an organization's services, actions or success" (BPEP 2015, 53)

standard deviation: a measure of the variability in a given dataset

standard work: "a process that has been broken down into a series of clearly defined tasks and is performed the same way every time by each individual involved in the process" (Lavallee 2011, 248)

structure: "the relatively stable characteristics of the providers of care, of the tools and resources they have at their disposal, and of the physical and organizational settings in which they work" (Donabedian 1980, 81)

system: "a set of connected parts that fit together to achieve a purpose" (Langabeer and Helton 2016, 477)

systemic structure: the interrelationships among key elements in the system and the influence of these interrelationships on the system's behavior over time (Senge 2006)

systems thinking: "a view of reality that emphasizes the relationships and interactions of each part of the system to all the other parts" (McLaughlin and Olson 2012, 39)

team: a group of people working together to achieve a common goal (Grumbach and Bodenheimer 2004)

teamwork: a team process involving the "knowledge, skills, experience, and perspectives of different individuals" (Health Resources and Services Administration 2011, 3)

tertiary prevention: intervention that "blocks the progression of a disability, condition, or disorder to keep it from advancing and requiring excessive care" (Merrill and Timmreck 2006, 17)

tightly coupled: relating to a system in which the parts "exhibit relatively time-dependent, invariant, and inflexible connections with little slack" (Scott 2003, 358)

total quality (TQ): "a philosophy or an approach to management that can be characterized by its principles, practices, and techniques. Its three principles are customer focus, continuous improvement, and teamwork . . . each principle is implemented through a set of practices . . . the practices are, in turn, supported by a wide array of techniques (i.e., specific step-by-step methods intended to make the practices effective)" (Dean and Bowen 2000, 4–5)

Toyota Production System: a common method of applying Lean in health services, first developed at the Toyota Motor Company

triggers: "clinical data related to patient care indicating a reasonable probability that an adverse event has occurred" (AAP 2011, 1206)

unobstructed throughput: elimination of bottlenecks in a process

value: the ratio of quality to cost (value = quality/cost)

value-stream map (VSM): a diagram that "graphically displays the process of services or product delivery with use of inputs, throughputs, and outputs" (Varkey, Reller, and Resar 2007, 738)

variable: number that "take[s] on different values on a continuous scale" (Carey and Lloyd 2001, 70)

violations: "deviations from safe operating practices, procedures, standards, or rules" (Reason 1997, 72)

vision: ideal future state

INDEX

ABOUT THE AUTHORS

Patrice L. Spath, RHIT, is a health information management professional with broad experience in healthcare quality and safety improvement. She is president of Brown-Spath & Associates, a healthcare publishing and training company in Forest Grove, Oregon. During the past 30 years, Spath has written numerous books and journal articles and presented more than 350 educational programs on healthcare quality management and patient safety topics.

Spath is currently an adjunct assistant professor in the Department of Health Services Administration at the University of Alabama, Birmingham; an adjunct professor in the College of Health Professions at Pacific University in Forest Grove, Oregon; and a guest lecturer in the Master of Science in Medical and Healthcare Simulation program at Drexel University College of Medicine in Philadelphia. She has previously taught at Oregon Health and Science University; Tougaloo College; Missouri Western State University; and Montana State University, Billings.

Spath earned a master's degree in management from American Public University and a bachelor of science in management and health information from Marylhurst University. She is a Registered Health Information Technician and a Certified Healthcare Technology Specialist in Implementation Management (CHIT-IM). She holds a Lean Project Leader certificate and serves as consulting editor for the monthly publication *Hospital Peer Review*.

Diane L. Kelly, DrPH, MBA, RN, is a seasoned professional who applies her expertise in quality and performance excellence along the continuum of healthcare delivery and public health organizations. Dr. Kelly has consulted with more than 100 hospitals and health services organizations in the United States, central and eastern Europe, and Bermuda. She currently works as a principal consultant with Quantix Health Capital, LLC.

Dr. Kelly has taught at the University of North Carolina at Chapel Hill, Duke University, and Weber State University. She has provided thought leadership for numerous healthcare organizations. She served as a member of the board of examiners for the Baldrige Performance Excellence Program. She also served on the editorial board of *The Joint Commission Journal on Quality and Patient Safety* from 2004 to 2008.

Dr. Kelly earned a doctorate in public health from the University of North Carolina at Chapel Hill, Gillings School of Global Public Health; a master's degree in business administration from the University of Utah; and a bachelor of science in nursing from West Virginia University. She is a certified National Committee for Quality Assurance patient-centered medical home content expert.

ABOUT THE CONTRIBUTOR

Naveen Kumar, PhD, is an assistant professor of business information and technology at the Fogelman College of Business and Economics at the University of Memphis. His interests include data analytics, with a focus on developing data science methods for contemporary big data applications in healthcare. Dr. Kumar has more than a decade of experience in applying advanced data analytics techniques to complex problems in healthcare, information, finance, and manufacturing. He has previously taught a variety of graduate and undergraduate courses in healthcare analytics at the College of Health Professions at Pacific University in Forest Grove, Oregon.

Dr. Kumar holds a PhD (2006) from the University of Washington, Seattle. He was a Boeing/GTTL scholarship winner for excellent scholarly achievement. One of his articles was selected for the best paper award at the 16th Annual Conference of the Society for Health Systems. He is an active member of the Institute for Operations Research and the Management Sciences (INFORMS). He is a Six Sigma green belt certificate holder.